Prince
of Quacks

T0276843

Prince
of Quacks

The Notorious Life of
Dr. Francis Tumblety, Charlatan
and Jack the Ripper Suspect

TIMOTHY B. RIORDAN

McFarland & Company, Inc., Publishers
Jefferson, North Carolina, and London

LIBRARY OF CONGRESS CATALOGUING-IN-PUBLICATION DATA

Riordan, Timothy B.
  Prince of quacks : the notorious life of Dr. Francis Tumblety,
charlatan and Jack the Ripper suspect / Timothy B. Riordan.
      p.   cm.
  Includes bibliographical references and index.

  ISBN 978-0-7864-4433-5
  softcover : 50# alkaline paper ∞

  1. Tumblety, Francis, 1830–1903.   2. Quacks and quackery—
United States—Biography.   3. Irish Americans—Biography.
4. Criminals—United States—Biography.   5. Lincoln, Abraham,
1809–1865—Assassination.   6. Jack, the Ripper.   I. Title.
CT275.T936R56   2009
615.8'56092—dc22 [B]   2009028704

British Library cataloguing data are available

On the cover: Tumblety in uniform from the 1871 biography
(collection of the New-York Historical Society); background
©2009 Shutterstock

Manufactured in the United States of America

*McFarland & Company, Inc., Publishers
  Box 611, Jefferson, North Carolina 28640
  www.mcfarlandpub.com*

To Tim and Phillip,
who have taught
their father much

Acknowledgments

One of the best aspects of doing research on Dr. Tumblety was that it brought me in contact with a number of truly friendly and wonderful people. They patiently answered my many emails and shared their enthusiasm for their diverse subjects. Without their help, this project could never have been done.

Much of the research required information from libraries and archives around the world. I appreciate the many reference librarians and archivists who graciously did so much work in response to my requests. In particular, three individuals went beyond what I asked and provided me with significant data. Christopher Hoolihan of the University of Rochester School of Medicine and Dentistry provided invaluable information on the medical background of Tumblety's preceptors. Wendy Thirkettle, archivist at the Manx National Heritage Library, sent a summary of the Tumblety-Caine correspondence which filled in many interesting aspects of that relationship. Sharon Shugart, museum specialist at the History Center of the Hot Springs National Park, gave me much data on this site so important to Tumblety's final years. Much of the research involved ads in newspapers scattered across the United States. Brenda L. Rodgers, Interlibrary Loan Specialist at St. Mary's College of Maryland, performed miracles in getting other institutions to lend microfilm for the research. This saved both money and time and added materially to the completion of the project.

The subject of this biography came to the attention of a modern audience as a result of his tangential relationship with one of the greatest mysteries of the nineteenth century—the Whitechapel murders of 1888. Today there are a large number of researchers who actively follow that case and my research was aided greatly by many of these individuals who shared their expertise and insights on Tumblety and other aspects of the case. I have come to think of some of them more as friends than colleagues. While all have generously shared their thoughts, several have given me significant documents or references which aided the research. In particular, I gratefully mention Joe Chetcuti, Christopher T. George, Stephen P. Ryder, Wolf Vanderlinden, and Adam Wood.

Throughout all of this, my family has been supportive and interested in what I was doing. Without this encouragement, I would not have been able to complete it. Mary Riordan, my sister, was not only supportive but did valuable research on Tumblety's time in Boston and incidents related to it. Overall, Tim and Phillip, my boys, kept me on track with their comments and questions. Thank you to all of you.

Table of Contents

Introduction

"Prince of quacks," "esteemed townsman," "charlatan," "modern Count of Monte Cristo," "public benefactor"—these and many other titles were bestowed on Francis Tumblety during his life. There seem to be few people who had a neutral opinion of the man. This diversity of opinion is a reflection of the dual nature of Tumblety's life. One part of him strove very hard to play the gentleman and fit in with the upper levels of Victorian society. The other part always ended up on the seamier side or was involved in something controversial. His need to keep the latter side of his personality hidden provided a dynamic that runs though all aspects of his life. A newspaper editor once remarked of him:

> The very curious fact about Tumblety is that he is two totally different men; that is, he has lived two totally distinct lives, and there are two irreconcilable histories given of him, each by witnesses who are positive they are correct.[1]

Despite his notoriety, after his death in 1903, he was almost completely forgotten. He would have remained in obscurity except for the discovery in 1993 of what is known as the Littlechild Letter, which named Tumblety as a "likely" suspect in the Whitechapel murders of 1888. Inspector John G. Littlechild was not directly involved in the Whitechapel case but he knew most of the men who were. The fact that a previously unknown person was considered a suspect by a top police official made headlines around the world. This evidence was reported in *The Lodger* by Evans and Gainey in 1995 and in *Jack the Ripper: First American Serial Killer* in 1998 by the same authors. The discovery that Tumblety was suspected of being Jack the Ripper brought him international fame of a sort not possible in his own day. One suspects, given his flair for self-promotion, that he would be rather flattered by the new attention.

It needs to be stated at the very beginning that this is not a book about Jack the Ripper, although the Whitechapel murders do play a part. I consider it highly unlikely that Tumblety was involved in the murders in any but the most peripheral way. That he was considered a suspect by Scotland Yard can not be denied. However, he was one of many false leads that were considered and later abandoned. There is an exhaustive literature on the "Ripper" murders and no purpose would be served in reviewing all the evidence here. Rather, those aspects which touch on Tumblety himself are reviewed.[2]

My interest in Dr. Tumblety was sparked by reading the 1998 Evans and Gainey book. The too brief sketch of his life presented in the book hinted at a much fuller and more interesting story. Although Tumblety is not the most sympathetic subject, he blazed an impressive path across the mid to late nineteenth century. Over the course of his 73 years, Tumblety had a knack for being in the wrong place at the wrong time. He also seems to have offended a number of powerful or vindictive enemies. At one time or another, he was suspected of being involved in the assassination of President Lincoln, being part of a plot to infect the North with yellow fever, participating in a Fenian plot to assassinate a high official of the British government, associating with the assassin of President Garfield and finally, being Jack the Ripper. Add to this an arrest for selling abortion drugs, an arrest for manslaughter, an arrest for pickpocketing and several arrests for homosexual activity. To say that he had a notorious reputation would be an understatement. During the 1860s, Tumblety became a sort of folk icon with his name appearing in ballads, humor magazines and, more than once, in caricature on stage.

But much of this reputation is based on hindsight and would not have been known to most of his contemporaries. When he was suspected of being the Ripper, newspapers sought out people who not only knew him but had interesting, none too flattering things to say about him. In 1888, the press had a grand time digging up every rumor they could about Tumblety and perhaps making up a few as they went along. Modern researchers have picked up these accounts, because they are the easiest to find, and accepted them at face value. A good example of this is the interview given by Col. C. A. Dunham in 1888. The information in this article is prominently repeated in every book or article about Tumblety. It has become the basis of what people think about Tumblety. There is some evidence that Inspector Littlechild knew of this report and it helped convince him of Tumblety's guilt. Charles A. Dunham, a.k.a. Sanford Conover, was convicted of perjury in 1869 for giving and arranging false testimony in the Lincoln conspiracy trials. When he was first caught in a lie, he offered to make up any lies the government wanted. Even as late as 1888, he was lying about his army career during the Civil War. His testimony on Tumblety should be considered suspect and subjected to close scrutiny.[3]

Much of the newspaper coverage of Tumblety, both in 1888 and at other times, needs to be taken with a grain of salt. Journalistic standards were not very high in the nineteenth century. Anecdotal stories were often more important than facts. For the study of any nineteenth-century figure, but especially for one as notorious as Dr. Tumblety, historians must view each piece of evidence critically and not accept at face value what was reported. In this case, much of what was written about Tumblety came out in the 1888 press frenzy but referred back to events that happened as many as 40 years earlier. Just because it was published does not make it true. Basic rules of evidence must be applied and facts need to be confirmed from independent sources.

If we are to understand Francis Tumblety and the life he lived, we must dig deeper than these obviously biased press accounts. He left us an extensive record of his medical practice in numerous newspapers across Canada and the United States. While this primarily informs us about his profession, some aspects of his personality can be gleaned. Tumblety was a natural showman and such an odd character that newspaper editors could not help talking about him. These asides give us invaluable details about his lifestyle. Fortunately, he was an active self-promoter and, while said to be virtually illiterate, issued nine well-written pamphlets about his life, some kind of medical pamphlet and a number of poems. His publications give us an idea of how Tumblety viewed the world. Like the press reports, these self-promotional autobiographies are biased and need to be carefully evaluated. Tumblety was not above lying about himself to increase his prestige and he was never afraid to plagiarize when he needed to do so.

Physically, Tumblety was an imposing presence in any gathering. People often commented on his height, said to be over six feet. Often people referred to him as being handsome or well-formed. In the early part of his life he wore his black hair long and flowing while later it was cut much more conservatively. The one thing that did not change was his moustache. Very early, he was distinguished by a large, impressive moustache which he maintained throughout his life. Later, it was reported that he dyed both hair and moustache to keep them black. For most of his life, he dressed in the latest fashions, often extensively reported by the press. During the last few years of his life, however, people thought him a pauper because of his shabby dress.

Dr. Tumblety was respected and sought after for most of his life. He had a way of getting prominent people to vouch for him and support him. Many people thought him charming, proper and well educated. His success at his profession allowed him to live a rich and easy lifestyle, including frequent trips to Europe. This hardly seems like the type of person on the run from the police or associating with the less respectable members of a community. The bad press he received in his later years could be matched by good press reports at other times.

While Tumblety's life is interesting, it is in the context of Victorian society that he becomes most important. Several of the themes of his life are deeply connected to the aspirations and fears of that society. How the doctor dealt with these issues, his successes and failures, say much about the society as a whole. His life provides a lens through which the image is made clearer.

One of these themes is the struggle to develop a professional medical practice. Today, we think of science-based medicine as the only rational choice. With the development of microbiology, genetics and a host of other sciences, medicine has made enormous strides and gained the faith of all but a small minority of the public. In the early nineteenth century medical practice was a lot more diverse. The "regular" physicians pursued a therapy that involved blood letting, blistering and the use of poisonous salts of mercury. They had no better idea of what caused disease than anyone else and the public perception was that they often caused more harm than good. In response to this, there arose several "alternative" medical therapies which involved vegetable remedies, sometimes as bad as the regular physicians' medicines. While both sides consistently called each other quacks and frauds, the truth is that neither had an effective therapy. In the early nineteenth century, the battle for control of the medical profession was not fought on the basis of effective treatment but on the idea of respectability. Reputation became the primary factor in choosing a doctor. Thus, getting and keeping the public's attention was an important part of a successful practice.[4]

Tumblety became an alternative physician and practiced for over 30 years. During that time, he fought several battles with the regular physicians, sometimes successful, sometimes not. He developed a public persona and a particular therapy. As part of this, he seems to have pioneered several of the aspects of advertising that would make patent medicine manufacturers millions of dollars later in the century. By modern standards, he was a quack in the sense that his medicines could not do what he promised they could. A harder issue is whether he knew this and perpetrated a fraud or if he truly believed he was helping people. Evidence can be found on both sides and that question may never be answered. His career is probably typical of this type of medical practitioner and allows us to see how the profession changed and developed over the course of the nineteenth century.

A second theme, important both to Tumblety and to Victorian society, was the issue of sex. In both his personal and his professional lives, the doctor found himself dealing with the less accepted side of the social divide. Despite occasional protests, Tumblety appears to have been an active homosexual. He is consistently described in association with handsome young men and seems to have had long-lasting relationships with several men. His dress and lifestyle is often described as extravagant. Several times he was arrested for what was euphemistically described as assault. These incidents were part of the risks associated with being a homosexual in the nineteenth century. Often, the only way to find a partner was to seek one in public places and these were infested with criminals who preyed on homosexuals. Of the crimes against Tumblety, one case was an attempt to blackmail him while two others were attempted robberies. When charged in England with "gross indecencies," he faced two years imprisonment and hard labor. As much of his practice depended on his reputation for respectability, evidence of this scandal could have had devastating consequences for him personally and professionally. The need to keep this secret was one aspect of the double life he lived for so long.

Professionally, Tumblety maintained a respectable practice dealing with skin problems, lung congestion and a number of other ailments. However, he also seems to have been involved in providing medicines for contraception, abortion, masturbation and venereal diseases. None of these latter issues enter into any of his advertising or his autobiographical pamphlets. Yet there is a continuous undercurrent of reports that link him to these issues. At one point, he published a "Guide to the Afflicted..." which dealt with diseases arising from the abuse of genital organs or sexually transmitted diseases. If it was like others of the same name, it had, for its time, frank discussions of sexual problems. While in New York, he was linked in a popular ballad with the well known abortionist Madam Restell. While he managed to avoid conviction for it in Montreal, it is likely that he sold a woman drugs with the intent to cause a miscarriage. Despite his best attempts to maintain a respectable façade, he seemed inevitably drawn to the seamier, and more profitable, aspects of his practice.

As a subject for a biography, Tumblety is ideal in many ways. His life was full of adventures and moments of high drama. His was a success story; beginning as a poor immigrant, possibly fleeing the potato famine, he overcame many obstacles and ended a wealthy and recognized, if not fully respected, man. He went through a major crisis in 1888. Not only was he accused of horrendous crimes but he was internationally exposed as a homosexual and the carefully constructed persona that he presented to the world was destroyed. The secrets that he spent so many years carefully hiding were splashed across newspaper columns from New York to San Francisco.

One can speculate that this was not unexpected. After balancing for so long on the respectability tightrope, was Tumblety bound to fall in the end? His life was spent running to keep ahead of his reputation. Nevertheless, he was successful for most of his life. It was his misfortune to be caught up in the most celebrated murders of the nineteenth century. And he was doubly cursed to be the only American suspect named. It is a curious fact that Dr. Tumblety is not mentioned in any British papers as a suspect. This may account for why he was unknown as a Ripper suspect for so long. The American papers, on the other hand, gave enormous attention to him in 1888. It is likely that, being caught on the sidelines for so much of the sensational story, editors of the American papers saw Tumblety as a way to become directly involved and, of course, to sell more newspapers. Once caught in that net, no matter his guilt or innocence, there was no escaping the exposure. For all of his faults, Tumblety was wrongly treated by the press and modern historians have only perpetuated those lies.

Emerging from this crisis, which would have made most people hide from the limelight, Tumblety went on the offensive. To regain his reputation, he began to use his considerable fortune to buy his way back to respectability. In the last decade of his life, he went out of his way to publicly contribute to charitable causes. Also, he updated and refocused his biography for at least five more editions from 1889 through 1900. Try as he might, after 1888 the newspapers consistently referred to him as the "notorious Dr. Tumblety."

My purpose here is not to defend nor to vilify Dr. Tumblety but rather to present the interesting story of a life lived fully. Like most people, Tumblety had good and bad qualities. Perhaps because of his personality and profession, these qualities seem exaggerated. One might not always understand Dr. Tumblety, but he always had the capacity to amaze.

1

~∞~

Early Life
(1830–1856)

The remarkable life of Francis Tumblety begins in an unremarkable way with his birth in or near Dublin, Ireland, in 1830. Like many Irish families of the time, the Tumblety clan was large. He was the youngest of 11 children with 8 sisters and 2 brothers. His father, James, was 54 in the year of his birth while his mother Margaret was 42. We know very little of their life in Ireland. Were they prosperous yeoman farmers or did they live on the edge of poverty, as did many other Catholic families? Were they long resident in one area or did they move every couple of years in search of lower rents and better fields?[1]

When Francis was in his mid-teens, this family was swept up and dispersed by the potato famine that ravaged Ireland. Several of his sisters, who were older, married and had families of their own, either staying in Ireland or ending up in Liverpool. Lawrence, his eldest brother, had migrated to Rochester, New York, as early as 1844. When the crisis struck, James and Margaret, along with their youngest daughter, Ann, and their youngest son, Francis, set out to join him in America. Along with many others, they made their way to Liverpool to take a packet ship for America.[2]

The family sailed in the *Ashburton*, a ship built in 1842 in Newburyport, Massachusetts, for the Red Swallowtail Line of Grinnell, Minturn & Co. The ship sailed under Captain William Howland on a regularly scheduled voyage between Liverpool and New York from at least 1846 to 1856. It carried about 400 passengers, with a dozen cabin passengers from England and the rest being Irish emigrants in steerage. The trip took about four weeks and the family arrived in New York on June 21, 1847. They soon traveled to Rochester.[3]

Like many Irish families, the Tumbletys followed the path already trod by a relative. Since Lawrence Tumblety settled in Rochester three years earlier, their movement there is understandable. Rochester in the 1840s was rapidly expanding and offered many opportunities for unskilled labor. Between 1840 and 1850, the city's population almost doubled. By 1846, 4,000 of the 7,500 households were foreign born. Of those, 45 percent were Irish immigrants.[4]

The family took up residence in a house on the southern end of Sophia Street, about a mile south of the town center and near the Genesee River. The Tumbletys would stay in this house throughout the rest of the century. In the late 1840s, the area was described as being sparsely settled with few houses nearby. The Rochester city directory for 1848 lists James Tumilty but gives no occupation for him. As he was 71 by this time, he probably had no job. The main support of the family appears to be his son, Lawrence, who worked as a gardener for Dr. Fitzhugh. Some additional support may have come from another son, Patrick, who had also located in Rochester and was working as a fireman in the gas works. In any case, the family must have been very poor.

Francis Tumblety, who was 17 in 1848, was not listed in the city directory. At a much later time, an acquaintance provided an unflattering portrait of the young man: "...he used to run about the canal in Rochester, N.Y., a dirty, awkward, ignorant, uncared-for, good-for-nothing boy. He was utterly devoid of education." Edward Haywood, who gave this description in 1888, was the nephew of Dr. Fitzhugh, for whom Lawrence Tumblety worked. The Fitzhugh family had helped to found Rochester and were at the center of its elite. Haywood's description of Tumblety may have been biased by their relative status. Nevertheless, "Frank Tumblety" does not seem to have been making a good impression.

Tumblety's connection to the Erie Canal, as it passed though the city, had an economic purpose. Another early Rochester resident, W. C. Streeter, who ran a canal boat, recalled Tumblety selling books and papers to the passengers. He was no ordinary paperboy, however. Streeter said that the books he sold were "of the kind Anthony Comstock suppresses now," and later he added, "I thought then that his mind had been affected by those books he sold."

Modern readers might not know who Anthony Comstock was, but in the late nineteenth century, he was a leading crusader against obscenity. In 1873, at Comstock's urging, Congress passed an act banning the mailing, importation and transportation of any obscene material. Obscenity was broadly defined to include anything involving sex, including contraception, abortion and sexual diseases. Comstock was appointed as a postal inspector with great powers to investigate and prosecute purveyors of obscenity. He used these powers not only to suppress obscenity but to persecute those who dared to talk openly about contemporary sexual problems.[5]

Researchers dealing with Tumblety have automatically assumed, based on Streeter's comments, that the books sold on the canal boats were pornographic. However, it is more likely that these books dealt with the other subjects banned by the Comstock Law. Throughout his later career and even here, early in Rochester, Tumblety seems to have been connected with issues of contraception, abortion and sexual activity. The first information about his association with medicine places him at a "hospital" that treated young men who injured their health by "secret habits." The owner of that establishment published his own advice book and it is likely this was what young Frank was selling.

The question of how this "awkward, ignorant" boy transformed himself into a gentleman and eminent physician in less than six years is central to the story. Before we can understand Tumblety's rise as a physician, there are two misconceptions that need to be dispelled. These involve questions of medical education and the very existence of a unified body of medical knowledge.

Today, doctors go to medical schools and serve time in hospitals under the direction of experienced physicians. In the early nineteenth century, most doctors did not go to medical school and those that did generally got only six months to a year of instruction. Most practitioners served an apprenticeship under a "preceptor," an older doctor who had an established practice. During this period, the candidate would learn about medicine but would also do menial tasks, like sweeping the floor and anything else asked of him. When the preceptor was convinced the student had learned enough, he sent him off with his recommendation. This was an ancient system and would not significantly change until the 1870s.

The second modern misconception is that there was, in the nineteenth century, a unified body of medical knowledge, as there is now. Today's medicine, regulated, licensed and built on experimental science, is a much different thing than nineteenth-century medicine. Throughout the century there were multiple competing medicines in the United States. Without scientifically established theories of the origin of disease, germ theory and tested therapies, medicine often did more harm than good to its patients. Using microbiology, rigorous testing of medicines and licensing, the "regular" doctors eventually established the medical profession we know today. However, in the early nineteenth century, the regulars, using therapies like mercury and bloodletting, were viewed by the public with despair. The public's dismay with their "heroic" treatments gave rise to several systems of medicine based on herbal and natural remedies. If these did not cure the patient, they were less harmful than the alternative. Today, herbal medicine is restricted by law and looked on as a fringe cult. In the nineteenth century, it was as respectable as regular medicine and more sought after by the public.[6]

Herbal medicine succeeded in the nineteenth century, but not because its therapies were better or more effective than those of the regular doctors. Rather, it took advantage of several weaknesses in medical knowledge and normal human frailties. The most important aspect was the fact, largely unknown or ignored, that the body will cure itself of most problems regardless of what treatment is given. The old adage that you get over a cold in seven days if you take medicine or a week if you do not, recognizes this process. Coupled with the tendency to exaggerate every minor ailment, this process guaranteed success. Thus, minor symptoms became major diseases which were therefore cured in time by the treatment of these doctors. Without recognizing it, these doctors counted on the "placebo effect" to aid in combating vague, often psychological symptoms such as tiredness, nervousness and other ill feelings. It should come as no surprise that the most common ingredient of most herbal medicines was a laxative. Demonstrating to the patient that the medicine was doing something went a long way towards ascribing the eventual cure to the herbal doctor's practice.[7]

Rochester, in the early nineteenth century, shows all of these trends. In a study of pre–Civil War medicine in the city, Edward C. Atwater reported that there were 374 physicians who practiced there before 1861. In addition to the regular doctors, there were botanic doctors, homeopathic doctors, eclectic doctors, Indian doctors, mesmeric doctors and "clairvoyant doctors." His study showed that over time, the status of doctors declined and competition for patients increased. Along with the decline in status came a decline in the training of physicians. In the 1830s and '40s, physicians made up a large proportion of the college educated in Rochester. By the 1850s, only a very small percentage of doctors could claim this education. The number of alternative physicians in Rochester markedly increased over time.[8]

For a young man looking to become a doctor, Rochester was full of opportunities and Frank Tumblety found a way to take advantage of them. We are fortunate that, in later years, several observers commented on his association with two doctors in the 1850s. One of these reports said he gained his medical knowledge at Lispenard's Hospital, which was in reality a doctor's office that specialized in treating sexual diseases. It was run by Dr. Reynolds and Tumblety was said to have worked there. The other influence on his medical training was an Indian herb doctor named R. J. Lyons. Aspects of Tumblety's later practice can be seen in the ads and descriptions of these two doctors and looking at their history provides insights on his development as a doctor.

Dr. Ezra J. Reynolds came to Rochester in late 1850 or in 1851. In the 1850 census, he is listed in Ward 4 of Albany and is described as 21 years old, a physician and single. Although Dr. W. C. (or C. W.) Lispenard does not show up in the census anywhere in New York, Reynolds managed an office known as Lispenard's Infirmary. Lispenard's name appears in the Albany city directories for 1852 and 1853 but Reynolds would later admit that this was a pseudonym. By 1851, Reynolds was established in Rochester but would keep the Infirmary in Albany until 1856.[9]

In the 1851 Rochester city directory, Ezra Lispenard is listed as a physician with an office at 14 Exchange Place and boarding at the New England House. Ezra J. Reynolds is also listed as a physician but no office is reported. Reynolds is also boarding at the New England House. By 1853, Dr. Lispenard's first name is "W. C." and, while he had an office at the same place, no home address is listed. Dr. Reynolds now lists his office as 14 Exchange Place and he has a house at 44 Franklin. Reynolds is listed again in 1855, 1857 and 1859 but Lispenard is no longer listed.

Dr. Lispenard's ad in the Rochester city directory of 1857. "Lispenard" was a pseudonym used by Dr. Ezra Reynolds to hide his treatment of sexual diseases. Dr. Reynolds was Tumblety's first medical teacher.

This seems like a straightforward history of a medical partnership. Certainly it is not unusual for two doctors to share an office. It is also not unusual that there might have been some mix-up in their first names as listed in the earlier directory. However, the evidence indicates that Dr. Lispenard, if he existed at all, was gone by 1855. This is particularly surprising since he had a full-page ad in the 1857 directory that states he is still seeing patients at his office. On the very next page, Dr. Reynolds has a full page ad saying that he continues to see patients at his old office. Lispenard is in 14 Exchange Place and Reynolds lists his office as 14½ Exchange Place.

Part of this deception may be Reynolds' desire to keep his name separate from the kind of practice that Lispenard was supposed to represent. The 1857 ad in the city directory touts a book entitled "Dr. Lispenard's Practical Private Medical Guide" which, in 224 pages of "PLAIN ENGLISH," describes the diseases of the genitals and how they are contracted and treated, as well as giving "important hints which will be found serviceable to those in married life." Subjects covered included midwifery, miscarriages, impotence and barrenness. It was available for 25 cents or five for a dollar. It is very likely that this was the book Tumblety was hired to sell on the canal boats. Lispenard's ad also stated that he was the only American agent for Dr. Vichois' Female Monthly Pills, which should not be taken by women "in a certain situation." It is generally believed that this is a euphemistic way of advertising these pills as an abortifacient. Atwater comments that prosecution for abortion was increasing in Rochester in the 1850s, so Reynolds' desire to separate his name from that end of the business may have been wise.

Dr. Reynolds' ad, appearing on the next page of the directory, is as grandiose if somewhat more discrete. He claims to be a specialist in diseases of a private or delicate nature. He then goes on to list over 30 parts of the body whose diseases he can cure. As Dr. Lispenard also advertised, he can cure problems of young men afflicted with "secret habits" (masturbation) and he can be consulted about diseases peculiar to the female (unwanted pregnancy). Dr. Reynolds reports that he has cured over 30,000 patients, more than half of whom had previously been treated with mercury. This claim plays into the public's dread of the regular physicians. Reynolds' medical knowledge was so immense that you did not even have to go to see him. All a patient had to do, from anywhere in the world, was send a letter, describing his age, symptoms and occupation, to the good doctor and he would prescribe a cure for them. All for the modest fee of one dollar enclosed with the letter.

The last part of Reynolds' ad is curious considering what is suspected of his use of Lispenard and other names as pseudonyms. He reports being reluctant to put his card before the public because he believes physicians should

Opposite: **Dr. Reynolds' ad in the Rochester city directory of 1857. This was Dr. Reynolds' own ad. He taught Tumblety about "secret diseases."**

not advertise. Nevertheless for the sake of the public he has done so. Reynolds warns about imposters who:

> ... with innumerable false names or combined quackshops, swarming large cities, advertising themselves as physicians; illiterate, shallow-brained fellows, too lazy to work at their original trade, with scarce two ideas above the brute, who for the purpose of enticing and deceiving, carry on five or six offices, under as many different names, so that the afflicted stranger, escaping one is sure to tumble head-long into the other.

The 1859 directory reveals that Reynolds had moved his office to 19 Exchange Place. There is no listing in this volume for Dr. Lispenard. However, in April 1858, Dr. Lispenard advertised his services in the local paper and reported that he could be found at his office at 19 Exchange Place. Apparently, Reynolds continued to find the pseudonym useful.

Whatever reluctance Dr. Reynolds had for putting his name before the public seems to have disappeared by 1859. In the city directory that year, he took out a full-page ad announcing the publication of "Dr. Reynold's [sic] Medical Guide." This was, almost word for word, the same ad as that for Dr. Lispenard's Medical Guide, published two years earlier. The only difference was that Reynolds inserted his name instead of Lispenard's. He also stated that he was the only American agent for Dr. Vichois' Female Monthly Pills, as was Dr. Lispenard earlier. Dr. Reynolds claims to have 30 years experience in his profession. He was a man of great talent since the 1860 census reveals that he was only 33 years old. Reynolds continued to advertise Lispenard's Hospital in the Rochester papers at least until 1865.[10]

Tumblety was not the only doctor trained by Reynolds. In his Albany office, Reynolds hired a man named J. V. C. Teller. When Reynolds moved to Rochester, Teller ran the Albany office. By at least the mid–1850s, Teller styled himself as "Dr. Teller." Around 1856, Reynolds apparently sold his Albany office to Teller and his brother Charles. In that same year, Charles Teller published "Dr. Teller's Pocket Companion," which was a duplicate of the book that Reynolds published. Teller's relationship to Reynolds is very similar to Tumblety's.[11]

It is not certain when Francis Tumblety worked for Dr. Reynolds. However, the 1850 census lists him as a laborer while the 1851 directory lists him as a peddler. Coming so soon after Reynolds' appearance in Rochester, this may reflect Tumblety's selling of books on the canal boats, as remembered by several people. Later, it was remembered derisively that Tumblety swept the floors for Reynolds. However, this was a normal thing for an apprentice to do. How long he stayed with Dr. Reynolds is unknown but it was long enough to pick up many of his advertising techniques. In his later career, he would issue his own medical guide, would promise to cure patients by mail, would make a specialty of female troubles and secret habits in men, could cure cases that regular doctors had given up on and would rail against imposters and quacks.

Whether he learned any medicine during this time is unknown. Dr. Reynolds seems to have taught him the mechanics of being an alternative physician but it was his other mentor who gave him the persona by which he would be known.[12]

The other major influence on Tumblety's medical career was Dr. Rudolph J. Lyons, a physician who pursued "the reformed Indian vegetable practice." Lyons, as evidenced by this description, was one of those physicians who understood the public's fear of mercury treatments and bloodletting and sought natural botanical remedies. He also appreciated his patients' belief that Native Americans were privy to a wealth of secret medical knowledge. Both of these beliefs, held by the public, ensured the success of the "Well Known and Celebrated Indian Herb Doctor." These herb doctors are often dismissed as frontier charlatans who disappeared with the arrival of regular doctors bearing medical degrees. Yet Lyons did well in Rochester and Tumblety later practiced this same kind of medicine in many major cities. It was not the lack of regular doctors that made these herb doctors successful, it was the conscious and knowing choice of the patients.

In the 1850 census, Lyons was living in Baltimore, was 34 years old and described himself as an herb doctor. He first shows up in Rochester in the 1853 directory where he is listed as a physician. There is a half-page ad that announces his practice and reports that he is from South America. Like Dr. Reynolds, he has a long list of diseases he could cure even though they had baffled other doctors for years. Dr. Lyons especially handled the complaints of woman and children. He offered free consultation and advice and had office hours from 8 A.M. to 9 P.M.

Lyons' ad lists his office location as "23 & 25 Reynolds Arcade over Mr. Appleby's Daguerrian Room." This location, no doubt consciously chosen, was at the heart of Rochester's commercial and social world. The Arcade, built in the late 1820s, was a four-and-a-half-story brick building with 86 rooms. It was designed like a modern shopping mall with a corridor through the middle of the structure and was lit by skylights. Shops and offices opened on the corridor on both the first and the second floor. It boasted many important functions. There was a hotel on the upper floors, an observation cupola 86 ft. in the air, the village post office and, from 1856 to 1866, the headquarters of the fledgling Western Union Company. Part of the building was set aside for the Rochester Athenaeum, an early form of a public library which featured newspapers and books from many cities and countries. The selection of this location gave him a fashionable address and exposed much of the city's elite to his advertisements. Lyons continued to practice in Rochester until the end of the decade. He is listed in the city directories in 1855 and 1857 but is gone in 1859. The 1860 census revealed him living in Cleveland, Ohio, with his occupation listed as physician.[13]

Unlike Reynolds, who apparently stayed in his office and waited for

DR. R. J. LYONS,

PHYSICIAN AND SURGEON,

FROM SOUTH AMERICA,

PURSUING THE REFORMED INDIAN VEGETABLE PRACTICE.

Would respectfully announce to the people of Rochester and vicinity that he cures all kinds of Complicated Chronic Complaints of years standing, which have baffled the skill of the most eminent Physicians of Europe and of this country, viz : Lungs, Heart, Liver, and Throat Diseases. Also Dropsy, Diseases of the Kidneys and Bladder, Rheumatism, Gout, Fits, Palsy, St. Vitus Dance, Dyspepsia. All sorts of Diseases of the Blood, such as Scrofula or Kings Evil, Erysipelas or St. Antony's Fire, Cancers, Salt Rheum. And lastly, all kinds of diseases of women and children.

☞ Consultation and advice given free of charge. Office hours from 8 to 9 P. M.

OFFICE NO. 23 & 25. REYNOLD'S ARCADE, OVER MR. APPLEBY'S DAGUERRIAN ROOM.

Dr. Lyons' ad in the Rochester city directory of 1853. Dr. Lyons was an Indian herb doctor. He taught Tumblety much about herbs and showmanship. Most of Tumblety's persona was taken directly from Dr. Lyons.

patients to come to him, Lyons traveled extensively over upstate New York. He advertised regular visits to 11 other towns. Each month, he spent 18 days in his Rochester office and 13 days on the road. The furthest he traveled was to Lockport, which was some 83 miles away. The average distance from Rochester was 47 miles. Most of these were overnight trips and the next day he was back in the Rochester office. From the 15th to the 17th of the month, he made a western swing through Lockport, Buffalo and Albion. Near the end of the month, from the 23rd through the 28th, he made an eastern trip through Canandaigua, Phelps, Geneva and Seneca Falls. These travels carried his medicine to a larger audience and increased his profits.[14]

Another difference between Reynolds and Lyons was in the importance of advertising. While Reynolds occasionally published an ad in the Rochester papers, Lyons was a regular contributor. His ads also show up in a number of newspapers outside Rochester. This may have been due to his need to announce himself when he came to town. However, Dr. Lyons was one of the first to take advantage of the dual aspects of the rapid expansion of newspapers in America and the increase in literacy in the nineteenth century. These trends would lead to an explosion of patent medicines and patent medicine advertising in the last half of the century.[15]

An important part of Dr. Lyons' practice, which Tumblety would use throughout his career, was a unique diagnosis method. Unlike the regular physicians, Dr. Lyons did not feel for a pulse, check for a fever or even ask the patient questions. His method was described well in one of his later ads:

> Dr. Lyons professes to discern diseases by the eye. He therefore asks no questions, nor does he require patients to explain symptoms. Call one and all, and have the symptoms and location of your disease explained free of charge.[16]

Tumblety was associated with R. J. Lyons sometime between 1853 and 1856. From him, Tumblety seems to have taken most of the style and polish which would characterize his practice in Canada over the next few years. While Tumblety is more often associated with Dr. Lispenard in later reflections, a comparison with Dr. Lyons' ads shows that Tumblety copied, borrowed and stole liberally from the public persona that Dr. Lyons projected in Rochester and elsewhere. When he shows up in Toronto in 1856, Tumblety was already referring to himself as the "Great Indian Herb Doctor," and located his practice in the heart of the elite social center of Toronto.[17]

Having served as an apprentice to two different doctors, Tumblety was ready to practice on his own. He would combine the showmanship of Lyons with Reynolds' concern for "secret diseases" and make himself into something bigger than either of his preceptors. When did he start to practice? Was it in Rochester or did he have to go where no one knew his origin? There is some evidence that Tumblety took the knowledge gained from Reynolds and Lyons and began practicing in Rochester.

An article published in a Rochester paper a decade later stated that Tumblety had opened an office in the Smith Block, a rival to the Arcade, where he worked under the name of Philip Steinburg and treated the same kind of diseases that Dr. Reynolds did. After 1853, when Dr. Lyons came to town, Tumblety associated with him. When he was ready to leave Rochester, the paper stated that he got a letter of recommendation from a number of prominent citizens. This brief outline of Tumblety's development is supported by the available documentation.[18]

Preserved in the Atwater Collection at the University of Rochester is a small pamphlet entitled, "Guide to the afflicted: containing at a glance, the most common symptoms of certain diseases which arise from the abuse of the genital organs, or contagion, together with the means of relief, being the result of great research and study by one of the most celebrated physicians of Germany," by Philip Steinburg. This was published at Rochester around 1853 and is supposedly the 27th edition. Tumblety was neither a German scientist nor over 50 years old. However, when in Toronto, a few years later, Tumblety published, under his own name, a "Guide to the Afflicted" which was the same as Steinburg's except that it did not list the German scientist nor was it called the 27th edition. It seems that he was using the name Steinburg in Rochester, but did he do this on his own? At the same time that Dr. Reynolds was still using the name Lispenard on his office, he opened another office run by a "Dr. Heneburger," who treated the same kind of secret diseases. When people called to see Dr. Heneburger, they found some young man running the office. It is likely that Tumblety filled this same role in the office of "Dr. Steinberg."[19]

Perhaps Dr. Reynolds had already cornered the market on secret diseases in Rochester. For whatever reason, Tumblety joined Dr. Lyons sometime after 1853. He learned a different kind of medicine and gained the public personality that he would use for the rest of his life. From Lyons, Tumblety also learned the value of moving from place to place. Unlike Reynolds, who stayed in Rochester for over two decades, Lyons, who in 1850 had been in Baltimore, moved to Rochester by 1853. He stayed there only six years and then moved on to Cleveland. Atwater commented that the medical profession was becoming very mobile by the 1850s. He reported that in an average five-year period, 45 percent of the doctors in Rochester moved on to other places. In contrast, the turnover for the general public was much less. This habit of moving from place to place, sometimes one step ahead of the law, would characterize Tumblety's life from now on.[20]

Tumblety's urge to travel began in 1855 when he contemplated going west from Rochester. In preparation for this move, he sought and obtained a testimonial from a number of prominent citizens of Rochester. According to his later publication of it, the testimonial said: "We the undersigned, Citizens of Rochester, N.Y., do hereby certify that we are acquainted with Dr. Francis Tumblety, an esteemed fellow townsman, and learning that he is about leaving for the West, feel desirous of recommending him as a gentleman entitled to public confidence." It is signed by the mayor, an ex-mayor, an alderman, two judges, three doctors and a number of other citizens. The testimonial is undated but Charles J. Hayden, listed as the mayor of Rochester, was elected in March 1855 and was not reelected in March 1856. This dates the testimonial and also suggests when Tumblety determined to leave Rochester.[21]

Certainly, if this is a true testimonial, it was strong support for Tumblety and the earliest identification of him as a doctor. But were these people real and did they actually sign such a document? Research in the 1850 and 1860 census of Rochester has identified 17 of the 22 names listed. Two of the others could not be identified because their names were commonly found and there was not sufficient information to identify a specific person. The average age of the 17 identified men was 43.25 in 1850 and all but one was married. On average, they were all wealthy men with 10 of the 17 declaring real property in excess of $1,500. By position, age and wealth, these men were at the top of Rochester society. Interestingly, neither Ezra Reynolds nor Rudolph J. Lyons are listed on the testimonial.

While it is easy enough to prove that these men existed, it is quite another thing to demonstrate that they actually signed such a document. A decade later, when Tumblety was in trouble, a newspaper in Rochester reported that the signatories were upset because they had set their names to it as a character reference, not as a testimonial to his ability as a doctor. Leaving aside the medical aspect, the reporter confirmed that 22 well-established, respectable citizens of Rochester did, in fact, sign this character reference. It seems then that Tumblety managed to impress some very important people in his home town. Without seeing the original, we can not be sure that he did not change the wording or add the title Doctor to his own name to make it refer to his medical ability. Genuine or not, the testimonial would be useful for Doctor Tumblety in establishing himself in his new practice.[22]

When Tumblety left Rochester has not been determined but it would have been after March 1855, when Charles Hayden was elected mayor. A much later newspaper report placed him in Detroit in 1855 where he was already practicing as a doctor. No evidence of his stay in Detroit has come to light but by early 1856, he crossed the border into western Ontario and began practicing in Canada. The earliest reference to Tumblety's practice as a doctor is a testimonial letter dated April 4, 1856, which was written in London, Ontario. From testimonials he later published, we can track his progress eastwards through Ontario. In April 1856, he is in London, by July he had moved to Hamilton, in October he went back to Brantford and by November he had arrived in Toronto.[23]

During his trip across Ontario, he seems to have followed the pattern established by Dr. Lyons. He would base himself in the main town then spend several days in the surrounding, smaller towns. An undated editorial in the *Paris Star* reported that Tumblety would be in town for only a few days. While in London, he visited such towns as Iona, Nissouri and Woodstock. From Brantford, he visited Ancaster and Paris. In each of the local papers he published testimonials to his cures and most of the papers gave him an editorial notice. These would later come in handy when he ran into trouble. He received favorable editorial notices in 13 newspapers in Western Ontario between April and November 1856. To get such favorable notice from so many editors, Tumblety must have been advertising heavily and this is an early indication of how successful his sales pitch was.[24]

The published testimonials show that Tumblety was beginning a practice he would continue throughout his career. There are 22 testimonials representing 15 diseases or complaints. Over half of these deal with skin eruptions, sore throat or lung problems and stomach upsets. On these complaints, Tumblety would build a fortune. There is only one testimonial for an unspecified female illness. In terms of how he treated patients, there is very little evidence. One editorial refers to "Dr. Tumblety's Vegetable Remedies." But it is unknown if he was developing a brand name. Another editorial refers to the application of an ointment to a patient's leg.

As would be the case through much of his life, Tumblety could not stay somewhere long without getting in trouble. In May of 1856 he was arraigned before the mayor of London, Ontario, for insulting a Mrs. Carden. Supposedly, on a professional visit to her house, he asked Mrs. Carden to brush the dust from his coat, which she did. Later she became convinced that this was an insult. The mayor agreed with her and fined Tumblety £5. This seems like an excessive fine for the offense and one wonders what else was going on here.[25]

Despite the last incident, within a short time, Tumblety seems to have become an experienced and respected doctor. He was now ready to try his act in a larger market. Sometime between October 28 and November 17, Tumblety packed his bags and set out for Toronto.

2

---◦◦◦---

Practicing in Toronto
(1856–1857)

Having been successful in many of the smaller communities of Canada West, Tumblety, at age 26, moved his operation to Toronto late in 1856. There, for the first time, we can assess his medical practice. Ample evidence exists, in his newspaper ads, to allow us to see what kind of doctor he claimed to be and how he approached his profession.

Newspaper advertisements would, in the mid to late 19th century, become the driving force behind a blossoming patent medicine industry. In the 1850s, it was still a novel technique, but Tumblety used it remarkably well. From November 1856 through September 1857, the *Toronto Globe* was published 286 times and Tumblety had ads in 172 of those editions. In November 1856, he advertised in 20 percent of the daily papers. In February this figure rose to 78 percent and by March, it was 85 percent. For the rest of the period, his ads were in 50 percent of the papers except for July, when he had ads in every single edition. Tumblety maintained a significant presence in the *Globe* right up to his move to Montreal in the fall of 1857.[1]

Keeping his name before the public in this fashion was not a cheap proposition. Based on the published rates for the *Globe*, Tumblety spent a minimum of £47 on newspaper advertising from January through early September 1857. There is no way to know how much of his income this figure represents; however, we can get a sense of the magnitude of this number by comparing it to other items advertised in the *Globe* during the same period. For example, a small house, in town, in a fashionable location near the post office, could be rented for £30 per year. The University of Toronto advertised a scholarship, to cover a year's tuition, at £30. A position for a grammar school teacher offered a salary of £100 per year. Based on these examples, the £47 Tumblety spent on newspaper ads represents a major expenditure and is a gauge of the success of his medical practice.[2]

By examining the ads in closer detail, a picture, not entirely flattering, emerges of Tumblety as a doctor. His first ad appeared in the *Globe* on Novem-

Physicians and Dentists.

The Indian Herb Doctor

F. TUMBLETY,

Will Remain at the

INTERNATIONAL HOTEL,

TORONTO, C.W.,

FROM 28TH NOV. 1856, TO

1ST MARCH, 1857.

Toronto, November 17, 1856.   2061-tf 886-tf

Tumblety's first ad in the *Toronto Globe* in 1857. No other ad published at this time included a picture. In his advertising, Tumblety always tried to catch the public's eye.

ber 17 under the title "The Indian Herb Doctor." It features a small woodcut of a man standing in a garden, holding a book under his arm and reaching out to a plant. This notice stands out from all of the other ads for physicians or surgeons for a number of reasons. Most obvious is the above mentioned graphic. Very few of the other medical ads during this entire period feature a graphic. Secondly, Tumblety's notice is much larger than other ads. Most doctors were content to use four to seven lines of large type, much like a business card, seldom filling more than two inches of column space. Tumblety's ad is at least twice the size of most other ads. The text of this first ad is simple and reports: "The Indian Herb Doctor, F. Tumblety, will remain at the International Hotel, Toronto, C. W. from 28 Nov. 1856 to 1 March 1857."[3]

By the end of the week, November 20, Tumblety ran a new ad, even larger than the first and giving a detailed picture of his practice. Like almost all of his ads, this new one features his woodcut. It begins: "Listen to the voice of truth and reason and be profited," and then quotes a verse from the bible referring to God's creation of "medicines of the Earth." The biblical reference not only describes his medicine but demonstrates his piety and therefore his respectability. Both were important issues for a new practitioner in any community. Next, he places himself in opposition to the regular doctors:

> The time has come that all who will, can escape the Iron grasp of Mercury, and other baneful poisons, by calling without delay to see the well-known and justly celebrated, Indian Herb Doctor, F. Tumblety,...

He goes on to report that he can be consulted at the International Hotel and that his medicines are herbal and safe. The ad includes an extensive list of diseases which can be cured by "Dr. T." and covers all parts of the body. Briefly, his medicines cure diseases of the lungs, heart, liver, throat, blood, stomach and skin as well as fevers, sores and "chronic complaints." He reports that he gives particular attention to those diseases peculiar to females and children. As a final aside, in keeping with his above stated piety, he states that "the poor will be liberally treated."[4]

This ad gives us the first opportunity to see Tumblety as a medical professional. Unlike other doctors who advertised in the *Globe*, he was making a statement about how and why he practiced medicine. Some of this echoes the physicians he is known to have worked with in Rochester. It also places him in a larger tradition, developed in the early 19th century, of alternative medicine.

In his reference to the "iron grasp of mercury," Tumblety has set himself up in opposition to the regular physicians and their use of this metal as a purgative. This, along with the title of the ad, "Indian Herb Doctor," announces to his potential patients that he practices a different system of medicine and does not rely on the "heroic therapy" normally employed by regular physicians. His mention of the organic nature of his "true and safe" medicines assures them that the cure does not have to be worse than the disease.

These statements clearly place Tumblety in the medical tradition known as Thomsonianism. Samuel Thomson was a New Hampshire farmer who, in the early 19th century, established a system of medicine based on herbal remedies rather than the then accepted regime of bloodletting and use of minerals like mercury. There was a strong sense of rebellious democracy in Thomson's attack on the medical professionals of his day. This is reflected in Tumblety's call to "listen to the voice of reason." Thomson couched his use of herbals as what God intended and Tumblety does this as well. Finally, Thomson argued that medicine should not be out of the reach of the poor. Several of the stories in his autobiography tell of patients who paid regular physicians large fees but were not cured. Thomson cured them for free. Tumblety's comment that the "poor will be liberally treated" is part of this aspect. This was what Dr. Lyons, in 1853, referred to as the "reformed Indian vegetable practice."[5]

When coming into a new community, a doctor would need to advertise simply to let potential patients know that he was available. Further, if that doctor believed that his system of medicine was different and better than the normal one, he would want to announce that to the public. Tumblety's ad, however, goes well beyond those simple needs. Clearly, with the publication of this ad, the citizens of Toronto were notified that a new and very flamboyant personality had come to town.

Business must have been good because on December 13, 1856, Tumblety, who had not had an ad for two weeks, published a modified version of the previous ad stating his intention to stay in Toronto until May 1 instead of March 1, 1857. At this time, he had opened an office at 111 King Street, opposite St. Lawrence Hall. The location was well chosen to place him at the center of activity in Toronto. St. Lawrence Hall had been built in 1851 as a public meeting space where large events could be held. The hall was the site for many exhibitions, balls, lectures and concerts. During this period, many famous speakers lectured at the hall and it was the main location for anti-slavery meetings in Toronto. It has been described as the "social center" of Toronto. Tumblety's choice of this location not only lent him the respectability of a prominent address but exposed a variety of educated visitors to his practice.[6]

In a later but unconfirmed story, it was reported that at this time Tumblety more fully developed his public image as an "Indian herb doctor." He never claimed to be an Indian himself but rather it was reported that he had been told great medical secrets by tribal members. His particular mentor was said to be Chief Sundown, a "savage of the Plains." To add to this image, he displayed a large pair of deer antlers in front of his office, which the chief had given to him.[7]

The ad announcing his new office, with minor revisions, appeared in the *Globe* through the end of March. In its simpler version, it begins, "The Indian Herb Doctor, F. Tumblety, after traversing the United States and Canada, has concluded to make Toronto, C.W. his home for the future." It continues to tout his natural medicines but drops the reference to mercury. As in the original ad, it concludes, "the poor will be liberally considered."

Not satisfied with this already excessive means of self-promotion, Tumblety soon began another type of advertisement—the testimonial letter. One of the first of these was published on January 6, 1857, and repeated on January 10. It was reportedly written on December 9, 1856, and was addressed directly to the editor of the *Toronto Globe* with the express intent of sharing with the public the "beneficial effects of his unrivalled medicine." Despite being addressed to the editor, these letters appeared correctly under the heading "New Advertisements."

This letter was written by a professor of music named Nelson Kneass, and it is typical of the genre. It reports a major and long-term health problem, in this case a painful disease of the hip, which the regular doctors could not cure. Kneass was coerced by his wife into going to see Tumblety, about whom he was very skeptical. In a very short time, two weeks, he was entirely cured of the affliction. He published the letter both out of a feeling of gratitude to

Tumblety and to share this important information with a needful public. Throughout the 19th century, thousands of testimonial letters follow this same pattern.[8]

Without considering the truthfulness of this letter, from the perspective of our time, we can see that such a testimonial is a contrived device for garnering publicity. Yet in the early 19th century it was an effective technique. As industries went from craftspeople producing for their neighbors to factories producing for a national market, producers had to advertise their wares to the public. Testimonials represented a mixture of advertisement and personal recommendation. People relied on them the way they used to rely on their neighbors' recommendations. Not only quacks used testimonial letters, most legitimate manufacturers either published testimonials or offered to send them to the skeptical. It was a standard part of most advertising in the 19th century. With no "truth in advertising" laws or other governmental oversight, there was no guarantee that they were true and it was this loophole that was exploited by the patent medicine men.

The effectiveness of testimonial letters would be enhanced if the author was known to the readers either from their local community or on a national level. Much as a sports figure advertises athletic shoes or hot dogs on television today, a testimonial letter from a nationally known person was a key to increasing sales. Kneass fit this purpose well.

Nelson Kneass began his career in New York as a music teacher. However, he became prominent as the composer of music for the poem "Ben Bolt" in 1848 (which is mentioned in the ad). This song was immensely popular throughout the rest of the century. He went on to write a large number of other songs and to found the Kneass Opera Troupe, which toured widely in the United States and Canada. At the time he wrote the testimonial for Tumblety, he was at the height of his popularity and such an endorsement would have carried a great deal of weight with the readers of the *Globe*.

In hindsight, the testimonial from Kneass may not have been entirely unbiased. It was later reported that when Tumblety came to Toronto, he was "with a strolling company of concert or menagerie folks." As Tumblety and the Kneass Opera Troupe show up in Toronto at the same time, it is not hard to make this connection. Professor Kneass's miraculous cure may be suspect.[9]

The Kneass testimonial was soon followed by two others in February. On February 13, the *Globe* published in its New Advertisements section, under the headline "Consumption in an Advanced State Cured," a letter from I. O'Brien to the *Hamilton Spectator* of Hamilton, Ontario. The letter had been written on July 8, 1856, and details how O'Brien's son had struggled with a severe cough. The doctors had said there was nothing that could be done but Tumblety's medicines completely cured him. The veracity of these statements were sworn before D. B. Galbraith, justice of the peace in Hamilton, on August 10, 1856.

The next day, Tumblety published an even more impressive testimonial. This appeared under the headline "Death Vanquished—The Grave Defied." Miss Charlotte J. Reynolds recounted, in a letter to the doctor, how she had hurt her leg the summer before and how it had swelled and caused her great pain. "The best physicians in Toronto" could give her no relief. One told her she had "galloping consumption" and would never get better. After but two days of treatment by Dr. Tumblety, she began to feel better and soon recovered. The truth of these statements was sworn on February 9 before John Hutchinson, mayor of Toronto. There followed a list of nine local residents who could testify to Miss Reynolds' truthfulness.

When one considers a testimonial of this type, the first question that comes to mind is Are these people real? No record of Charlotte Reynolds has been found but an Asa Reynolds, listed as a tavern keeper on King Street East, is mentioned in the 1856 Toronto city directory. As she is listed as Miss Reynolds, it may be his daughter. All of the male witnesses were real and were found in the 1856 city directory. J. W. T. Green was a tinsmith working at 113 King Street East, next door to Tumblety's office. In addition, the list includes a retired colonel of artillery and a telegraph superintendent, both higher statuses, as well as tinsmiths, grocers, a clerk and a butcher. Taken together, this is probably a good cross-section of Tumblety's clientele in Toronto. The ad was a very powerful endorsement for Tumblety. Although the mayor may only have been performing his duty as a justice of the peace, being able to list him in the ad gave the doctor an air of respectability he could not otherwise hope to obtain. Also, using local, well-known citizens as witnesses provided credibility to the claims in the letter. In a small community, personal testimony would prove to be good for business.[10]

Business must have been good because in early March, Tumblety published the largest ad for any purpose seen in the *Globe* during this entire time. It took up the width of two normal columns and ran the length of the page. This ad first appeared on March 6 and ran for a week. It begins with the same material as the other ads, reporting Tumblety's fame and his desire to settle in Toronto. Twice it decries the use of mercury and extols the use of natural medicines. It lists an even larger number of diseases that can be cured by his treatment. For the first and only time, it relates that he is from Rochester, New York. This is the first recorded printing of the Rochester testimonial discussed in the last chapter. The first part of the ad includes a small poem that describes the Doctor's attitude:

> I desire your prostrate hearts to lift,
> Your bleeding wounds to cure,
> And with the treasure of nature's gift,
> Relieve the rich and poor.

The ad includes appeals to two specific groups of patients, young men and females. The appeal to young men refers to those with "hollow cheeks, pallid countenances and attenuated forms." While that addressed to females refers to "any disease peculiar to your sex." Several researchers have suggested that these are code phrases for masturbation, sexual diseases, contraception and abortion. As we have seen in his time in Rochester, he was already involved in this kind of medicine. It is reported that he was distributing at this time a pamphlet entitled "Dr. Tumblety's Private Medical Treatise" which spoke frankly about sexual issues. No title of this type is known to survive but a copy of a "Guide to the Afflicted," similar to that published in Rochester, but with Tumblety as the author, is preserved at the Toronto Public Library. Whichever it was, it was said to contain things "no parent would want his young children to peruse." This sort of reputation will soon land the doctor in a lot of trouble.[11]

Most of the rest of the ad is taken up with testimonials. The three previously mentioned testimonials are included as well as a number of new ones. John Magee swore before the mayor of London, Ontario, on April 11, 1856, that he had been cured of scurvy. Miss B. Ready (there's an interesting name) swore before the mayor of Hamilton, Ontario, on July 19, 1856, that she had been cured of a "disease peculiar to her sex." Mrs. D. Chambers swore before a justice of the peace of Hamilton, Ontario, on August 16, 1856, that she had been cured of a skin disease. Anthony Bird swore before the mayor of Brantford, Ontario, on October 27, 1856, that he had been cured of epileptic fits. John Riordan testified before the mayor of Toronto on December 23, 1856, that Tumblety had cured the incurable ulcers on his arm.

While these are typical of many such letters, there is one testimonial in this ad that deserves more attention. It is from Hamilton Hunter, editor of the London, Ontario, *Atlas*. The letter generally comments on the success of his treatments and on his "urbanity and gentlemanly character." Whether or not Hunter was a personal friend of Tumblety's cannot be determined on the present evidence. Nevertheless, he was the first of many people to comment on these qualities in the doctor's character and manners which are so out of step with the description of him growing up in Rochester.

Near the end of the ad is yet another piece of poetry extolling the Doctor's medical ability:

> Come and see for yourselves, ye lame and suffering,
> Oh! ye rheumatic and dying, come and see,
> Light shall again the fading eyes illume,
> And rosy health the pallid cheek resume,
> Thousands rescued from disease and death,
> Invoke God's blessings on Tumblety.

Finally, Dr. Tumblety opened a new branch of his practice by soliciting mail orders for his medicines. He realized that while seeing patients was profitable, getting them to send you money greatly expanded that profitability. His ad suggests that those who lived too far away to visit his office send a letter containing one dollar and he would send them the medicine with full directions for its use.

This is a very early example of a mail order fraud that will, later in the century, become very common among patent medicine makers. Dr. Reynolds had made the same claim in Rochester while Tumblety worked for him. It relies on the tendency of people who order things by mail not to demand their money back. Should a problem arise, it could be claimed that the instructions were not properly followed.[12]

On March 28, Tumblety published a new ad that clearly indicates either a delusional state or an outright attempt at fraud. It is again much larger than most ads, has the familiar graphic, and is headed "Good News for All." What makes the ad stand out even more is that it is printed not in a standard font but in a cursive style, which no other ad ever used. In the text, he announces:

> The Indian Herb Doctor, F. Tumblety, has discovered an Herb, the medical properties of which were hitherto unknown to the medical faculty, that will cure any case of Fever and Ague in twenty four hours, by applying it externally.

The likelihood of Tumblety having discovered an unknown herb is extremely slight and, even if he thought he did, an herb that by external application can have an effect on a fever is still unknown. By claiming to discover a new medicine, Tumblety could show his superiority to the regular medical practitioners and appeal to those people who followed new trends. It was an appeal which would become part of the standard pitch for medical quacks throughout the 19th century.[13]

The herb ad ran until early May, when it was replaced by an ad which was printed in the same unusual typeface but repeated the text of his original ad of December. It ran for a week and was replaced by his smallest but most common ad. This was his final version, which ran in 69 editions from May 30 through September 17 and was by far the simplest. It contains the woodcut, a brief sentence about his natural medicines and the address of his office.

The ads tell us only what Tumblety wanted the people of Toronto to know about him but we have little else to know him by. From these, we can not see him as a person or as others might have seen him. Was he a respected member of the community or was he viewed as a disreputable quack? The only evidence of this sort appears to be an unsolicited comment in the *Toronto Globe*, whose editor said "We know nothing of his method, and of the results only from the patients themselves, but there remains very little room for doubt that he has been remarkably successful in a number of cases."[14]

"From the patients themselves," we can get a snapshot of Tumblety's practice in Toronto and the surrounding area. At various times, he listed 17 testimonials dating to this period. Based on the testimonials, his practice was more used by males than females, with 12 men and only five women represented.

Only one of the women was treated for a "female problem." All but two of the patients were adults. As might be expected, he treated a variety of diseases. There were four testimonials each for consumption or cough, three for ulcers on various parts of the body and two for scurvy. The other maladies cured by the doctor were paralysis, blindness, scrofula, skin disease, female problems, cancer, epilepsy and hip pain.

In Toronto, and throughout his career, Tumblety will make good money off two sets of conditions which were the bread and butter of patent medicine in the 19th century: consumption and skin disease. Consumption was a wasting away disease, most often associated with tuberculosis. However, the vagueness of diagnoses at this time led to many false claims of consumption. Any heavy cough or congestion had the possibility of being termed consumption. There was a natural inclination on the part of patients to view their maladies with great concern and to amplify the seriousness of them. Most of these cases of "consumption" would have gotten better on their own without the treatment of any doctor. If patients were being treated by someone like Tumblety, their recovery from this deadly disease was attributed to the doctor's skill and medicines. In the same vein, poor diet and hygiene often led to skin diseases. As with the other disease, these most often cured themselves. Some quacks recognized this process but many did not. They honestly thought their medicine was doing some good. Because they were easy to treat and success was frequent, testimonials regarding these two conditions are common in patent medicine advertising.[15]

Sometimes the conditions did not get better and the patients began causing trouble. It is from incidents like this that a true picture of Tumblety's medicine emerges. During December 1856, a patient, Adolphus Binkert, who was otherwise in good health, came to Tumblety with eruptions on his face. In the office, the doctor "felt his pulse, shook his head and said, 'Poor fellow, it is all over with you and you must die very soon.'" Tumblety told Binkert that he was in the last stages of consumption. While this may seem like a severe diagnosis, it was the stock in trade of the medical quack. It was important to lure the mark in on some excuse and then "discover" that he was much sicker than he thought. Tumblety told him that he could cure him at a cost of $50 but Binkert did not have the cash. With Tumblety continuing to make dire predictions about his health, they finally agreed that the doctor would accept a gold watch, valued at $36, and a note for the rest.[16]

This expensive treatment consisted of a box of pills, a bottle of brown liquid and a set of printed directions. At the time, Tumblety also gave him a lecture about God and the devil. In several subsequent visits, he got additional medicine but the treatment did not seem to be working. When he asked the doctor about this, Tumblety asked his religion. Binkert was a Catholic and Tumblety told him that the medicine would not work unless he went to see a priest and got absolution. Soon thereafter, Binkert saw an article in a newspaper that called Tumblety "an unprincipled and wicked imposter." Angry at being duped, he went to Tumblety and demanded his watch and money back. According to Binkert, Tumblety told him he would keep the watch and make him pay the note. Because of the perceived deception, he charged Tumblety with false pretenses.

Tumblety, his accuser and their lawyers appeared before G. S. Gurnett, a police magistrate in Toronto in late March. The article that reports this hearing has an extensive section presenting Binkert's testimony. Dr. John Grant, a licensed physician, gave testimony in support of Binkert. He made a point to say that he was "perfectly satisfied" that Tumblety was not a licensed physician in the province. He reported on an examination he made of Binkert, in company with two other doctors, saying that his lungs were sound and would have been sound even before Binkert sought out Tumblety.

As part of his testimony in this case, Binkert reported on an analysis of the medicines. The pills were reportedly made of flour, sugar and cayenne pepper. The liquid was an infusion of a flower called "Lyons Teeth." There is no indication of who produced the analysis or how it was produced. While it is simplified, the purpose of the medicines was similar to that of a medicine tested in Montreal. The "Lyons Teeth" is dandelion and it functions as a laxative. The cayenne pepper is to stimulate the appetite. According to this theory of medicine, bad blood expresses itself in a number of different symptoms, skin disease being one of them. The doctor must first clean the system and then get the patient to eat regular food. As late as the 1870s, Tumblety advocated this theory as the basis of his treatment.

There is not much in the article from Tumblety's side. His lawyer, Mr. Eccles asked for a postponement until March 31, 1857, saying that evidence for the defense would be offered at that time. Tumblety was granted bail of £100 along with two sureties of £50 each from George Cary and Patrick Heaney. The outcome of this case has not been determined and it is possible that the parties made an out of court settlement.

However, Dr. John Grant was not finished with Tumblety. He filed a complaint against Tumblety for practicing physic without a license. Evidence in the case revolved around a man name Thomas Mullen who came to Tumblety, after having consulted other doctors, to be treated for general debility. Tumblety agreed to treat him for $20 and an additional $10 when he was cured. The doctor gave him the same type of pills, bottle of liquid and printed instructions that he gave his other patients. Mullen came back to Tumblety for more medicine for seven weeks. There is no mention of additional charges and it is likely that the fee included a course of treatment rather than one dose of medicines. When Mullen complained about his lungs, Tumblety had a plaster applied to his chest which cleared up the problem. On cross-examination, it was revealed that Mullen was reporting to Dr. Clark as well. This case was set to be tried at the assizes and Tumblety was given the same bail as in the previous case. Neither case seems to show up again and Tumblety continued to practice in Toronto with seemingly no hindrance.

The only other contemporary mention of Dr. Tumblety in the newspaper, outside the ads and testimonials, is in relation to an accident that occurred shortly after his arrival in Toronto. On December 6, 1856, between three and four o'clock in the afternoon, Tumblety was making his way along Wellington Street in a cutter, a one-man sleigh pulled by one horse. Some boys were running a dog sled which somehow scared Tumblety's horse, which ran off with the cutter attached. Soon Tumblety was thrown from the sleigh and the horse broke away from the cutter, dragging its whippletree behind it.

On the west side of St. Lawrence Market, a group of people were standing outside an auction house as the horse headed straight for them. Daniel O'Brien, a resident of Newmarket, saw the horse coming and moved to push a woman out of its path. He was successful in saving the woman but the horse knocked him over and the whippletree hit him in the face. He lost a considerable amount of blood and was under a doctor's care for the next few days.

Dr. Tumblety was brought before the police magistrate's court on a charge of neglect and leaving his horse unsecured on a public street. O'Brien testified about the events and his injuries. Joseph T. Kirby, Tumblety's lawyer, argued that his client was not responsible and had suffered considerable injuries of his own as a result of being thrown from the sleigh. When the horse ran away, he had no way of restraining it and the charge of neglect should not stand. The lawyer stated that although Tumblety admitted no responsibility he was willing to pay any medical expenses for O'Brien. The magistrate "thought this was a fair proposition," and dismissed the case. Tumblety was assessed £14 5s in fees and fines.[17]

One other aspect of Dr. Tumblety's medical career in Toronto has come to light. In 1856, he took Charles P. Jones as an apprentice. A one-paragraph biography of Jones, published in 1884, reports both that he stayed with Tumblety for nearly four years and that he attended the Toronto Medical Institute, graduating in 1859. It should be pointed out that Tumblety's ads refer to his office as the "Medical Institute" during 1858–1859. Jones later moved to Ohio and practiced in the community of Nevada, Ohio, for over 20 years. He was a well-respected physician, belonged to the Northwestern Medical Association and was financially successful. His association with Tumblety was proudly recorded in this biography. At least in this instance, Tumblety passed on his medical knowledge in the way that it had been passed to him.[18]

There is no way to know how Tumblety met Jones or if they had a relationship other than professional. Jones was only 21 when he met Tumblety. He had been a salesman in Cleveland before moving to Canada and studying medicine with the doctor. As we shall see, it was Tumblety's habit to surround himself with young men, many of whom he picked up by starting conversations with them and offering them a job. Jones may be the first of these young men.

Later in Ohio, Jones married the daughter of a judge and they had three children.

One account of Tumblety's approach to meeting young men was written by Lt. Col. Denison some 60 years after the event. When Denison met Tumblety he was in his late teens. He was riding home after being at the Carlton Racecourse in Toronto when Tumblety rode up behind him and began a conversation. The doctor started by praising the horse Denison was riding and they talked about horses and other subjects. Apparently, Tumblety talked a lot about himself, which he is reported to have been very fond of doing. Even after so many years, Denison commented on how Tumblety was dressed: "He was flashily dressed in a black velvet coat with side pockets, a showy waistcoat and a black velvet cap. He wore a large, gaily-colored necktie." Despite his young age (or because he was remembering it in old age), Denison saw right through Tumblety. Although Denison does not report meeting Tumblety again, he apparently kept up on the events of his life.[19]

Sometime near the end of July 1857, for unknown reasons, Tumblety began planning to move to Montreal. For two weeks in mid August, he had no ad in the *Toronto Globe*. He started advertising again on August 26 and on September 17, the last ad for the Indian Herb Doctor was published in Toronto. By this time, he had already started publishing ads in the *Montreal Pilot*, the first being on September 14, in which he reported his intention to stay in Montreal from September 1, 1857 to May 1, 1858. Despite his intention to move to Montreal, there is evidence that Tumblety did not close his Toronto office.

Beginning in June 1857 and continuing through 1858, including the time he was in Montreal, he had an ad running in the *Boston Pilot* which listed his office on King Street. This ad was very similar to those he published in Toronto, including the woodcut, and offered to send medicine to anyone for a fee. The *Pilot* was a weekly paper run by and catering to Irish Catholics in Boston. It is not known if he chose this paper for those reasons or if it was part of a much larger campaign. That Tumblety was advertising in a paper as far away as Boston suggests his mail order business was larger than previously thought and must have been quite profitable.[20]

During his stay in Toronto, Dr. Tumblety continued and expanded a successful medical practice. Regardless of the value of his treatment, people were paying him well and financially he was well established. He was getting respect from the public if not from the regular physicians. Thus far, the regular physicians were too weak to do anything against Tumblety. However, he was moving to an area where the regular physicians were of high status and well connected to the legal establishment. Dr. Tumblety was about to face the first crisis of his life.

3

Montreal Troubles
(1857–1858)

After spending almost a year in Toronto, Dr. Tumblety moved to Montreal in September 1857. While the move was only approximately 300 miles east, he was entering an entirely different cultural situation and that would soon cause him great trouble. This episode in his life was summarized in a 1993 article on the development of the medical profession in Montreal and was published before any other information about Tumblety was known.[1]

A central issue in the article is the perceived difference between Toronto and Montreal in its treatment of doctors in the early 19th century. In Toronto, the regular doctors had lost political power by associating themselves with a rebellion in the 1830s. This, coupled with the development of alternative medicines and the increase in the number of practitioners, trends noted for nearby Rochester at the same time, led to a loss of status for the regular physicians. In Montreal, however, the regular physicians had been able to establish themselves as strong supporters of the government and maintained an elite status. As part of the professional class, regular physicians played an important part in municipal politics and, with the devolution of police powers to the municipalities, were in a good position to regulate their profession. While Tumblety prospered in Toronto, he was about to meet a professional jealousy that could land him in jail for a long time.

On September 14, 1857, Tumblety began advertising in the *Montreal Pilot*. He had already secured an office on Great St. James Street and, with his assistant John Guy, had opened for business. There is no reason to believe that his business was any different or any less busy in Montreal than it was in Toronto. The ad is almost identical to his first ads in Toronto, including the small graphic of the doctor in the garden. It rails against mercury, describes the diseases he can cure, intimates that women and children are given special attention, offers advice to the poor for free and promises that he will consult by mail for a dollar. All of these claims had served him well in Toronto. This ad appeared in the *Pilot* every day from September 14 to December 22, 1857, most of the time on the front page.

33

Tumblety's advertisement seemed to have struck a sore nerve with someone. On September 16, a letter written by a person only identified as "Civis" appeared in the *Montreal Pilot* and suggested that the medical men of Montreal have the right to regulate their profession. He states that if a new doctor arrives in town without any credentials, he should be reported to the authorities. If that does not have any effect, they should find one of his patients who "has been made miserable for life by swallowing some horrible mixture." The quack could then be prosecuted and the profession upheld. The letter was dated September 14, the same day that Tumblety's ad first appeared, and was an omen of future trouble.[2]

To be truly effective at discouraging unwanted doctors, however, it would not be sufficient to simply find a patient who was harmed by some medicine. Medical mistakes were not exclusive to the alternative practitioners. The use of mercury and excessive bloodletting, the therapy used by the regular physicians, left its own wake of maimed and dead patients. Instead, the regular physicians chose to fight the battle on the basis of respectability and looked to find a way to discredit their rival. Tumblety's practice depended to a large extent on public trust and on the perception that he was not just another quack. If he could be tainted as less than respectable, his patients would disappear and the challenge to medical orthodoxy would be ended. In this type of battle, Tumblety was his own worst enemy.

It was reported that Tumbley was distributing pamphlets with remedies for various diseases but particularly for those associated with females, the implication being that they were recipes for contraceptive or abortion drugs. Further, he was reported to have actually administered these abortion drugs to several female patients in Toronto. No evidence of this has come to light, but it was a powerful canard. The administration of drugs to a woman with the intent to induce a miscarriage had been considered a felony in Canada since at least 1841. Conviction carried a sentence of at least seven years hard labor in the penitentiary. However, no one seems to have been prosecuted under this law in Montreal or anywhere else. Whether the rumors were true or not, this was the battleground that was chosen.[3]

Less than five days after the letter in the *Montreal Pilot*, a man named Simard visited Tumblety in his office. He later testified that he asked the doctor if he could get medicine that would cause a miscarriage. Tumblety reportedly stated he could provide such medicine but wanted to know whether the girl was a Catholic or Protestant. Simard assured the doctor that she was Protestant and they agreed on a price of $20 for the medicine. Simard left, promising to be back the next day to pick it up. Detective Simard of the Metropolitan Police had just set the trap which would soon ensnare Tumblety.[4]

The following morning, Simard returned and stated that the girl was nervous about taking the medicine and wanted the doctor to be present when she did. Simard left to bring the girl to Tumblety. He went to the police magistrate's office to make final plans to entrap Tumblety. At the office, Simard met with Charles Joseph Coursol, the police magistrate, a Dr. Jones, probably the city coroner, and Philomene Dumas, a 17-year-old prostitute whom Simard had recruited for the plot. Dumas would later state that she had only been in Montreal for a month yet Simard knew her from two visits he made to the brothel where she worked. There is no indication whether those visits were in his professional capacity or not.[5]

The plot to destroy Tumblety may have begun with the "Civis" letter but it could never have been carried out without the aid of the supposedly neutral Coursol, the police magistrate. It was in his office that the plotters met beforehand and it was before him that Tumblety would be examined. To understand Coursol's position in this affair, we need to know something of his life.[6]

Charles Joseph Coursol was 38 years old at the time and was well connected in the provincial hierarchy by both politics and family relations. He had a history of direct action in political matters. In 1841, he led a mob of 600 armed men in support of the Reform candidate and again in 1849 was at the head of a mob defending his political ally. He has been described as "desperately ambitious" and "attracted by the more physical, organizational side of the struggle for responsible government." In short, he was an activist who clearly felt that the end justified the means. He had been police magistrate since February 1856 and took that duty very seriously. Whether he was the originator of the plot can never be known, but he clearly supported it.

In the magistrate's office, Dr. Jones instructed Dumas on what to say and then she and Simard set off for Tumblety's office. When they arrived, Dumas told Tumblety that she was pregnant and he asked her a number of questions about her condition. Sometime during the conversation, Tumblety reportedly told Dumas that the easiest way for her to get over her "condition" was to get Simard to marry her. The doctor gave her a bottle of medicine and a box of pills. She drank some of the liquid, Simard paid Tumblety $20 and the couple left. As they were leaving, Tumblety reportedly said, "Come back in a fortnight, and you will find all has disappeared." Shortly thereafter, Tumblety was arrested and brought before Coursol for an examination. Not surprisingly, considering Coursol's involvement, he was denied bail and put in jail. With the law conspiring against him and the testimony of Simard and Dumas, it seemed certain that Tumblety would be convicted.[7]

To defend himself, Tumblety hired two of the most prominent lawyers in Montreal, Bernard Devlin and Lewis Drummond. Devlin was born in Ireland and studied medicine with his uncle and later in Dublin. When he arrived in Quebec in 1844, the medical board would not allow him to practice as he was a minor (he was 20 at the time). Having experienced the closed nature of medicine in Quebec, Devlin never went back to it. Instead, he became a journalist and a lawyer. By 1847, he was recognized as a skilled lawyer and soon had a large practice. Devlin was also active in politics, particularly in organizing the Irish in Montreal. At the time of this trial, he was actively forging an alliance between the Irish and the Reform candidates, which would soon result in a change of government. Lewis Drummond had for a long time been on the other side from Devlin. He had been attorney general for Canada East until 1856. When he was not appointed co-premier after the election of 1856, he resigned and began to actively work for the opposition. He would become attorney general in the new government in 1858. The involvement of these two men has been seen as a reflection of the political nature of the prosecution of Tumblety.[8]

There can be no doubt that these two lawyers were well-connected political activists who would soon help to shake the Canadian establishment. However, it is likely that their connections have been overstated in this case. A review of the newspaper reports of legal action at the Queen's bench in September and October 1857 reveals only a handful of defense attorneys, of which Devlin and Drummond are the most frequently listed. During this term, they not only defended Tumblety against these charges but also a wide range of people against charges of forgery, assault, murder and receiving stolen goods. For any particular case, there was a better than even chance that Devlin, Drummond or both would be listed as defense attorneys. Given this, there is no reason that the case was in any way different than any of the others and we should not overstate the political angle.

On September 26, Tumblety had his first hearing in front of Coursol. Tumblety's lawyers painted a sinister, and most likely true, picture of conspiracy and entrapment. Devlin expressed outrage about a "doctor, pretending to respectability, closeted with a prostitute, and in place too which ought to be the Sanctuary of Justice, planning the destruction of a fellow man." The bail hearing and, ultimately the entire case were based on two issues: whether Tumblety promised that the drugs he sold would produce an abortion and what those drugs were.[9]

Simard and Dumas testified, as they had previously, that Tumblety was asked for drugs to produce an abortion and sold them medicine for that purpose. However, John Guy, Tumblety's assistant, testified that he was present during the discussion and reported that the doctor said the medicine was for headaches, nervousness and backaches. With diametrically opposite testimony, the issue came down to who was more believable.

The physical evidence, the drugs that Tumblety sold, produced no clearer result. John Birks, a chemist hired by the government, testified that he had been given a box of pills and a bottle of medicine by a "Dr. Jones." He said that the bottle contained black hellebore, an herb that in large doses is a poison and a violent narcotic. In smaller doses it was used to increase menstrual flow. This, plus its toxic nature, was thought to produce miscarriages. The pills were said to contain oil of savine and cantharides which acted in a similar fashion to produce toxic results which could lead to an abortion.

Devlin challenged this evidence on several counts. He argued that Birks had relied on smell alone to determine the composition of the bottled medicine. This does not seem to have been rebutted. He further stated that there was no way to know if the bottle passed to Birks by Dr. Jones was the same as that sold to Simard by Tumblety. He implied that there may have been a switch made between Simard's getting the medicine and Dr. Jones presenting it to Birks. Finally, he called to the stand the druggist who made the pills for Tumblety. He identified the pills and testified they were composed mostly of aloes, with smaller amounts of steel cast soap, gamboges, colocynth, gentian, mandrake, capsicum, and oil of peppermint. Specifically, he said they did not contain oil of savine and cantharides, as Birks had testified.[10]

The composition of the pills, as described by the druggist, tells a lot about what they were intended to treat. The aloes, gamboges, colocynth and mandrake all have strong laxative properties. Together these items make up almost 70 percent of the recipe. Most 19th-century medicines had laxatives in them if for no other reason than they convinced the patient that the medicine was being effective. The oil of peppermint and the steel cast soap are used for relieving pain, particularly abdominal pain, which the first set of drugs tends to cause, but also headache pain. Finally, the capsicum stimulates saliva and appetite while the gentian stimulates menstrual flow and appetite. Stimulants for the appetite made up over a quarter of the pill recipe. According to the ingredients, these pills would not produce an abortion but would cure headaches and abdominal pains, as the doctor's assistant had said they were intended to do.[11]

Kenneth Campbell, the assistant druggist who made the pills, further testified that he did not make the liquid for Tumblety. However, he did examine some fluid said to have been analyzed by Birks. He testified that he could find no black hellebore, by either smell or taste, in the liquid. The prosecution did not ask any questions of this witness so his testimony ended.

Using the confused evidence of the nature of the medicines, Devlin made a case that the police had conspired with unnamed persons and falsified evidence. Despite these arguments, Coursol, who was involved in the trap to begin with, decided that there was enough evidence to warrant a trial and that Tumblety, as a stranger in the community, was a flight risk. He denied bail and sent him back to jail.

Devlin immediately filed for a writ of *habeas corpus* at the Queen's bench and on September 28, Justice Aylwin decided that the case was strong and denied Tumblety bail for the second time. In his printed opinion, he was afraid that because of the publicity, Tumblety would have many women flocking to him for similar services were he allowed to continue to practice. His reasons for doing so suggest the gravity of the crime which Tumblety was charged with:

To protect society, therefore, and to take care that such publicity should not be taken advantage of, he considered it his duty to keep the prisoner where he was until the day of his trial. If, indeed, his drugs and instruments could be seized, and the possibility of his repeating the offense wherewith he stood charged, could be thus made certain of, if a policeman could be stationed at his door to interrogate females seeking his aid, and see for what disease he treated them, the man might fitly be allowed to go at large.

Not to be deterred, Devlin filed his request for a writ with another justice of the Queen's bench, Justice Gray, on the same day. On September 30, a hearing was held and the *Montreal Pilot* reported Devlin's speech in detail. He again made an impassioned plea against the conspiracy and flung the respectability issue back at the accusers:

He believed that during his Honour's long professional experience, he had never before known of professional medical men in Lower Canada, and particularly men of presumed respectable standing and sworn officers of Justice associating themselves with the debased patrons and debauched inmates of a low brothel for so ignoble a purpose as has been attempted in this case.

Devlin went on to ask the question why, if the accused was a quack, he was not prosecuted for practicing without a license? Instead the conspirators set up a trap to induce an innocent man to commit a serious crime. Next, he reviewed the conflicting testimony about the nature of the medicines and the intentions of their prescription. He ended by saying that with this much uncertainty, Tumblety should, at least, be granted bail. These tactics were sufficient to convince Justice Gray, who granted Tumblety bail on October 1, 1857. The hearing before the grand jury was set for October 24, 1857. After a ten-day stay in jail, Tumblety was once again a free man.[12]

The Montreal press treated Tumblety's case in a sensational fashion. Numerous editorials were published covering a wide range of opinion. All were united in the idea that sellers of such drugs should be prosecuted. Some felt the police tactics were perfectly acceptable while others raised questions about entrapment. On October 2, the *Montreal Pilot* published an extensive editorial which commented on all sides of the case and probably summarizes the feelings of most people at the time. It begins by mentioning that public opinion was highly divided. The idea that an innocent man would be enticed by the authorities to commit a crime is described as "generally as dangerous as it is immoral." But the editor goes on to ask if there are any circumstances where it might be appropriate. He suggests that if the London police had word of a plot to assassinate the Queen, they would not wait till the deed was done but would take active measures to trap the plotters. Next he goes on to report that Coursol had word that Tumblety had sold drugs for abortion in Toronto and that Tumblety's pamphlet had immoral advice in it. Given these supposed facts, the *Pilot* said that the police were justified in laying a trap. Expressing a certain amount of justified skepticism, the editor commented:

There is strong evidence that it was given for the purpose of procuring abortion, and it requires some faith to suppose that he charged a person in the humbler walks of life twenty dollars for a few pills and a draught to cure a temporary pain in the back.[13]

As Devlin argued in court, this dispute was about respectability and Tumblety began a defense in the media. During his ten days in jail, his main ad was published in six of the possible editions. On September 30, he began publishing in Montreal many of his earlier testimonials that had appeared in the *Toronto Globe*. From this point on, there will hardly be a day when some testimonial to Dr. Tumblety does not appear in the newspapers. However, this was part of his normal business practice. When coming to a new place, he would begin with ads announcing who he was. Within a few days he would begin to publish testimonials. The normal process had been disrupted by his sudden arrest and time in jail. An unexplained and curious pattern is noted in the testimonials. Although he got testimonials from citizens of Montreal dated as early as October 4, none of these were published until December. The ads from October and November were all from Toronto or earlier in his career.

Unlike his earlier practice, during October, Tumblety published a large number of testimonials not to his cures but to his character. Clearly, he was trying to influence the people who would eventually sit on the jury and decide if he should be indicted. In the next few weeks, many columns of print were used to publish notices from at least 12 Canadian newspapers in Brantford, London, Paris, Woodstock, Hamilton and Toronto which all reported that Tumblety was a gentleman and an excellent physician. These were editorial notices published by the papers themselves, not advertisements paid for by Tumblety. However, the fact that Tumblety had spent so much money advertising in their papers should not be forgotten. Typical of these is an editorial published in the Woodstock *Sentinel*:

> We have much pleasure in intimating to our readers, in town and country, that Dr. F. Tumblety has taken rooms in Mr. Norton's hotel, in this town, where he intends to stay for two weeks. His unparalleled success in the treatment of those diseases, generally considered incurable, has caused and sustained for him the reputation of being a gentleman well skilled in his profession and the most successful medical practitioner of the age.[14]

Probably the most important newspaper editorial appeared in the *Montreal Pilot* on October 21. It reported that Tumblety continued a successful practice and directed readers to testimonials in the paper. The editor added, "We can ourselves testify to another instance where a young lady, far gone in consumption, ... by the treatment of the Doctor is now well." This endorsement came from a paper which had editorialized, barely three weeks earlier, that Tumblety either cheated Dumas or intended to cause her a miscarriage! But he was advertising heavily and business was always good. Such apparently unsolicited testimony as this was bound to have an effect on the populace.[15]

While waiting for the Grand Jury hearing, Tumblety showed up in the newspapers one more time in one of those coincidences that make life so unpredictable. On October 10, the *Pilot* reported, under the title "Ran Away," that Tumblety had been involved in an accident. He and his student were proceeding down Notre Dame Street in a buggy when something scared the horse and Tumblety lost control. The buggy eventually hit some wood and broke its axle. The doctor and his student were thrown into the street and he suffered a slight injury. Who should be passing by but C. J. Coursol, the police magistrate, who then assisted them. It must have been an interesting meeting between Tumblety and the man responsible for having him thrown in jail. The reference to Tumblety's student suggests that he was continuing his role as teacher for medical students. The doctor seems to have had really poor control of his horses since a similar incident had already been reported from his stay in Toronto.[16]

While Tumblety was boosting his image in the papers, the prosecution was readying its case. Stung by Devlin's attack on their evidence, Sir Henry Driscoll, Queen's counsel, arranged to have a professional analysis completed on Tumblety's medicines. On October 3, 1857, a bottle of liquid and a box of pills were delivered to Professor Larue, of Laval University, by M. Delille, grand constable of Montreal. Larue was described as a professor of legal medicine, toxicology and hygiene. Mindful of Devlin's questions about the chain of evidence, both Larue and Delille signed their names to the evidence and then locked it in an iron case. Larue went to great lengths to prove that the medicine he analyzed was the medicine that was delivered to him and that there was no chance of contamination.[17]

The results of the analysis were mostly negative. The pills contained a high proportion of iron and Larue ruled out the significant presence of any other minerals, metals or acids. He agreed with earlier reports that there was cayenne pepper in the pills. He took some of the medicine and reported no ill effects. Dr. Larue said that given the state of chemistry at the time, it was not possible to determine chemically the identity of organic substances in the medicines. In his report, there was no indication that either the pills or the liquid could cause an abortion.

More importantly, for our purposes, Larue described in detail the way the medicines were packaged and what they looked like. He reported that the bottle was a vial containing about two ounces of liquid. When he received it, it was stoppered with a cork but not sealed. There was a white label on the bottle but he did not describe what it said. The liquid was reddish brown in color and had a sugary, unpleasant taste. There were ten pills in a white cardboard box. Each of the pills was about five grains in weight and greenish yellow in color. He said they were round, well made and smelled of mint. When broken, the pills had a homogeneous paste of a reddish brown color with distinct small red grains. These grains he tasted and identified as cayenne pepper. He described the taste as very bitter, a little sugary and very hot to the tongue, requiring him to, "rinse [his] mouth several times to get rid of it, and it was only by constantly applying cold water to the tongue that [he] managed to make it stop." These two medicines, the bottle of liquid and the box of pills, would remain the basic therapy of Dr. Tumblety over the next few years.

The Grand Jury hearing commenced on Friday, October 23, 1857, before a panel of 18 jurors. For all of the sensation the case caused, the result seems underreported. On October 24, the *Pilot* simply said, "The Grand Jury returned to-day a 'No Bill' in the case of Dr. Tumblety." Similarly, the *Toronto Globe* repeated the same message on October 27, without further elaboration. Apparently, the papers had decided this was no longer newsworthy.[18]

While the papers were ready to let it go, Tumblety needed to rehabilitate his image. He continued to publish testimonials to both his cures and his character. On October 30, he published an address to the citizens of Montreal which reflects his thoughts about the case:

FELLOW CITIZENS:

In Consequence of the foul and criminal conspiracy by which it was sought to ruin my character and degrade me in your estimation, I have felt it my duty to appeal to those who have had ample opportunity of judging my conduct as a private citizen and as a medical practitioner...

The indictment of the conspirators, as you are aware, was rejected by the Grand Jury, although I should have wished it otherwise, so as to have given me the opportunity of fully exposing the infamous designs of my accusers and the utter worthlessness of their characters.[19]

In the same light, Tumblety solicited and received character references from several groups of people. In a testimonial dated October 9, 1857, 53 citizens of Toronto praised him as a respectable and legitimate physician. Previous research has demonstrated that the men who signed this testimonial were primarily non-professional middle-class individuals, including such professions as merchant, grocer, printer, hotel keeper, shoemaker and bookseller. These were the type of people who were his main clientele. It is also not surprising that many of them have addresses listed near his Toronto office and probably did non-medical business with him. They said:

We consider him a gentleman in every sense of the word. He enjoys the reputation in the art of healing the sick by means exceedingly simple and effective. He has been extensively patronized and many of his patients speak very highly of his ability in the practice of his profession.

A more relevant character reference came on October 10 from a Toronto business familiar with Tumblety's medicine:

Dr. Francis Tumblety has been in the habit of purchasing medicines at the store of Lyman, Brothers & Co., since he came to this city, and has got nothing from them specially calculated to produce abortion.

Since his residence in this city he has had a very successful practice, and I have never heard of anything prejudicial to his character, and do not think he would be guilty of the charge preferred against him in Montreal.

The letter is signed by James C. Thomson. Below his name is a subscription from Lyman, Brothers & Co. which identifies Thomson as the "principal assistant in the dispensary department" and says his testimony is reliable. Lyman, Brothers & Co. was a major importer of "drugs, chemicals, medicines perfumery, etc." located at 106 King Street, a few doors away from Tumblety's office.

Following his acquittal, Tumblety continued his practice as before. His main ad was published every day and he kept various testimonials before the public. It has been suggested that while Tumblety was acquitted, the bad publicity from the trial ruined his practice and forced him to leave Montreal in January. Based on his advertising, it is hard to believe this hypothesis. There were 33 testimonials that Tumblety published from Montreal patients. If we look at the dates of the testimonials, we can see a clear trend. In October and November, he had 10 and 9 testimonials respectively. In December, there were 13 testimonials. No doubt these are self-serving promotions, but they do indicate a steady flow of patients.

There is a distinct difference in the Montreal testimonials after his acquittal. Prior to the trial, including his time in Toronto, the testimonials refer to the failure of the "Medical Faculty" or the "physicians" to treat a specific patient. They do not mention any doctors by name. Following Tumblety's run-in with Montreal's medical establishment, he was ready to name names. One testimonial, dated April 6, 1857, but published first on October 30, lists three Toronto doctors—Drs. Hodder, Buchanan and Widmer—as being unable to cure a patient whom Tumblety easily cured. These doctors were prominent members of their community and founders of both the Toronto Hospital and the Medical School. Another testimonial, dated December 10, 1857, mentions a Montreal doctor named Howard. Finally, a testimonial printed on February 6, 1858, reports: "...was told three years ago by Dr. Sutherland, of Great St. James Street, that my complaint was hereditary and could never recover: but twelve days ago I called on Dr. F. Tumblety.... I am now a great deal better." In Sutherland's case, there may have been a personal motive—he had testified against Tumblety before the Grand Jury. These testimonials represent one of the few times that Tumblety took on the regular physicians by name.[20]

The trial testimony provides several important insights on Tumblety as a doctor and on the kind of treatment he offered. In an earlier chapter, Tumblety's medical training was discussed. It was informal at best and did not include class work or a degree. This seems to have been a sore point with Tumblety and he seems to have purchased a degree from one of the many diploma mills. One of the Montreal newspapers reported that Tumblety claimed to have a medical degree from the University of Paris. It is possible that Tumblety made this claim but it is not repeated in any other paper at the time. The lack of a formal medical education would be a problem throughout Tumblety's life.[21]

The testimony also shows the development of the doctor's therapy for the first time. Prior to this, his ads and testimonials usually mention his herbal medicines but do not elaborate on what they were or how they were used. Occasionally, they refer to a bottle or draught of medicine. The trial testimony refers to a bottle of medicine and a box of pills. These will become known as "Dr. Tumblety's Vegetable Remedies," and will receive prominent notice in the next few years. It is possible that Tumblety was trying to establish his own brand of patent medicine but his itinerant lifestyle made this unsuccessful.

There is an interesting footnote to Tumblety's abortion case. After the verdict, Devlin, one of the doctor's attorneys, gave him a bill that asked £125 for services rendered. Tumblety considered this an outrageous price and refused to pay it. On November 2, 1857, Devlin sued Tumblety and the case was heard in the Superior Court, with Drummond, Tumblety's other lawyer, defending him. Devlin alleged that, in addition to activities for which fixed charges were used, filing writs, etc., his consultations with his client were valuable and he deserved to be compensated for this advice. In part, the total was based on the fact that Tumblety was a wealthy man. He claimed that Tumblety had only given him £25 and wanted another £100. For his part, Tumblety claimed to have paid Devlin £32 10s and deposited with the court another £17 10s to bring the total up to £50, which is what he considered a fair price for the services.[22]

The court found that it could not put a price on intellectual property but that it was not a good idea to set charges based on the supposed wealth of the client. In the end, it advised lawyers to make a contract for services on the basis of a set fee before taking a case. In this particular case, the court found for Devlin but accepted the total of £50 as a fair price. As Tumblety had not proved the payment of £32 and Devlin said that he only received £25, the court required Tumblety to make up the difference and to pay about £5 in costs. This was an important decision which shaped the lawyer-client relationship in Canada for the rest of the century.

It is important to note that throughout the proceedings, everyone admitted that Tumblety was a wealthy man. This is only two years after he left Rochester to begin his practice. Within that short time, he seems to have become very successful and well paid.

At least two other events indicate some of Tumblety's impact on Montreal. The first occurred in November during the annual Montreal Hunt Club races. The Hunt Club was founded in 1828 to foster fox hunting and horse racing. It was a prestigious institution and the *Montreal Pilot* prominently reported the hurdle races on November 19. The second or "green" hurdle race was for new horses. There were three entries and one was named Tumblety. No owner is listed but it must have been entered either by the doctor or one of his friends. The horse was ridden by "Mr. Macdougall," who was a celebrated Montreal jockey. At the first hurdle the horse balked but soon recovered and reportedly took the rest of the jumps "in great style." It was close right up to the end but

"Tumblety" prevailed. Given Tumblety's lifelong penchant for both good horses and self-promotion, the horse may have been his.[23]

While it is not possible to directly associate Tumblety with the horse race, the other incident shows his direct involvement, if only to decline the honor. Late in 1857, Montreal was preparing for an important election and the Irish community, long feeling underrepresented, decided it should field a candidate for parliament. Montreal was entitled to three representatives and the Irish declared that one of those should be from their community. A meeting of Irish electors was held in Bonaventure Hall on December 1, 1857, to select a candidate. Mr. Thomas D'Arcy McGee was selected. In his acceptance speech McGee said that he did not want to be just a sectional candidate and would represent the interest of Montreal in general. He went on to win the election and played a major part in establishing the modern Canadian government.[24]

Not all of the Irish Catholics supported McGee and they sought another candidate. As early as December 3, there were rumors that Tumblety was going to be asked to run against McGee. The Montreal papers reported on December 5 that Tumblety had received a petition from numerous electors to run in opposition to McGee. By December 8, Tumblety reported that while he was honored to be considered, he could not accept the nomination. This was probably one of the wisest things he ever did. The *Montreal Pilot* reported that at the December 1 meeting where Magee was nominated, "Sharp threats were held out to all Irishmen who should differ from the decision of the meeting and so split up the Irish interest."[25]

Ad for Tumblety's practice published in the *Montreal Pilot* in 1857. This was the title of a full-page ad that Tumblety published to increase his respectability after his arrest for selling abortion drugs. It was full of testimonials from Canadian newspaper editors praising his medical skill and identifying him as a gentleman.

This incident is often seen as another example of Tumblety's self-promotion, yet the evidence suggests otherwise. There was an active group in the Irish community that was in opposition to McGee and looking for a candidate. From the newspaper accounts, it appears that a petition was delivered to Tumblety asking him to run. At least part of the community must have thought he had a chance to win. This is another indication of the status that Tumblety had achieved in Canada

When and why Tumblety left Montreal is not at all certain. An earlier researcher suggested that he was disgraced by the trial and that patent medicine advertising provided the last blow. However, his flow of patients seems to have maintained its previous level. Since numerous citizens were willing to make him their candidate in the election, he does not seem particularly disgraced. On December 21, 1857, Tumblety published his largest and most impressive ad. It comprised an entire page and had at the top a banner headline: "News to the Afflicted!!! Certificates from the Citizens of Montreal to Dr. Tumblety." This ad contained 32 dated testimonials spanning October through December 1857. Of these, there are 9 dated to both October and November but there are 14 dated in December. This is an indication of an increasing practice rather than a shamed and disgraced one.[26]

Another possible reason for Tumblety's exit from Montreal was an affair stemming from a satirical theater performance. James B. Prior performed a skit at the Theater Royal where he parodied Tumblety's appearance and profession. It is reported he dressed in a very long "claw hammer" and that Tumblety's own dog had been enticed onto the stage with him. He sang a comic song of which Tumblety was the main topic. The beginning of the song was said to be:

> I am the famous medicine man
> My name is Tumble Tie
> And I can cure all diseases
> In the twinkling of an eye

Unlike his response to a later, more famous performance, Tumblety is said to have taken more direct action. He hired a couple of toughs to beat up the actor. When they tried to surprise him, the theater's property man joined in and they sent the toughs running. According to a report published in 1888, arrests followed and Tumblety slipped out of town. There is very little evidence that this actually happened, but Tumblety was shifting his base back to Toronto.

It appears that Tumblety intended to maintain a presence in both Montreal and Toronto. After an absence of three months, his ads begin appearing in Toronto on December 19. This is two days before his biggest and most detailed Montreal ad. It is interesting to note that his Toronto address did not change. It is possible that assistants carried it on while he was away. Reportedly, Tumblety was in Toronto by January 2, 1858. His testimonials continued to run in Montreal through January and early February. The last one occurs on February 12, 1858. Interestingly, while there was occasionally a testimonial in the Toronto papers after this date, his ads there stop at about the same time. Whether he maintained an office in Montreal during this time is uncertain but his emphasis certainly shifted back to Toronto.

The *Montreal Pilot* provided one parting shot at Tumblety. It published a satiric poem on January 4 with the title of "Carrier's Address." Supposedly written by a newspaper boy, the poem reviewed the events of the previous year, including the Crimean War and the Sepoy Rebellion. It then went on to discuss the election and to lambaste another paper, the *Montreal Witness*, for its switch of allegiance. The editor, John Dougall, was a noted temperance leader and rabid Protestant but he and his paper supported the radical candidates, including McGee, in the election, much to the annoyance of the *Pilot*. The poem describes Dougall as reeling from the smell of alcohol and Rome (the Irish) and invokes Tumblety's name because of his many cures:

> When, by good fortune, came round Tumblety
> Beheld the excited crowd, and quick drew sigh:
> He felt the pulse, then scan'd his tongue and face
> Look'd wise, and then exclaimed—a hopeless case:
>
> •••
>
> Ah! lucky doctor you—the prince of quacks—
> Guess'd John's disease, and raised him off his back;
> Quick he improves and shows his hearty thanks,
> By jumping headlong into Luther's ranks.[27]

4

—ↄ◍ↄ—

Back in Toronto
(1858–1859)

It appears that Dr. Tumblety came back to a well-established practice in Toronto. Although there had been no advertisements in the Toronto newspapers over the past six months, the ad which appeared on December 19, 1857, mentions that his office is at 111 King Street East, where it had been before he left. Mail orders had been sent to this office during his entire sojourn in Montreal.

Despite his recent troubles, Tumblety came back to Toronto full of confidence and the next month would see the greatest development of his medical enterprise, including, perhaps his attempt to portray himself as a legitimate practitioner. The first significant change was that he became simply Dr. F. Tumblety. There was no longer any mention of "the great Indian herb doctor." Perhaps the Montreal experience taught him the value of respectability and an association with the medical profession. For whatever reason, all previous references to Native American medical knowledge were removed from his ads. His first production begins with the headline: "Wonderful Cures by Dr. Tumblety." It goes on to list a host of diseases that his medicine can cure and most of these are the same as in earlier ads.[1]

Prominent in this ad, about in the center, is a headline in bold type: "Dr. Tumblety's Vegetable Compound." This is the patent medicine that he began to develop in Montreal and that was now the centerpiece of his advertising campaign. Below the headline is a quote proclaiming "its efficacy has been fair tested and its virtues pronounced unparalleled." The medicine was put up in bottles in "highly concentrated form" and was for sale in three sizes: 25 cents, 50 cents and one dollar. The medicine was accompanied by printed directions. It is unfortunate that no example of these instructions seems to have survived. The ad reports that the compound was for sale at the doctor's office but could be sent by freight anywhere in the world. One wonders if this is the same bottled medicine that Detective Simard paid $20 for in Montreal. With this ad, Tumblety was ready to carry on his old practice but also to participate in the rapidly growing patent medicine business. The "Wonderful Cures" ad ran for about a week.

His next ad appeared on December 24 under the headline, "The Only Sure Remedy." It features the woodcut, used previously in Toronto, and combines it with the text from the previous ad, including the list of diseases and the description of the Vegetable Compound. To this is added the headline, "Dr. Tumblety's Vegetable Pills." Here is the second part of the therapy offered in Montreal. The pills are described as cathartic and purifying and were available for 25 cents or 50 cents a box.[2]

In keeping with the doctor's new image, the last part of the ad reports that these remedies are not crude and untried but rather the result of science, skill and experience. It goes on to state that "hundreds of Physicians now use them and acknowledge them to be the most scientific and wholesome preparations ever offered to the public." They could be had either wholesale or retail. The call to science is again part of a change in how Tumblety promotes his medicine. Earlier in Toronto, he relied on the Thomasonian tradition of secret Native American knowledge and opposition to the medical establishment. He took his first steps away from this tradition when he claimed to have discovered an unknown herb and to have tested its medical properties. Soon, he would be calling himself an "eclectic" physician who relied on science and testing as opposed to folklore. In the traditional sense an eclectic physician used the best of both natural and regular therapies. There is no evidence that Tumblety ever used anything but vegetable remedies. Nonetheless, this was the image he portrayed through his ads. The "Sure Remedy" ad ran almost every day through late December and January.

On January 15, along with the "Sure Remedy" ad, Tumblety published another ad with an elaborate border that began with the headline: "A Card— A Public Invitation to All Who Suffer Pain." The border was unlike anything else in the newspaper and, even today, immediately draws the eye of the reader to that part of the page. It extols the virtue of Dr. Tumblety's Vegetable Compound for the immediate relief of pain and reports that "if you are suffering any acute pain, this Vegetable Compound is warranted to stop it before you leave his office." This must have been amazing stuff to be so effective. It ends with a piece of poetry which he had used before in Toronto and again in Montreal. The ad ran with the "Sure Remedy" ad through the end of January.[3]

While his new image was being honed and polished in Toronto, the mail order ads in the *Boston Pilot* continued to reflect the old persona. They did not specifically mention any patent medicines but continued to simply say that "medicines" would be sent. While the Toronto ads show that Tumblety was trying on a new image, the mail order ads show that he was not fully committed to it.[4]

During this time, Tumblety published very few testimonials. Only three were seen in the *Toronto Globe*, on January 22, February 6 and March 6, 1858. For most of February and March, there were no ads of any kind. It was at this time that he made his first recorded trip back to his boyhood home in Rochester. It was a very different Frank Tumblety who entered the city on March 11, 1858. The *Rochester Daily Union and Advertiser* reported, "The celebrated Dr. Tumblety, one of the most famous characters who has figured in recent Canadian history, has arrived in this city today." Whether this was a paid notice or not cannot be determined.[5]

People who had known him earlier were surprised by his success. W. C. Streeter, a canal boat captain who knew Tumblety when he was growing up, later described an encounter with the doctor at this time:

> He returned to Rochester as a great physician and soon became the wonder of the city. He wore a light fur overcoat that reached to his feet and had a dark collar and cuffs, and he was always followed by a big greyhound.... When I met him on his return, having known him quite well as a boy, I said, "Hello, Frank, how d'ye do?" and he merely replied "Hello, Streeter," and passed on.[6]

Captain Streeter was clearly upset by this apparent snub from Tumblety. He attributed it to the doctor's becoming "very aristocratic" during his time in Canada. Streeter was correct in his assessment, even if he did not fully understand the implication. Tumblety had transformed himself into a medical professional and tried hard to be accepted into respectable society. He certainly did not want to bring up his origins or his association with the canal boats. Tumblety had changed but Streeter had not.

His stay in Rochester was brief and he soon returned to Toronto. On March 24, he published two new testimonials under the headline, "Most Remarkable Cures, Let the Sick Rejoice for Immediate Relief Can Be Obtained by Using Dr. Tumblety's Vegetable Compound and Pill." About a month later, on April 20, 1858, Tumblety began a new phase of his ad campaign. In the Special Notices section, the *Toronto Globe* published a testimonial to the doctor's herbal medicines. However, it is the description of the business that is most striking: "Everlasting fame belongs to the 'MEDICAL INSTITUTE,' No. 111 King-street, east, Toronto and its successful principle, F. Tumblety, M. D." This passage contains two elements that are vital to understanding what Tumblety was trying to achieve.[7]

In the battle for respectability, appearances were more important than substance. It is unlikely that any major change was made in Tumblety's office or practice. However, giving it a more prestigious name lent it an air of greater respectability. Patients no longer called at the doctor's office but rather at the "Medical Institute." The term "Institute" carried with it meanings of science and education. It implied an organization dedicated to these things. The use of this term may also imply that Tumblety had several associates in this practice. Someone had to have kept the Toronto office open while he was in Montreal. Later sources suggest that he opened branch offices in Montreal and Quebec. These would have to be staffed as well. In any case, the "Medical Institute" represents a major part of Tumblety's new strategy.

The second important aspect of this passage is Tumblety's use of the abbreviation "M.D." for the first time. From the beginning, he had called himself a doctor but the use of these letters implied a greater degree of training and education. It advertised that he had attended a medical college, completed a course of study and received a medical degree. This is part of Tumblety's attempt to move from being perceived as a quack to a more secure place in the medical community. The term "M.D." occurs in only two ads, the testimonial dated March 6 and the Medical Institute ad of April 20. In the first case, it was in the salutation of a letter written to the doctor and he could not be held responsible for it. However, in the April 20 ad, he claimed a medical degree for himself.

In his rush to become a "regular physician," Tumblety was courting disaster. His presence was already resented by the medical faculty. This claim to the title "M.D." may have set off a legal reaction. George S. Gurnett, former mayor of Toronto and longtime police magistrate, said that Tumblety was again brought before him on a charge of practicing medicine without a license. In his defense, Tumblety presented a diploma from a Philadelphia medical college as evidence of his training.[8]

Six months earlier, during his trial in Montreal, Tumblety had claimed to have a degree from the University of Paris. Since that time, he seemed to have acquired a diploma from an American medical college. It is unlikely that Tumblety did any studying in Philadelphia. The chronology does not permit him even the time to complete the abbreviated course of study offered by some institutions. However, then, as now, there were many way to obtain a medical degree. Philadelphia in the early 19th century was home to a number of "diploma mills," where, for a fee, one could get a certificate stating that the named individual had completed a particular course of study. Prominent among these was the Eclectic Medical College of Pennsylvania, run by Dr. Joseph R. Buchanan. As Tumblety later claimed to be an eclectic physician, his degree may have been from this school.[9]

The college was chartered in 1850 and trained eclectic physicians on site throughout its history. In the 1850s, a course of lectures ran three to four months with five or six lectures a day. The lectures covered a wide range of medical issues, all from the eclectic perspective and against the regular physicians. The education that students received was a respectable, if biased, one. To graduate, a student had to prove that he had studied medicine for three years with a reputable physician, had a good moral character, a "fair English education" and two courses of lectures at a medical school with at least one at the Eclectic College. Further, he had to submit a thesis on some medical topic and pass an examination. The standards for graduates from the Eclectic Medical College were very high and at least as good as those at many regular medical colleges.

All of the students' hard work was cheapened, however. by the sale of bogus diplomas. "Dr." Buchanan is reported to have been a porter in Philadelphia in 1850. Soon thereafter, he became a professor at the Eclectic College and by 1853 was selling medical degrees. Reportedly, he did so with the knowledge and aid of the rest of the faculty. Buchanan sent agents throughout the United States, Canada and later Europe, seeking doctors who did not have medical degrees. For as little as $50, a practitioner could get a medical degree, never having even seen the college. By 1866, the college claimed to have graduated over 1,000 students, far more than are recorded in its records. It would be another 20 years before these diploma mills would be exposed for what they were.

It is not hard to imagine the attraction that this offer would have to a doctor in Tumblety's position. He had just been humiliated by the regular physicians in Montreal. Here was his chance to be able to prove his medical knowledge at a slight cost to his time or business. The police magistrate found Tumblety guilty of practicing without a license and fined him $100. To obtain a license Tumblety would have to be examined by a panel of regular physicians. It was an examination he would not pass, so he was forced to drop his claim to the title M.D. There is no indication that his diploma was questioned or that he was not a doctor. His fine was for not following the procedure to obtain a license.

Ads that mention the Medical Institute, in the form of testimonials, were published sporadically through April and May 1858. All of these mention Dr. Tumblety and the Medical Institute. They do not term him "M.D." nor do they term him an "herb doctor." However, all of the later ads strongly suggest that the power of Tumblety's medicines comes from nature and that the regular doctors are not aware of the usefulness of these medicines. Prior to this, the ads, while mentioning herbal medicines, made no reference to other doctors. This may have been Tumblety's way of getting revenge on those who indicted him. The last ad of this type appears on June 8 and, while it does mention the Medical Institute, Tumblety's name is not even listed.[10]

It is likely that Tumblety was reconsidering the direction of his career at this time. He was now aware that the regular physicians would never accept him, no matter how scientific he claimed to be. Being a patent medicine salesman was less flamboyant than his previous roles. Without that special edge and secret Native American knowledge, he was just another doctor. This too may have affected the number of patients that came to see him. Whatever the reasons, after half a year, the Indian Herb Doctor reappears in full regalia.

The first indication of this shift is a large ad, taking up a whole column of the page, that was published in the *Toronto Globe* on June 24, 1858. This ad goes back to many of the devices first seen when Tumblety arrived in Toronto. It begins with the familiar "Listen to the voice of truth and reason," and includes the familiar wood cut. Several places in the ad refer to him as an herb doctor or "the Indian Herb Doctor," phrases that had been conspicuously absent from his ads since his return to Toronto.

Still, Tumblety would like to have the best of both personae. The ad still mentions the Medical Institute and several testimonials extolling the scientific basis of his medicines. According to one testament, "Nature's remedies in scientific hands have cured her perfectly." At the bottom of the page is a paragraph extolling the virtues of herbal medicines and suggesting that the regular doctors did not know the value or power of these medicines. It ends by suggesting that they will entirely replace the mineral medicines. The ad ends with the usual offer to treat patients at a distance and to send medicine by freight to any destination. The letters are to be addressed to the "Indian Herb Doctor, F. Tumblety, Toronto, C. W." Clearly, Tumblety was once again identifying himself with this persona and had begun to abandon the pretense of being a scientific practitioner.[11]

There are several aspects of this ad, beyond the change in his public presentation, that inform us of his practice and his patent medicine business. The ad contains 34 brief testimonials from all over Ontario. Of these, seven are from Toronto and may be patients Tumblety saw at the Medical Institute. The other 27 come from a wide variety of places, some at a considerable distance from Toronto. The distances range from 13 to 339 miles and the average distance from Toronto is 83 miles. While it is possible that Tumblety traveled to all of these places, there is no indication of his actual presence there. Rather, these testimonials are more likely from his mail order business, which he was rapidly trying to expand in the summer of 1858.

An example of Tumblety's mail order advertising was published in the *Perth Courier*. The town of Perth is 207 miles east of Toronto. Dr. Tumblety published ads in the *Courier* from October 15, 1858, to February 18, 1859. These ads look and sound like the early Toronto ads and have the famous woodcut. However, there is no indication that the doctor is visiting that location. It lists no office or hotel where he may be found, nor does it mention his being in town. What it does have is an extensive pitch for mail order medicines. As before, the letters are addressed to the Indian Herb Doctor in Toronto. A very similar ad was published in the *Markham Economist* from November 1858 through July 1859.[12]

Another aspect of Tumblety's practice evident in the *Toronto Globe* ad of June 24 is the first exposition of his ideas concerning disease and pain. Dr. Tumblety was what historians of patent medicines call a blood doctor. He believed that many, if not all, diseases and pains stemmed from impure blood. His medicines were designed to clean the blood, clearing the underlying problem and thereby eliminating the overt symptoms. Several large fortunes were made in the 19th century selling blood purifiers. As one of the testimonials reported: "The humor was removed from his blood, his cough cured, his body strengthened and he is now a healthy, strong man." This theme will be repeated in many of his ads over the years.

The final aspect of Dr. Tumblety's treatment is the length of care needed to complete a cure. Of the 34 testimonials, ten make some comment on the course of treatment. In two cases, the patient was cured after ordering one package of Tumblety's medicines without specifying how long they took them for. The others report taking the medicine for periods ranging from one month to three months. Half of those who listed a time specified a period of treatment of six weeks and this may have been Dr. Tumblety's standard prescription. This represents multiple bottles and boxes of medicines and, consequently, quite a bit of money.

Tumblety must have had a staff in Toronto to handle the mail order business. By the time the *Toronto Globe* ad was published on June 24, 1858, Dr. Tumblety was already on the road. He may have been in Ottawa and Montreal but by late May he was in Quebec. He established an office there but the length of his stay in Quebec cannot have been long. Of all the places mentioned in his autobiography, Quebec has the least detail and the fewest testimonials.

There are only two testimonials from this period, one for blindness and one for epilepsy. These testimonials are distinguished by their harsh criticism of the regular physicians. In total, these two ads mention five prominent doctors in Quebec and their failure to provide a cure. One individual testified that, despite having been under their care for a long time, he had not received "the least particle of relief from these medical gentlemen." It is possible that Dr. Tumblety ran into the same kind of opposition in Quebec that had troubled him in Montreal.

Tumblety's whereabouts for the last part of 1858 are obscure. He may have come back to the United States because of a family tragedy. Patrick Tumblety, brother of the doctor, had moved to Rochester about the same time as most of the family. In 1848, he began working at the new Gas Works as a fireman, one who kept the fire going. His house was on Andrews Street close by the Gas Works. On September 20, 1858, Patrick Tumblety was killed in an accident. Whether Dr. Tumblety was able to attend the funeral or not remains unknown.

In any case, he was in upstate New York by the beginning of 1859. After a brief visit to his home town, Tumblety was on the road to Toronto by way of Buffalo. He placed an ad in the *Buffalo Express* on January 12, 1859, announcing his arrival and his intention to remain until April 12, when he would return to Toronto. The ad begins with the now familiar title, "Listen to the voice of truth and reason." It is essentially the same as his early Toronto ads without the woodcut. He describes himself as "the well-known and justly celebrated Indian Herb Doctor, F. Tumblety of Toronto, C. W." He includes the mail order business with letters to be directed to him in Buffalo.[13]

The ad reveals that Tumblety rented space at 157 Main Street for an office. He was located in a structure known as the "Concert Hall Buildings." As he had done in both Toronto and Montreal, his choice of location reflected a desire to be in the middle of the most important and fashionable district of the city. He relied on walk-in traffic as much as that brought by advertising. Being located by the area where crowds gathered for entertainment was sure to add to the number of his customers.

His medical practice in Buffalo was no different than in previous locations. His ads decry the use of mercury and praise herbal medicines. The same list of diseases cured by the doctor is presented, he reports particular attention to the diseases of females and children and again says that the poor will be liberally considered. Finally, he adds a line that will be used repeatedly over the years: " 'A good tree is known by its good fruit' and a good Physician is known by his successful work." This ad ran almost every day until February 16.[14]

In Buffalo, we first see a report that Tumblety added several accoutrements to his public persona which would raise eyebrows and elicit comment for the next decade. The first of these new items was a beautiful black mare which he rode prominently up and down the streets. In pervious descriptions, Tumblety's mode of transportation was described as a carriage or, in the winter, a sleigh. From now on, people would comment on his horses and his excellent riding ability. In his rides, the doctor was followed by his valet, also riding on the beautiful horse. As a marketing technique this worked very well. When people remembered Tumblety, even decades later, they invariably talked about him riding through the streets and on his excellent horses. Finally, Tumblety was followed through the streets by two greyhounds. The dogs, as much as the horse, would stick in people's memories. His appearance and parade made a big impression on the citizens of Buffalo as it later would in most large cities on the east coast over the next decade.

On the same day that his first ad appeared in the *Express*, the editor inserted a small notice among items of local interest. It calls attention to Tumblety's ad and reports that he will be practicing in Buffalo for only a short time. The editor comments, "He comes to us well recommended." A few days later, the editor inserted another notice giving Tumblety's address and saying that the "circular we enclose this morning speaks volumes in the Doctor's favor." While this circular has not been preserved, it was most likely similar to that published by the *Montreal Pilot* in December 1857 with the title "News to the Afflicted." It consisted of testimonials from cured patients and complimentary notices from Canadian papers. In an era when most people found out about new businesses and products from their neighbors, this was an effective means of advertising.[15]

This ad campaign continued late in January when Tumblety published similar "editorial" notices from Canadian newspapers. These favorable notices, originally published in response to Tumblety's paid advertising, would be republished many times in the course of his career. Such notices served both to establish his respectability and to demonstrate his successful cures. What better recommendation could any suffering prospective patient want than that written by the editor of the *Christian Messenger* when he wrote,

Crowds of people are resorting to him for advice, and many are already experiencing considerable relief from using his medicines. Nearly every disease to which the human system is subject, seems to give way under Dr. Tumblety's treatment.[16]

As useful as these editorial comments were, they did not have the impact that local testimonials would. After only two weeks in Buffalo, Tumblety had letters and certificates from satisfied patients. Every few days, he would publish two or three new testimonials from gratefully cured individuals. Without going into excessive detail, his patients included a house painter, a worker in a shipyard, a ship's captain and a collector in a freight yard. They were mostly men but a few women were included. Neither the type of patients nor the diseases mentioned are any different from those treated in Canada.[17]

The advertisements seem to abruptly stop in mid February. The last of the testimonials came out on February 15 and the original ad finished on February 16, 1859. For about a week, there was no mention of Tumblety in the *Express*. You would think he slipped out of town unannounced. There are at least two other newspapers contemporary with the *Buffalo Morning Express* and Tumblety may have been advertising in them.

On February 21, Tumblety published a notice that on the next day he would meet any merchant of the city at the Liberty Pole on the Terrace and would freely distribute 20 barrels of flour to the poor. One of the local editors, being suspicious of this unusual charity, telegraphed the Bank of Toronto, asking about Tumblety's solvency. The answer came back saying that he was quite solvent and that "his check is good for $60,000 in the bank."[18]

Let us stop for a minute and consider the implication of that statement. The bank said Tumblety was worth, at a minimum, $60,000. This is a remarkable amount of money for the time. Just four years earlier, Tumblety had left Rochester with nothing. The medical business was proving quite profitable. If we average this sum over the four years, Tumblety made at least $15,000 a year as a doctor. While this may not seem like much in today's economy, a few comparisons will allow us to understand the magnitude of this figure. In 1860, the average farm laborer made a yearly salary of $200, a Baptist preacher made $350 and the average annual salary in New York City was $500. By this standard, Tumblety's average salary made him a very wealthy man. This also gives us an idea of the scope of his practice. The $60,000 represents a large number of one-dollar bottles of medicine and 50-cent boxes of pills. He may have been a quack and charlatan but he was a rich quack and charlatan!

The flour distribution was made on February 22 at the Liberty Pole on the Terrace. This was a traditional gathering spot for public rallies and political speeches. Crowds of as many as 15,000 reportedly attended some of these events. There is no estimate of the crowd on this day except that it was "immense." The following day, the *Buffalo Express* published a less than flattering review of the whole affair:

> The crowd collected was very immense, and very little discretion was used in regard to the actual necessities of the poor. The whole thing, as our readers already know, was an advertising dodge, and reflects no credit on the originator. Had some discretionary power been, the food distributed might have been of some lasting benefit; but as it was, the street beggars—the busiest of jaws got the whole lot.[19]

Whether it was the nature of this report or other issues, Tumblety never advertised in the *Express* again. Later reports state that he had handbills printed and continued to advertise but no evidence has yet come to light. It was reported that in the few months he spent in Buffalo, he made $20,000. Not a bad return for the $100 he spent on 20 barrels of flour. Presumably, Doctor Tumblety finished his stated engagement in Buffalo and returned to Toronto in May 1859. His office in Toronto was still functioning and the mail order business was being carried on while he was in Buffalo. He was in Toronto until at least July 1859.

Despite a few minor brushes with the law, Francis Tumblety had made a remarkable success of himself in the four years since leaving Rochester. He had a steady stream of patients at his Toronto office, he may have maintained a Montreal office and seems to have had a flourishing mail order business. Even if some newspaper editors and town officials thought of him as a quack, he had many acquaintances and achieved a certain amount of respect. He had come a long way from the so-called "dirty, awkward, ignorant" boy who grew up along the Erie Canal.

5

—⊷⊷⊷—

Manslaughter in St. John
(1859–1860)

Seeking new territory, Tumblety gave up his Toronto office after three years and traveled east, perhaps visiting relatives in Rochester. His destination, however, was Boston, where he had been advertising his mail order medicines since 1857. Why he chose Boston is as obscure as the reasoning behind any other destination in his life. In coming to Boston, he reverted to his earlier persona as the Indian herb doctor and stripped away any pretense at science. Also gone was the patent medicine type of advertising that characterized his recent ads in Toronto.

His first ads, as a resident, appeared in other Boston papers, not just the *Pilot*, in September 1859. These ads are identical to those in Toronto and include the familiar woodcut. His first office was at 360 Washington Street but by the middle of the month, he had moved to the Montgomery House at the corner of Tremont and Bromfield Streets. This structure had been an elegant hotel but by the time Tumblety arrived, the ground floor housed the printing plant for *Gleason's Pictorial Companion* and Tumblety took an office adjacent to the printer.[1]

His ads appeared in various Boston newspapers from late 1859 through early 1860. The content of the ads was the same as those from his early days in Toronto. He continued to advertise against the use of mercury, to claim particular attention to the diseases of women and children, and to maintain his mail order business from his new office. By the end of September, Tumblety makes two changes in his ads that would stay with him for years to come. The first of these is the inclusion of a poem entitled "Our Motto":

> We use such Balms as have no strife
> With Nature or the Laws of Life;
> With blood our hands we never stain
> Nor Poison men to ease their pain.
>
> Our Father—whom all goodness fills
> Provides the means to cure all ills;

The simple Herbs beneath our feet
Well used, relieve our pains complete

A simple Herb, a simple Flower,
Culled from the dewy lea
These, they shall speak with touching power
Of change and health to thee.

This poem first appears in Boston on September 30 and will be repeated in his ads and biographies until his death. The poem neatly summarizes his approach to his profession. It emphasizes the herbal nature of his medicines and their association with God. Importantly, it shows that his cures are in harmony with nature, not at war with it. This reflects his, and the herbalists' in general, belief that nature provides the answers to all medical problems. The line "With blood, our hands we never stain" shows his abhorrence of surgery and bloodletting, a feeling he would loudly proclaim for the rest of his life. The poison referred to in the next line is mercury. The poem is most often signed "F. Tumblety, M. D.," which he hoped would add to his respectability. For all of his time in Boston, Tumblety added "M. D." to the end of his name with no apparent opposition.[2]

The other change in his ads was a focus on a cure for consumption. He claims to have a theory and certain cure for consumption but does not elaborate in his ad. As previously discussed, any cough or congestion was considered to be the first stages of deadly consumption when, in reality, like most colds, they would go away in time. Curing consumption was a mainstay of the medicine business and Tumblety exploited it fully. By mid–October, he settled on a very simple ad which featured his woodcut and simply offered to diagnose patients with no information from them. This ad ran in the Boston papers through early 1860.[3]

All we know of his time in Boston, aside from his ads, is what he chose later to publish. In his later autobiography, Tumblety reports that he met several captains of the Cunard steamship line while in Boston. In the 1840s, the Cunard line had secured the British mail contract, with its large subsidy, and had selected Boston as its terminal. Tumblety mentions meeting Captain James Anderson at this time. Anderson knew Tumblety's uncle, who worked for the Cunard line in Liverpool for 20 years. As a favor, Anderson carried a daguerreotype of Tumblety to his uncle. Anderson would later become famous as the captain of the *Great Eastern*, which laid the first successful transatlantic cable.[4]

In the same source, Tumblety refers fondly to his time in the "Old Tremont." this was the Tremont House, the first luxury hotel in America. It opened in 1829 and it established most of the traits we associate with a modern hotel, including bellhops, private rooms, running water and luxury appointments. The hotel featured a 200-seat dining room which served above average meals. As would be his practice, Tumblety sought to establish himself in a prestigious location.[5]

A report from the press craze of 1888 stated that he had an office in Horticultural Hall on Tremont Street at this time. This was right in its location but the reference to the Hall is an anachronism. The original Horticultural Hall in Boston was built on School Street in 1844. It was replaced by a new building on Tremont Street at the corner of Bromfield Street in 1865. The 1865 building was built in the same location as the Montgomery House, where the doctor's office was located. Another report from the same time period stated that he had an office in the North End but none of his ads reflect this.[6]

An informant for an article in the *Chicago Tribune* in 1888 reported that the doctor purchased a quantity of ground gentian from him. This was a major ingredient in the pills he had made in Montreal and may indicate a continuation of that practice. It was also mentioned that he often wore several medals that Tumblety claimed were given him by the colleges where he studied. Finally, the informant offered a comment on the doctor's personality which may relate to his homosexuality or other practices. He reported, "He liked the slums, notwithstanding the fact that he always had plenty of money, and could have entered, if he had been inclined, into good society." This may be the earliest reference to Tumblety's habit of picking up young men of limited circumstances.[7]

In a later context, Tumblety published 35 testimonials from Boston and the nearby vicinity. As was seen in Canada, the majority of his patients were men, although women make up about a third of the sample. Of the 11 women mentioned, only two were suffering from specifically female problems. He treated the usual range of diseases, including consumption, debility and a host of other problems. There were 15 separate conditions mentioned for the patients. In light of his later development of Dr. Tumblety's Pimple Banisher, it is interesting to note that nine of the patients, a quarter of the sample, were treated for pimples or other skin diseases.[8]

Tumblety may have been traveling a lot at this time as his testimonials show a broad distribution. Most are from Boston but surrounding towns are well represented, including Charlestown, Chelsea, Watertown, Cambridge and Roxbury. He also reports patients from other parts of Massachusetts and New England. In Massachusetts this included South Reading, Sharon, and Lynn. Patients from outside of Massachusetts included some from Portland, Maine, and Newport, Rhode Island. Most of his patients are working-class people but they also include a Reverend and someone identified as "Esq." Probably his most famous patient was Alonzo Lewis, known as the Bard of Lynn. Lewis was a well-known writer, poet, intellectual and editor. Tumblety reportedly treated him for dyspepsia in 1860 and proclaimed him cured. It was probably just coincidence that Lewis died on January 21, 1861.[9]

Tumblety continued to advertise in Boston through January 1860 but he was in the city until late June. In a letter to Amy Kirby Post of Rochester, who apparently knew Tumblety, William C. Nell, newspaper editor and abolitionist, wrote on July 8, "Dr. Tumblety has recently left Boston—he remained here about eight months—and created quite a sensation with his Hounds, His Indian Signs." This supports previous stories about his greyhounds but leaves us to wonder about the last part. Perhaps the story of Chief Sundown from Toronto was still in use in Boston. The doctor was on his way to New Brunswick and a new adventure.[10]

We can not say for sure why Tumblety decided to go to New Brunswick. Perhaps interest in his medicines had dried up in Boston or other, personal reasons led him to seek a new location. Whatever his reasons, the Indian herb doctor arrived in St. John, New Brunswick in July 1860. As in his earlier career, this guise brought him commercial success and professional conflict. Medical practice in New Brunswick was even more controlled than in Toronto or Montreal and this would cause Tumblety much trouble during his brief stay in St. John.

As was his practice, Tumblety sought a prominent address from which to make his show. On his arrival, he engaged two rooms at the American House, a relatively new but prestigious hotel on King Street, run by Samuel B. Estey. One of these rooms would serve as his office. The exact date of his arrival is not certain. One report states he arrived on June 28 while Estey's later testimony suggests it was the first week of July.

Unlike in most places, the practice of medicine was already highly regulated in New Brunswick. The Medical Act required all physicians to register with the common clerk and obtain a license. Tumblety either knew this or was made aware of it soon after his arrival. It is reported that his application identified him as an "Indian Herb Doctor." At some point, that was crossed out and replaced with the word "Druggist." This probably reflects an uncertainty over just what kind of medicine Tumblety practiced. His emphasis on herbs as medicines may have suggested that he dealt in them. Perhaps it was an obfuscation on his own part. Whatever the description, he was not registered as a medical doctor. Apparently he was granted a license and was free to practice.[11]

The problem, as always, was to get patients to come and see him. Tumblety sought to gain the public's attention in two ways. The first was his traditional advertisements. One of his earliest ads appeared in the *Morning Freeman* on July 3 under the bold title "The Indian Herb Doctor." It announced that he had arrived from Canada, interestingly omitting his time in Boston. At this time, "Canada" was composed of Upper and Lower Canada (Ontario and Quebec) and the maritime provinces were independent. New Brunswick would not become part of Canada until the Confederation in 1867. Tumblety further stated he had taken rooms at the American House and could be consulted free of charge. As he had done in the past, the doctor advised potential patients that he could tell them what their ailment was without their saying anything.

Within the next few days, he began publishing local testimonials. These follow the same form and cover the same diseases as he had treated before. Although no specific doctors are mentioned, many of the testimonials contained a statement that the testifier had been given up by the best local physicians and only Tumblety's medicine was able to save him. This most likely reflects a vestige of Tumblety's anger against the regular physicians who gave him so much trouble in Montreal. But in this environment it was a dangerous tone to maintain.

At the same time that Tumblety was publishing his ads, the *Morning Freeman* took an interest in him. On the editorial page there was often a small note praising his medicines, extolling his cures and suggesting that the reader look at the testimonials on another page. It is possible that the editor appreciated the amount of advertising Tumblety was giving his paper and sought to aid him. Whatever the reason, the backing of the newspaper gave Tumblety a credibility with the citizens of St. John that he could get in no other way.[12]

In addition to the newspaper notices, Tumblety began to make himself familiar to the people of St. John. He continued the practice of making a grand show on the streets. In St. John, he rode a beautiful white horse with a long tail. Along with the horse came a riding outfit that was variously described but always included high leather boots. As usual, Tumblety was followed through the streets by two greyhounds. The show had its desired effect and, judging by the increased number of testimonials, his business was beginning to flourish.

This new persona was aptly summarized in a poem entitled "Dr. Tumblety," that was published in the *Albion* in St. John. The authorship of the poem is open to question. Tumblety claimed that it was written by "his friends in the press." However, the poem is so self-serving that it is likely Tumblety either wrote it or had it written. It is a long poem but we need only quote a small part that deals with his public face:

> Dr. Tumblety rode a white steed
> Into St. Johns in its time of need
> Determined to cure with herbal pills
> All the ailing of all their ills
> Dr. Tumblety had a greyhound
> A beautiful animal I'll be bound
> The dog looked up in the Doctor's face
> As he rode along at a slapping pace.
> Tumblety had a killing air
> Though curing was his professional trade
> Rosy of cheek and glossy of hair
> Dangerous man to widow or maid

Summarized in this poem is the person that Tumblety wanted the citizens of St. John to know and recognize. As stated above, the horse and the greyhound were an important part of the public image. They gave him the air of a gentleman and a sportsman. These aspects are intimately tied with the issue of respectability and that was vital to attracting patients. He manages to get in a line about the herbal nature of his practice and its effectiveness. The final part of the quote makes him out to be a handsome ladies' man. As one of his specialties was dealing with "female diseases," the ability to attract members of that sex was important to the business. Whatever his personal preferences may have been, women were some of his best customers. This poem was a way of reinforcing the public perception of Dr. Tumblety.[13]

On July 26, he published an ad which included the poem entitled "Our Motto," first seen in Boston. The poem appeared with the signature "F. Tumblety, M. D.," and was about to cause a major problem for him. Most of the testimonials mention "Dr. Tumblety" in the text, clearly indicating that he was known as a doctor. However, the initials "M.D." specifically mean medical doctor and this was apparently too much for the regular physicians. A Dr. George Keator made out a complaint against Tumblety before the police magistrate for misrepresenting himself as a medical doctor registered under the Medical Act. The case came to trial before the magistrate on July 30, 1860. Tumblety was represented by David S. Kerr. As was his practice when in trouble, Tumblety had sought out the best legal talent available. Kerr had come to St. John in 1855 and rapidly established himself as the most prominent defense attorney in the city. According to a later biographer, one of Kerr's favorite themes was "the individual's right to be protected against arbitrary action on the part of the state." This case fit well with that philosophy.[14]

Because of the specialized nature of the case, Dr. Keator, the informant, was required to hire his own attorney to present the evidence. He chose Andrew R. Wetmore, another prominent counsel who would eventually become premier of New Brunswick. It was alleged that by calling himself "doctor" and using the initials "M.D." Tumblety sought to deceive people into thinking that he was registered as a doctor under the Medical Act. Like the police magistrate in Montreal, this judge had nothing but contempt for Tumblety. In finding him guilty, he said:

> I have carefully weighed all of the evidence in this case, and consider that the defendant, by his representations and practice, has brought himself within the 22nd section of the Medical Act; that the "Indian Herb" prefixed to the Doctor is nothing but a delusion and fraud, while at the same time the word "Doctor" and letters "M.D.," falsely assumed by defendant, are admirably calculated to deceive the weary and unsuspecting.

Tumblety was fined and, presumably, required to stop misrepresenting himself. His lawyer made plans to appeal the decision. Nevertheless, the verdict made little difference in his advertising. Throughout August, his testimonials still referred to him as Dr. Tumblety. The only difference is that he did not again add "M. D." to his name. On the editorial page of the *Morning Freeman* there were frequent notices in praise of Dr. Tumblety and his medicines, larger and more convincing than before. A good example of the tenor and tone of these editorials was published on August 2, shortly after the verdict:

That vegetable medicines are most natural is evident, and as to their safety and efficacy there can be no doubt. These remedies are compounded upon principles not known to the mineral doctors and are entirely different in their operation, acting in perfect harmony with the laws of life they are adapted to all constitutions and diseases, and every day adds new evidence of their virtues; their destiny is a virtuous one, possessing not only power over disease, but principles which will continually supersede the whole mineral practice of medicine.[15]

Coming so soon after the verdict against Tumblety, this seems a very powerful recommendation. It would be more convincing if this same paragraph had not already appeared in one of Tumblety's ads in Toronto two years earlier. However, it was published on the editorial page and carried the weight of the paper behind it. It strongly suggested that the regular physicians or "mineral doctors" were behind the times and would soon be swept away by this new medicine. To make things worse, the paper still referred to him as "Dr." Tumblety in defiance of the verdict of the police court.

Through early September, Tumblety continued to do business as usual and made no change in his ads. It is clear that the regular physicians had not given up the fight, however. On September 17, a "T. W. Smith, M. D." wrote a letter to the editor of the *Morning Freeman*, which the newspaper published the next day. Dr. Smith stated that Tumblety had been heard saying that he had cured Dr. Smith's son of lameness. Smith indignantly reported that his son had never been under the care of Tumblety and he was writing the letter to put a stop to such rumors. Appended to the letter was a statement by Frank Smith saying the same thing as his father.

The significance of this letter is not that Tumblety may have lied. It would not be the first or last time he had been caught extending the truth. Rather, it was in the way the newspaper treated the letter. It was published under a large headline that read "Advertisement." No other letter to the editor had such an endorsement as this even though some clearly were attempts to advertise. None of the published testimonials relate to this Francis Smith and the only evidence that Tumblety claimed to have cured him is the word of this Dr. Smith. The editor of the *Morning Freeman*, no friend of the regular physicians, may have had his own doubts about this letter.[16]

However, a later source suggests that there may be more to it than at first appears. It is reported that Tumblety, in addition to his newspaper ads, had circulars printed with his testimonials in them. There is no way to know if the ads in the newspaper were the only testimonials or if others were privately printed. In at least one case, Tumblety reportedly treated a ship's pilot for a tapeworm. When he was cured, Tumblety published a testimonial without the patient's knowledge. When the pilot found out, he threatened to come after the doctor with a club. Apparently this was not the only time such an incident occurred, which throws suspicion on many of his "testimonials." Others treated this way were said to be mortified and angry to have their illness advertised to the world. While no one assaulted Tumblety, someone did stab his dog while in St. John and was never caught.

On September 10, 1860, the Supreme Court of New Brunswick reviewed the case against Tumblety. The defendant was still represented by attorney David Kerr, while Dr. Keator was now represented by Mr. Bayard. The judge, Robert Parker, found that Tumblety had not misrepresented himself under the narrow confines of the law:

> ...it appearing to me that the Magistrate was not warranted in implying that the defendant by taking and using the name and title of Doctor of Medicine meant to assert and signify that he was duly registered under the Medical Act of the Province of New Brunswick, when he was not so registered, and that consequently the evidence was not sufficient to sustain the information *on that particular charge* which the Defendant was summoned to answer...[17]

The italics are in the original article and were meant to suggest the Parker had no illusions about Tumblety's qualifications. Nevertheless, he reversed the verdict of the police magistrate and awarded costs to the defense. Dr. Keator was required to pay Tumblety a little over £20. Tumblety promptly announced, as was reported in the newspapers, that this money would be distributed to the poor.

With all of this publicity and his other advertising, Tumblety's business was going well. Around this time, he met a young man on the steam ferry, struck up a conversation and offered him a job as a clerk. William Hamilton later testified that his job was to meet patients in the hall and to offer them a chair if the doctor was busy in the office. He also said that he was to do any writing if required but that all he did was copy some advertisements. When more medicines were needed, Tumblety would send him to the druggist to pick them up.[18]

Around the same time that Hamilton was hired, early in September, James Portmore, a carpenter and longtime resident of St. John, came to see the doctor. He was 59 years old and had been suffering from kidney and bladder problems for ten years. According to his wife, the condition had worsened so much that he was unable to work at his trade. Since June, Portmore had been under the treatment of a Dr. Humphrey, who determined that he had a liver ailment and a stone in the bladder. He did not prescribe any treatment, believing that when the stone passed, he would be cured. In pain and encouraged by the ads he saw in the papers, Portmore came to Tumblety to see if he could do what the other doctors failed to do. The doctor gave him two bottles, each containing about four ounces of a clear liquid. He instructed him to take a teaspoon of the medicine mixed with water, three times a day.[19]

Portmore's wife testified that when he brought the medicine home and first took it, he said, "that would burn the heart out of a man." He took the liquid as instructed for nine or ten days. During that time, he complained of the burning in his stomach each time. The medicine had some unintended consequences in that it made his stomach hurt, his bladder condition worsened and he lost his appetite. On September 17, Portmore went to see Tumblety again and brought home another bottle of medicine. According to his wife, this medicine did not look any different from the first one. However, after he took it, he vomited and got much sicker. He went to bed and could eat nothing thereafter.

Alarmed by her husband's worsening condition, Mrs. Portmore sent for Dr. Tumblety to come to their home. Tumblety, accompanied by his assistant Hamilton, went to the Portmore house on September 19. With Hamilton waiting outside in the buggy, Tumblety went into the house and found a very angry Mrs. Portmore. She accused him of killing her husband by giving him the wrong medicine. Tumblety asked the patient how he felt and Portmore said he was a dead man. Mrs. Portmore continued to rail against Tumblety and threatened to hit him with a chair. According to Tumblety, Portmore said, "Mary, don't blame him," while Mrs. Portmore recalled him saying simply, "Mary, hold your tongue." Mrs. Portmore reported that she and her husband had determined to show the medicines to other doctors and have Tumblety charged. When she told this to Tumblety, he went over to the table where the bottles were, picked one up and smelled it. Replacing the bottle, he told Mrs. Portmore to apply "hot water fomentations" to her husband's stomach. This was, as it sounds, the application of cloths soaked in warm water to ease the pain. When she went to heat the water, Mrs. Portmore said Tumblety deftly pocketed the three bottles. After having the cloths applied, Tumblety said that he would send a balsam to ease the stomach by four P.M. and left the house. It was soon after when the Portmores discovered that the medicine bottles were missing. Portmore reportedly told his wife, "Let the villain take them." Tumblety never sent the balsam and sent word that he was busy and could not come.[20]

Finding no help from one doctor, Mrs. Portmore called for Dr. Humphrey, the original doctor, to come and see her husband. He reportedly found Portmore in a semi-conscious state and suffering from severe stomach pains. Dr. Humphrey prescribed a standard treatment which involved bloodletting and mercury. He had leeches applied to Portmore's stomach to draw off the bad blood and gave him purgative pills to clean out his system. A major component of these pills was calomel or mercury chloride. As one of the effects of calomel was to irritate the stomach, it is not surprising that Portmore could not keep this medicine down. The patient continued to decline and Dr. Humphrey told Mrs. Portmore that there was no hope of a recovery.[21]

According to the *Morning Freeman*, Mrs. Portmore called for the police chief, Mr. Scoullar, on Wednesday night, September 26, who found Mr. Portmore speechless and barely alive. Mrs. Portmore said that on the advice of Dr. LeBaron Botsford, an associate of Dr. Humphrey, she wanted the policeman to arrest Tumblety for poisoning her husband. Mr. Scoullar declined to make any arrest until a proper warrant was sworn. Soon after he left, James Portmore died. The next day, the mayor of St. John asked Dr. William Bayard, the

coroner, to conduct an inquest. The fact that Dr. Bayard was the brother of the
lawyer who had just prosecuted Tumblety before the Supreme Court did not
seem to bother anyone. That same morning, Thursday, September 27, Drs.
Humphrey and Botsford conducted an autopsy on Portmore.

The inquest began Thursday afternoon at the Portmore house. Dr. Bayard
convened a "most respectable jury" and testimony was taken. Mrs. Portmore
presented her testimony as described above. Tumblety asked her about Portmore saying "don't blame him," and, not surprisingly, she replied that he simply told her to hold her tongue. After taking the widow's testimony, the inquest
was adjourned until the next day.

The inquest was reconvened on Friday morning at the Court House. Drs.
Humphrey and Botsford both testified concerning the autopsy. They reported
that Portmore had healthy lungs, and "disordered" kidneys, and suffered from
a "calculus or stone." The conclusion of the autopsy was that Portmore died
of an acute inflammation of the stomach. They reported that this condition was
not related to his earlier disease and did not arise from it. In their opinion, the
inflamed stomach was the result of an acid or other irritant but would not swear
to it. Nor did they find any such substance in the stomach during their examination. The coroner, Dr. Bayard, assured the jury that he agreed with the opinion of his colleagues.[22]

Dr. Tumblety did not ask any questions about the autopsy because he was
conspicuously missing from the inquest. The coroner attempted to find out
where he was. S. B. Estey, proprietor of the American House, testified that the
last time he saw Tumblety was 9 P.M. on Thursday when Tumblety came down-
stairs, lit a cigar and went out. Estey was not aware that he was gone until the
next morning when Tumblety's clerk came and paid his bill.

Next to testify was William Hamilton, the aforementioned clerk. He
reported that he accompanied Tumblety out of town on Thursday night as he
headed south. Tumblety was described as being on his white horse and dressed
in "cloak, cap and grey trousers.' He was accompanied by his hound. Hamilton did not know where they were going but assumed they were on their way
to make a house call. When they had gone some way out of town, Tumblety
asked him which was the road to Calais, at the American border. He gave
Hamilton $100 and told him to pay his bills. Tumblety would telegraph him
and let him know where to send his trunks.[23]

It is clear that Tumblety was very worried by the way the inquest was going
and had determined much earlier to leave St. John. W. Jask, who was connected
with the Commercial Bank in St. John, stated that Tumblety withdrew "a large
amount of specie" before he left. He also said that Tumblety boasted in Eastport of the large sums he carried away. Apparently, Tumblety's practice in St.
John had been a financial success. Much later in time, other people remembered Tumblety's flight from St. John in more dramatic fashion. It was said
that he fled St. John

...with the haste of Paul Revere in his Midnight ride. Farmers along the road were startled from their sleep by the sound of furious galloping.... The driver of the mail stage on its way to St. John, turning a curve in the road, saw a man urge a white horse into the bushes where he remained hidden until the stage had passed.[24]

Tumblety's flight would not stop the inquest and the final witness provided invaluable insight on his medical practice at the time. The coroner called Mr. Barker, an apothecary who supplied herbs and drugs to Tumblety. He testified to supplying Tumblety with a wide variety of herbs and drugs. One of the most important was called Irish moss, which Barker sold in quarter-pound packages. Tumblety reportedly purchased 70–80 pounds of this material. That is an incredible amount for the three months that he was resident in St. John. Next most common among Tumblety's purchases was a six-ounce combination, in equal proportions, of balsam copaiba and sweet spirits of nitre. For coughs, he got a mixture of balsam of fir and balsam of Tolu. Barker also made pills for Tumblety which had cayenne pepper in them. Tumblety also ordered quantities of commercial products like Perry Davis Pain Killer and something called Russia salve. Barker swore that Tumblety never got any ammonia or mineral salts from him. Finally, Barker reportedly told many people "that the medicines Dr. Tumblety got would do no harm if they did no good."[25]

This is a much more complex medical practice than was evident in the two nostrum descriptions in Montreal. It is possible that Tumblety had been using these all along but they were simply not mentioned. It seems that the same pills as in Montreal were made here. Their purpose was purgative and for pain relief. The rest of the medicines are new and need to be looked at both to identify what Tumblety used them for and to assess what happened to Portmore.

Given the quantity purchased, Irish moss was an important part of Tumblety's therapy. One of the things that he would comment on several times in his published statements was how important it was to get a patient to eat normally. Irish moss, which is really seaweed, was a very nutritious herb and a decoction of this, mixed with water or milk, was considered good medicine for helping to restore the appetite. A secondary use for Irish moss was to treat irritations of the bladder and kidneys. In a later article, Tumblety claimed to have been treating Portmore with a "parsley tea," and it may be this herb he had in mind. However, there is nothing in this that would make a man's stomach burn.

The next medicine was composed of copaiba and nitre in equal proportions. Copaiba normally was used to treat gonorrhea but was also used for irritations of the bladder and the urinary tract. In its effect, it is a laxative, a stimulant and a diuretic. If the dose is too large, copaiba will cause "warmth in the gastric region," belching, nausea and vomiting. This medicine has an odor and a bitter taste. Nitre is a strong diuretic but also soothes irritations of the stomach and nausea. Finally, it was used to relieve pain in urination. This formulation seems clearly designed to fight the effects of gonorrhea.

The symptoms described for overdoses of copaiba seem very similar to those experienced by Portmore. The burning of the stomach and the vomiting certainly could result from large doses of the drug. The fact that Tumblety smelled the bottle before he took it is very suggestive, as copaiba is said to have a distinctive odor. Also, copaiba is said to be absorbed and therefore would not be found in the stomach, especially after not taking it for a week. If, in addition to his other ailments, Portmore had an ulcer, this could have made the effect of the medicine worse. We can never know if Tumblety gave him the wrong medicine or if it had been mixed in the wrong proportions. What seems clear is that his condition worsened when he began to take the medicine.

The other medicines that Barker describes are important for understanding the full extent of Tumblety's practice. His use of balsam of fir and balsam of Tolu for coughs is in line with standard practice 19th-century medicine. One of Tumblety's repeated claims is that he cured consumption. Very often a bad cold was diagnosed as consumption and this medicine would work wonders. Perry Davis Pain Killer was mostly alcohol and opiates. It was effective in killing pain if it did nothing else. Russia salve is an ointment used in treating skin conditions. As this was a big part of Tumblety's business, it is likely he used a lot of this commercial product.

What these medicines tell us about Tumblety is that he had at least rudimentary knowledge of herbal medicine. By this time, Tumblety had been involved in herbal medicine for almost a decade. He must have picked up enough knowledge to order what he needed. However, he might not have had enough knowledge to know the effect his medicine would have on Portmore.

While Tumblety may have been responsible for Portmore's death, it is also possible that Dr. Humphrey caused or aided that death. Portmore was already in very bad health and the only thing Humphrey told him to do was go home and wait for the stone to pass. There is no sure evidence that any of the medicine that Tumblety prescribed to Portmore would have killed him. When he returned to Dr. Humphrey's care he had severe stomach pains and the doctor gave him pills whose known effect was to irritate the stomach! Humphrey also bled an already weak Portmore, which was a recipe for disaster. Portmore was under Dr. Humphrey's care for almost a week after Tumblety's final visit. Dr. Humphrey bears at least as much responsibility as Tumblety, yet he was not prosecuted or questioned.

After the testimony was completed, the coroner "addressed the jury at length." They withdrew and deliberated for 30 minutes. On returning, they found Tumblety guilty of manslaughter. The case was passed on to the circuit court for trial. There is no evidence that the case was ever tried.[26]

Meanwhile, Tumblety was across the border in Maine, presumably await-
ing word of the verdict. By chance he met William Smith, a resident of St.
John, who was waiting out a storm. Years later, when Tumblety was accused
in the Whitechapel murders, Smith remembered this meeting in a letter to a
friend, "When I was in Eastport in 1860 ... I met him there and spent part of
the day with him. He was very agreeable and intelligent. I do not think he could
be the Whitechapel fiend." On October 1, Tumblety sent a letter to the *Morning Freeman*, saying that he was informed of the verdict and that, when he
finished his business in Maine, he would return to defend himself. Perhaps to
add a final twist, he signed the letter "F. Tumblety, M. D."[27]

Sometime in the second week of October, the *Eastport Sentinel* published
an article on Tumblety that was reprinted, in part, in the *Morning Freeman* on
October 16. It is clear that the doctor was telling his story as he saw it. But it
does give a perspective on his mind at the time. He described the regular physicians as conspiring against him and made sure to report his donation of the
court costs to the poor. He claims that he told Portmore he could not cure him
but could give him some medicine that would ease his pain. According to Tumblety, the medicine, a parsley tea, worked well and he listed several people who
could testify that Portmore told them it was effective. One of the regular doctors convinced Portmore to stop taking Tumblety's medicine and to take his
medicine. Of course, he died from this new medicine. With definite echoes of
the Montreal case, Tumblety commented on what happened next:

> Over their wine the doctors planned. Portmore was dead. He had taken Tum-
> blety's medicine. These were the materials. A coroner's inquest was held, presided
> over by one of the doctors, a bitter enemy of Dr. Tumblety's. Three brothers of the
> Coroner were on the jury. A post-mortem examination was had. No traces of poi-
> son in the stomach, not the slightest indication of any deleterious drug.
> But Portmore was dead, that was certain, what killed him was not so certain,
> but they would charge it to Tumblety. The Coroner, therefore put on a solemn
> face, and told the jury they should bring in a verdict of manslaughter. The jury
> knew what they were empanelled for and obeyed.[28]

During the five years Francis Tumblety spent in Canada, he built a
profitable medical practice and became relatively well known. The indictment
for manslaughter threatened all of that. His stay on the border may have been
in hopes of saving what he could. Although there is no evidence that the indictment was ever brought before the circuit court, the threat was enough to get
Tumblety to move on. Soon, he would set off for New York and begin a new
and equally troubled part of his career.

As is usual with the doctor, later recollections add a few details about his
life in St. John that did not make it into the public record at the time. These
are unsubstantiated and generally undated. Nevertheless they tell us something of the perception of Tumblety and add to the overall impression of his
personality. According to a much later report, at the inquest into Portmore's

death, the doctors presented the deceased's heart and liver for the coroner's examination. While the organs sat on the table, Tumblety's dog tried to eat them. It is hard to reconcile this with the testimony presented at the time. The first day of the inquest was held at the Portmore home and did not include any testimony about the autopsy. That information was presented the next day, but by then, Tumblety and his dog were gone.[29]

The same article stated, "The vile character of Tumblety was fully shown at another time by an assault which he attempted on a young drug clerk who came to him as a patient." Again, there is nothing in the papers to support this allegation. That Tumblety might have made sexual advances to a young man and that they were rebuffed is not unusual. It is the type of thing that may have been talked about in the community without actually resulting in any public record. It is in sharp contrast to the image of Tumblety as a "dangerous man to widow or maid."[30]

6

———❦———

Travels in the East
(1860–1861)

After his escape from New Brunswick, Tumblety was in Maine and may
have visited Boston. However, his ultimate destination was New York. Tumblety was in New York sometime in December 1860 and took up residence at
the Fifth Avenue Hotel. As suggested for Boston, the doctor chose to live in
the most prestigious hotel in the city. The Fifth Avenue Hotel was opened in
1859 and soon became "the social center of New York." The building was constructed of white marble in the Corinthian style, boasted the first elevator in
a hotel in the United States, and had 600 guest rooms. A later reference from
1908 describes the clientele:

> From the visit of the Prince of Wales in 1860 to the present day, this hotel has
> been the resort of the titled, and the distinguished, presidents, senators, governors,
> foreign noblemen and ambassadors, famous politicians, admirals, generals and
> emperors have stopped at the Fifth Avenue.[1]

Such an address demonstrated both Tumblety's status as a gentleman and his
success as a physician. It also undoubtedly appealed to him personally. That
he could afford to stay in such a hotel suggests his practice was paying very
well.

Perhaps because of his recent troubles in New Brunswick, he sought some
legal recognition of his status. On March 18, Louis E. Hopkins, of the Board
of Health, sent him the following message:

> Dear Sir: Herewith do I transmit a copy of the Health Laws and Ordinances,
> published under the auspices of our commission. Inasmuch as you are a member
> of the medical fraternity, I have no doubt that it will prove valuable to you.[2]

Despite Mr. Hopkins's generous inclusion of Tumblety in the "medical
fraternity," the only thing the note really says is that he was sent a copy of the
laws. While this is hardly a ringing endorsement of his medical credentials,
Tumblety used this, both in New York and later, to demonstrate that he was
accepted as a regular physician.

To begin his practice, Tumblety engaged an office at 933 Broadway. This was described as a half-minute walk from the Fifth Avenue Hotel. It was located in a building that had Dressler's Music Store on the ground floor, offices on the second and rooms on the upper stories. While this office was close to his residence, it may not have attracted enough walk-in traffic, being located in a relatively quiet neighborhood. The doctor soon moved his office down in the heart of the commercial district at 499 Broadway. This structure was described as a first-class, four-story building with a full basement. Like many structures in the area, the upper stories were used for offices and apartments.[3]

His practice in New York seems no different than it had been in Toronto, Montreal or Boston. In his autobiography, Tumblety states that he has testimonials "without number" from this time. He later published 39 testimonials from New York and the vicinity, however all but 12 of these date to his residence in Brooklyn in 1863–1864. Those that date to this period are a smaller, more focused group. There were, of course, no references to abortion drugs or contraceptives. Consumption and lung complaints were the most common and made up over 40 percent of the sample. The number of patients suffering from skin diseases continued at 25 percent of the testimonials but none reported being treated for pimples.[4]

Shortly after his arrival in New York, Tumblety deposited funds in the Chemical Bank. This was one of the oldest and most stable banks in New York City. In the recent financial crisis of 1857, it was the only bank to continue paying its notes in gold, earning it the nickname "Old Bullion." Given the reputation of the bank, Tumblety was shocked to find that they had accepted a forged check on his account. The account was short $400 from a check that Dr. Tumblety alleged was a forgery. The bank president, John Q. Jones, claimed that the signatures were genuine. To recover the money, Tumblety sued the Chemical Bank.[5]

This was shaping up to be quite a battle. To sue the bank, Tumblety hired A. D. Russell, who was a prominent lawyer and a city judge living at the Fifth Avenue Hotel, as well as E. B. Shafer. The defendant hired Robert B. Roosevelt, uncle of the future president and one of the most powerful lawyers in the city, and William Mackellar, lawyer, detective and advisor to the *New York Daily News* and publisher of the *National Police Gazette*. As part of its defense, the Chemical Bank decided to put Tumblety's life on trial. In late January 1861, they collected information about his practice and life in other cities. They found out about his manslaughter indictment in St. John and some of his troubles in Toronto.[6]

Lawyers for the bank requested to examine seven men. These included individuals from Toronto, Boston, Buffalo, St. John and Detroit. Of the seven listed, only five could be identified either in the census or other sources. G. S. Gurnett was a former mayor of Toronto and, more importantly, a longtime police magistrate. It was in his court that Tumblety was arraigned for claiming to be a regular physician. G. W. Lefavor was the paying teller of the Revere Bank in Boston. He could identify Tumblety's signature. George Henson was a justice of the peace in Buffalo and probably had much to say about Tumblety's time there. W. Jask was connected to the Commercial Bank in St. John. William Champ was a deputy sheriff in Detroit. According to the defendants, the man was not even Dr. Tumblety. They reported that his real name was Sullivan and that he had been a servant of Dr. Tumblety. When Dr. Tumblety died, Sullivan assumed his name and practice. They also stated that he had been charged in Nova Scotia, a few months ago, with a serious offense. The Chemical Bank's preparations were made in early in February 1861. A paper commented at the time "when the case comes up for trial it promises to be exceedingly interesting if not spicy."

This is one of those times where we must use the information from a newspaper story with great care. One of the defense attorneys, Mackellar, was also an editor of the paper that published these "facts." Tumblety was not dead in 1861 and would continue to be recognized by friends and relatives for many more years. Sullivan could be a name he assumed at some point but it is hard to see when or where. In both New Brunswick and in Boston, he was known by his own name. Further, he was charged in New Brunswick, not Nova Scotia. This same information was apparently published in an article entitled, "How an Irishman Becomes an Indian Doctor," which appeared in the *National Police Gazette,* of which Mackellar was publisher, sometime between January and March 1861. Unfortunately, no copy of this issue seems to exist today.[7]

It may be that Sullivan was an alias adopted by one of the young men that Tumblety lured into a relationship. Over the long course of his career, Tumblety was in the habit of picking up young men, offering them jobs, giving them presents and eventually propositioning them. Sometimes these contacts would develop into long-lasting relationships, but just as many times, the young men would react badly to his advances and a court case would result. So far, he had not had that problem. John Guy, in Montreal, and William Hamilton, whom Tumblety met on a ferry in New Brunswick, had not caused him problems.

Apparently, Charles Whelpley was another one of these young men. In the 1860 census, he is listed as a 17-year-old clerk, living at home with his father and siblings. Early in the next year, he was living at the Fifth Avenue Hotel. One way his fortunes could have changed so quickly would be if some one else was footing the bill. Tumblety seems to have used him, as he always did, as companion and secretary. It is reported that sometime in January, Tumblety told Whelpley to fill out a check for $100 from his account at the Chemical Bank. When the check was ready, the doctor signed it and got the money.

It was alleged that three days after Whelpley filled out the first check, he completed another one, this time for $400. Forging Tumblety's signature, he took and cashed the check. Shortly thereafter, he fled the city. Discovering that he had no money in the account, Tumblety swore out a complaint against the bank for accepting a forged check. Within a few days, the bank had hired Mackellar to investigate the case. Tumblety came to his office and swore an affidavit charging Whelpley with fraud. In the next few weeks, he came back several times to see if the bank was going to take action against Whelpley.

Mackellar was informed that Whelpley had returned to the city in late February. On the 21, Whelpley was arrested for forgery and brought before a judge. He was ordered held until an examination could be made. Although the details are unclear, apparently Whelpley was granted bail on the condition that he be available for the examination. Mackellar conducted this interrogation without informing the plaintiff and Whelpley became a defense witness.

The trial began on April 1, 1861, and the first witness for the plaintiff was Jacob C. Parsons, the paying teller of the Chemical Bank. He testified that he had paid out the check and "believed" the signature on the check was that of Dr. Tumblety. What he did not say was that he paid it to Tumblety. Such a statement would have ended the case right there. While it was not published, we have to assume that someone else cashed the check, presumably Whelpley.

Next, Tumblety took the stand, testifying that he was an Irishman and had opened an account with the bank in December 1860. Subsequently he had withdrawn all but $400 from the account. He stated that he was in the habit of cashing all checks drawn on the account personally and he identified a number of checks which he had cashed. He flatly denied signing or cashing the check for $400 and said that he had made a complaint against Whelpley for forgery. Whelpley then took the stand for the defense and stated that he had not forged nor cashed the check. He admitted that he had filled in one check for the doctor in his room. After Whelpley's testimony, the court adjourned till the next day.

The only witness specifically mentioned the next day was Mackellar, who described his various roles as defense attorney, detective and newspaper editor. Apparently there was some confusion about who hired Mackellar and Tumblety's lawyer made several points about his not informing Tumblety that he was working for the bank. He was grilled hard on the point of not notifying the plaintiff about the examination of Whelpley. In the end, Mackellar's reported testimony added little to the case. The paper next said, "A number of witnesses were then called who gave the plaintiff a good character, while a similar number gave him a bad reputation." Clearly, the dual nature of Tumblety's reputation was already established. The judge instructed the jury, which then retired and "in a few moments brought a verdict for the defendant."[8]

This case, as reported in the newspapers, is difficult to understand, yet may provide important insights on Tumblety's personality and life. It is certain that Tumblety did not present the check to be cashed. Parsons, the teller, never stated who did cash the check and Whelpley testified that he did not do so. Tumblety swore that he had not signed the check while others said the signature was his. The jury sided with the defendant, believing the signature was genuine. Why would Tumblety charge Whelpley and sue the bank, if it could be proved that the signature was his? There were a number of episodes in Tumblety's life where he gave some valuable piece of property to a young man only to turn around and go to the police when the young man disposed of it. Perhaps this is the earliest of those cases. On the other hand, it is clear that the Chemical Bank chose to fight this battle not on the evidence but on the issue of respectability. Tumblety's reputation was already iffy and they sought to exploit this. Neither side comes out well in this event.

While his experience with Whelpley may have turned out badly, his relationship with Mark A. Blackburn, whom he met about this time, would be long-lasting. Blackburn was a 17-year-old tinsmith living in Brooklyn with his family. He was the second son of Mark and Martha Blackburn. Mark, along with his parents and three siblings, immigrated to New York about 1850. It is not known how Tumblety met Blackburn but he would later state, in 1865, that he had had only one man in his employ for the past five years. This suggests that they met late in 1860 or early in 1861. For the next two decades, Tumblety and Blackburn would be in and out of each other's lives. Blackburn would name one of his children after Tumblety and, when Tumblety died in 1903, he left a substantial bequest to Blackburn.[9]

The exact nature of their professional relationship is unknown. It is likely that Tumblety taught Blackburn the herb trade, as Reynolds and Lyons had taught him. Later, Blackburn would call himself a doctor and practice the same kind of herbal medicine that Tumblety did. In the 1860s, Blackburn probably kept an eye on the office when Tumblety was out and it was he who was described as following behind Tumblety in various places. In some cases he had the doctor's dogs on a leash while in others he was said to follow behind on horseback when the doctor went riding. There is no way to know if the two had a physical relationship as well as a professional one. Blackburn was clearly the kind of young man Tumblety liked to pick up and promise a better life. In other cases, this resulted in altercations and accusations of improper suggestions or advances. Blackburn and Tumblety lived together for long periods in the 1860s and 1870s without any reported difficulties. Blackburn would marry twice during this time. Based on Tumblety's history, it is hard to imagine that he did not have a physical relationship with Blackburn. They were too close not to have had one.

An important question for many aspects of Tumblety's later history is how long and when he was in New York City and when he moved to Washington. In his 1872 memorial to the Joint High Claims Commission, Tumblety states that he moved to Washington in April 1861, back to New York in May 1863 and to St. Louis in 1865. There is no evidence that places Tumblety in Washington earlier than November 1861. This does not mean that he could not have taken trips there but it suggests that he was not living there during this time.[10]

On the other hand, a number of indications place Tumblety in New York during most of 1861. Twice, in the *Knickerbocker Magazine*, the editor pokes fun at Tumblety and his medicines. In May, he comments that he

> makes quite a "splash" in the advertising columns of our daily contemporaries. He wants no pay for consultations; he stipulates no description of symptoms: all he desires is the patient. *That* desideratum supplied, he *looks* at him—and the *diagnosis* of his complaint is established. Tumblety may not be a humbug: it would perhaps be ungracious so to term him...

The editor then goes on to describe the Tumblety bug as being fussy and "pompious" while rolling a small ball along the ground. Perhaps a literal use of the term pill-pusher? The *Knickerbocker*'s editor returned to this subject in the July issue, where he "commends" Dr. Tumblety and states the doctor knows the infallibility of his own cures. The editor recommends a few folk cures that would aid Tumblety's practice: "A load-stone, put on the place where the pain is, is beautiful for them as has the rheumatiz." He comments that it is not necessary for the doctor to see the patient for it to work. The editor is implying that Tumblety's cures have no more value than these obviously silly ones.[11]

At the same time, Tumblety's fame brought him ridicule in other magazines and from the stage in New York. On August 3, 1861, *Vanity Fair*, published in New York, presented the following: "Q.—Why is the Champion of the Prize Ring like Professor Tumblety, or any other quack? A.—Because he travels on his Physique." Dan Bryant's Minstrels, playing at a theater at 473 Broadway, beginning on August 31 and continuing through April 19, performed a burlesque entitled, "Dr. Tumblety Outdone." This same skit would later be performed in Washington after Tumblety moved there. New York audiences were familiar enough with Tumblety to laugh at him. If Tumblety were not living and advertising in the city, why would these publications be making fun of him?[12]

A more important indication that Tumblety was still in New York was his ads. In July 1861, Tumblety started to peddle his medicine in the pages of *Harper's Weekly*, a periodical based in New York but with national circulation. As one of the leading publications of its day, *Harper's* was aimed at an upper-middle-class audience and offered the Doctor unprecedented access to the upper reaches of society. The publication was careful not to print anything but that which would be considered family fare. Tumblety chose to advertise only his "Pimple Banisher," and to do so in a restrained manner. The earliest ad appears on July 13 and has the title "To Be Good Looking, Old Faces Made to Look Young and Beautiful." The ad was accompanied by a picture of a young man with a severe case of acne. It promised that Dr. Tumblety's Pimple Banisher would produce a complexion free of pimples or blemishes. The price was one dollar per bottle and could be sent to any address from the doctor's office at 499 Broadway. This was the greatest development of Tumblety's mail order business. Versions of this ad ran until October 19, 1861. Similar ads were also run in *Frank Leslie's Illustrated Newspaper* and the *New York Illustrated News* from July through October.[13]

Further, Tumblety's only ads in the *New York Times* occur during this period on August 2–3, 1861. The Pimple Banisher was also sold wholesale and was advertised at least in Philadelphia up to October 12. It seems very unlikely that Dr. Tumblety started such a major and new ad campaign in New York while he was living in Washington. The cessation of his advertising in both *Harper's* and the Philadelphia papers is an indication that he was getting ready to move.[14]

Even though he was still advertising in New York, he was already traveling down the East Coast. On September 17, 1861, he began advertising in the *Baltimore Sun*. This ad included two elements that he used in other places. The first is the combination of his name and the poem "Our Motto" along with his usual claims. This is the same ad that ran in Boston with only the place changed; his office is listed at 220 W. Baltimore Street. Above this was a large copy of the testimonial by citizens of Toronto, dated October 6, 1857, which he first published in Montreal. He advertised in Baltimore for a little less than a month—his last ad was published on October 7. Whether he returned to New York or went to Washington has not been ascertained but his destination would soon be Washington.[15]

Before we go on, we need to look at one more story told about Tumblety's time in New York. It was recounted by Fred H. Hart in an article published in 1888. Hart was a well-known newspaper editor out West, an author, and a friend of Mark Twain. He claimed to have known Tumblety in New York in 1856 when Hart was 21 years old. According to the story, Tumblety had an office on Thirteenth Street, east of Sixth Avenue. There was a drug store in the area run by a man named Giles who had angered Tumblety somehow. The doctor sought to embarrass Giles by having a "scurrilous and obscene" poem written about him. Hart refused to participate but Tumblety enlisted the aid of another young man, identified as the stepson of a Presbyterian minister who would become famous for "Blaine's ruin with his three R's." The stepson was said to be within months of his majority. Together they finished the poem, had it printed and distributed it to every house in the Ninth Ward. The stepson escaped but Tumblety was arrested and given a year in the Tombs jail. Hart said he went to California the next year.[16]

There are a number of problems with this story. Census data reveals that Hart would have been 21 in 1857. Yet in that year, Tumblety was clearly in Toronto and Montreal. The key to this mystery may be Hart's statement that he left for California the next year. His own writing shows that he traveled west in either 1861 or 1862. In the 1860 census he is living in Albany with his mother and his occupation is listed as clerk. By 1862, Fred H. Hart is listed as working as a clerk in a store in Virginia City, Nevada, where Hart began his journalistic career. Further research in the 1860 census showed that a George Giles was living in the Ninth Ward of New York City and was listed as a physician. Like Tumblety himself, he could have been described as both a druggist and a physician.[17]

The description of the Presbyterian minister who would be known for "Blaine's ruin with his three R's" refers to Samuel D. Burchard. At a political rally for James G. Blaine in New York City during the presidential campaign of 1884, Burchard described the Democrats as the party of "rum, Romanism and rebellion." This remark is credited with influencing the Irish vote in New York City against the Republicans and costing Blaine the election. In the 1860 census, Burchard was living in the Ninth Ward and did have three stepsons whose name was Leeds. Henry Leeds turned 18 in 1856, William in 1858, and James in 1862. If Hart was 21, then the incident can only have occurred late in 1857 or early in 1858. If James Leeds was the stepson referred to, he could have been almost 18 in 1861, when Tumblety was in New York.[18]

Hart's story has the feel of something that Tumblety might do but there is no way to prove it refers to him. No evidence has been located in the New York papers to shed light on the issue. During his long career, Tumblety used poetry as part of his advertising. The association with young men certainly fits the profile. There is, however, no way he spent a year in jail at this time and I find it hard to believe that in the press blitz of 1888, no one else mentioned his time in jail. Finally, Hart comments that the doctor's real name was made public in the newspapers but he cannot remember it. To me this suggests that Hart is mixing up Tumblety with someone else.

Though the evidence is slim, it suggests that Tumblety was still residing in New York City as late as October 1861. There is no evidence that Tumblety was living in Washington before November 1861. When he finally did make the trip south is uncertain. However, the lure of easy money and thousands of young men were too strong for Tumblety to resist for long. It is also possible, as we shall see, that Tumblety went to Washington in anticipation of getting a lucrative position in the government. When he did go, he seems to have gone alone. There is no indication that Blackburn went with him. When people recalled Tumblety in Washington, they do not mention anyone following him. It may be that Tumblety kept his New York office open and that Blackburn ran it while the doctor was in Washington.

7

⤜⟨∞⟩⤛

Civil War Washington
(1861–1863)

With the beginning of the Civil War, there was a great rush of men who came to Washington. Some came out of patriotism and duty, some to make a quick buck. The town was soon overflowing with anonymous young men brought together by the necessity of the times. Without well-established social networks, each person had to be judged on his own apparent merits. It was a place for new starts or to continue well-established falsehoods. One author neatly captured the flavor of the capital during the Civil War:

> Washington was packed with the varied concourse of people attracted by the great army. Contractors, inventors and cranks infested the bureaus. Officers used their furloughs to seek promotions.... Correspondents were there to scribble, and artists to sketch. Soldiers' relatives mingled with sight-seeing tourists.... Counterfeiters and confidence men assembled from all sections of the country. Petty thieves and pickpockets ... slid through the crowds and kept the Metropolitan Police on the run.... To entertain the legions ... came dancers and singers and comedians, prize fighters and gamblers, vendors of obscene literature and proprietors of "rum-jug shops." Apparent on every street was the secret invasion of the women of the town.... In the wake of the women, followed doctors, blatant in their promises....[1]

Such a situation was ideal for Dr. Tumblety and he decided to capitalize on it. Leaving New York late in 1861, Tumblety soon arrived in Washington. In the large congregation of soldiers and officers, the doctor soon found some old friends. He would later state that he was accepted by General McClellan and his staff and had decided to offer his services as a surgeon, only being prevented from doing so by a change in his health. We could dismiss this story as another of Tumblety's fantasies except that there is evidence that some of it is true.

An unnamed officer in the Army of the Potomac, arriving home in Buffalo in November 1861, told the editor of the *Buffalo Express* some startling news. He reported that the notorious Dr. Tumblety "actually held the position of Senior Surgeon on the staff of General McClellan." The officer stated that he often saw Tumblety in the retinue of the general. This report went out over the wires and caused considerable consternation in some places. The *British American Medical Journal*, published in Montreal, reprinted the article and, with very evident condescension, commented, "It is almost incredible that the foregoing should prove true, but the high positions that the commonest quacks have obtained in the army of the North, render it by no means impossible."[2]

This attitude raised the ire of the *Boston Medical and Surgical Journal*, which stated that the idea was too ridiculous to comment on and then extensively commented on it. First, they said, there was no position of "staff surgeon" in the army, confusing the terms senior and staff. More importantly, they mentioned that doctors needed to pass a rigorous examination to be appointed an assistant surgeon and had to have been in that position for five years to be appointed a surgeon with the regular army. Almost as an aside, they stated that doctors in the volunteers also had to pass an examination. The only concession they were willing to make was an admission that in some of the three-month regiments, raised at the very beginning of the war, there might have been some less qualified doctors.[3]

The war between the North and the South was not the only battle going on during 1861, as the regular doctors fought hard to keep all other practitioners out of the service. The Civil War was the biggest medical event since the cholera epidemics of the 1840s. If the homeopaths, eclectics and botanics were shut out of military service, it would greatly restore the prestige of the medical fraternity. At the beginning of the war, regular physicians held all 155 positions in the medical department and they were determined to keep it that way. For a federal appointment, a doctor had to take a five-hour examination detailing knowledge of anatomy, surgery, chemistry and general subjects. Even experienced regular physicians had a hard time passing this exam. In the volunteer regiments, things were less strict but the established state medical societies lobbied hard for similar examinations and to recognize only university-trained physicians. Because of this, Congress required the Secretary of War, in July 1861, to see that surgeons assigned to the volunteer brigades take an exam of "practical character."[4]

But the alternative doctors were not idle. In December 1861, Senator Grimes of Iowa presented a petition to the Army Medical Board to allow homeopathic physicians to practice in the army. The following month, the board rejected this petition, stating that it would open the army to all sorts of quacks. Not to be deterred, Grimes introduced a bill to allow homeopathic doctors to practice in the army. When this bill passed, early in 1862, it allowed homeopathic physicians to practice in some of the general hospitals and gave the president the authority to appoint doctors directly without an examination. In May 1862, Ohio removed all restrictions on the appointment of alternative healers. In late 1861, it was not unreasonable that Tumblety could have sought an appointment and been encouraged to think it was possible.

A more pertinent aspect of this debate has to do with General McClellan himself. In late December 1861, while attending a review of troops in Virginia, McClellan contracted typhoid fever. Although McClellan came from a family of highly respected regular physicians, he was treated by Erastus E. Marcy, his wife's uncle. Marcy was one of the leading homeopathic doctors in the country and editor of the *North American Homeopathic Journal*. McClellan's use of an alternative physician led some of his subordinates to question his leadership and his judgment. This may go a long way to explaining Tumblety's association with the general's staff.[5]

Tumblety reportedly attributed his hope of getting an army commission to his acquaintance with Robert Lincoln, the president's son. He had met him the previous summer at a resort and treated him for a sprained ankle. Supposedly, Lincoln gave him letters of introduction and Mrs. Lincoln used her influence on his part. As of late November, he was still in anticipation of a commission. It is known that Mrs. Lincoln and her son took a vacation trip to Long Branch, New Jersey, in August 1861. Tumblety was in New York and is known to have frequently visited resorts, including Long Branch. Whether they met is unknown.[6]

Not all of Tumblety's problems were with the medical press. In a news report, published in 1888, Edward Haywood commented on Tumblety's association with General McClellan. He said that Tumblety wore a military fatigue "costume" and let it be known that he was on McClellan's staff. One day, according to Haywood, the doctor was confronted by Lt. Larry Sullivan of one of the Rochester regiments, who, being familiar with McClellan's staff, told Tumblety he was a liar. It would seem that Tumblety got what he deserved.[7]

However, there is no record of this "Lt. Larry Sullivan" in any of the four regiments raised in Rochester. No Sullivan whose name begins with L (Lawrence, Laurence, Lafayette, etc.) nor any Sullivan with a middle initial of L was carried on the muster rolls as an officer. There is a Larry Sullivan listed in the 1860 census of Rochester, but he was a 12-year-old living in the Western House of Refuge for Juvenile Delinquents. No other Sullivan in Monroe County had a name beginning with L or a middle name with an L. This story is part of a larger article containing C. A. Dunham's recollections and may suffer from the same problems. Like so many things in Dr. Tumblety's life, we are left more questions than answers.

General McClellan's illness and subsequent withdrawal from public places, the rejection of the Grimes petition and the uproar in the press about his supposed position may have convinced Tumblety that he would never be accepted in the army. In any case, he decided to stay in Washington. In keeping with his presentation as a well-known and respected gentleman, Tumblety chose the most famous and prestigious hotel for his lodgings. Checking into

Washington Buildings, location of Tumblety's office during the Civil War. This multistory office building was built in the late 1850s and boasted all the latest conveniences, including gas lights and running water. It was located in the heart of Washington's social and business districts. ("The City of Washington: Bird's-Eye View from the Potomac—Looking North," c. 1880, Currier & Ives, Library of Congress, Geography and Map Division.)

the Willard Hotel on Fourteenth Street and Pennsylvania Avenue, he was immediately placing himself in the midst of Washington's elite. Beginning in the 1850s, the Willard brothers expanded and redecorated their hotel, making it the largest and best in the city. Nathaniel Hawthorne commented that the Willard "more justly could be called the center of Washington than either the Capitol or the White House." The bar at the Willard was the favorite resort of all the gentlemen of Washington. In this very fluid society, seeking a badge of respectability, Tumblety could not have chosen a better place to live.[8]

To conduct his practice, Tumblety rented a room in the Washington Buildings, an office building located on the north side of Pennsylvania Avenue near the corner of Seventh Street. This location was well chosen to attract customers and to demonstrate his prestige. Pennsylvania Avenue, known in Washington as simply "the Avenue," had, on the north side, the only brick sidewalk and served as the town's "promenade." In this location, he was assured that Washington's elite would pass his office every day. The major hotels were located along Pennsylvania Ave., as well as the theaters. This road also served as a boundary between respectable Washington on the north side and the less respectable on the south side. By locating "on the Avenue," Tumblety gained a measure of respectability. In addition, Seventh Street, north of Pennsylvania, was the heart of Washington's business district. Tumblety's office straddled the social heart and economic center of the city.

Because the location and nature of Tumblety's office later became an issue, it would be good to consider what evidence of the building exists. The 1862 Washington city directory lists: "Tumblety, Francis, physician, 344 Penn. Av., h. Willard's Hotel." By his first ad in the *Washington Star*, his office is described as being in the Washington Building at the corner of Pennsylvania Avenue and Seventh Street. These were the same location and Tumblety only had one office during his time in Washington.[9]

The building in which he chose to locate his office was, and is, a landmark in the District of Columbia. In 1859, the firm of Murray & Semmes acquired the land from Charles Stott and began building a large store and office building. It was to be a five-story brownstone building. The ground floor would contain two large rooms for stores while the four upper floors were for offices. In its original condition, each of the upper floors had six rooms, equipped with gas and water. While the stores on the ground floor were always referred to by their street addresses, 344 and 346 Pennsylvania Avenue, the offices above them were referred to as the Washington Building and were numbered 1 through 24.

Tumblety's office was number 11 and was located on the third floor. Other offices were then occupied by doctors, a dentist, a sewing machine agent, attorneys, insurance agents, a stencil cutter, a portrait painter and a watch repairer. One of the doctors, M. La Bonta, had his office on the same floor as Tumblety and advertised that he treated a variety of sexual diseases. When Tumblety moved in, Dr. La Bonta moved to an office on a lower floor. Interestingly, after Tumblety was long gone from Washington, in 1864, a Dr. H. C. Lispenard moved into number 16 and advertised to treat private diseases. He was still there when Tumblety was in the Old Capitol Prison. The ads in the *Washington Star* indicate that this building was entirely commercial and no living space was provided or offered.

By this time in his career, Dr. Tumblety was well experienced in setting up practice in a new place. Although he may have been in Washington earlier, his first ad does not appear in a newspaper until January 10, 1862, and he began advertising in both the *Washington Evening Star* and the *National Intelligencer*. It introduced him to Washington and continued a pattern that would last well into the 1870s. The ad begins with the title, in large block letters, "The Indian Herb Doctor from Canada," and, as he had done in St. John, announced that he can tell the illness of a patient without any information from them. He continued to claim that he could be consulted free of charge. The ads include the poem entitled "Our Motto," which he first used in Boston. Through all of January and February, this ad remained his only public presentation. On February 14, 1862, with the same ad, he included a list of Canadian dignitaries as references, including the governor of Canada and the mayors of Toronto, Montreal, Quebec, Hamilton and Brantford, among others. Within a few days, he added a list of local names and the diseases he had cured. These diseases included scrofula, nervous debility, consumption, fits, dyspepsia, pimples, etc. None of these ads mention his name but refer to him only as the Indian Herb Doctor.[10]

Beginning on March 21, all of his ads feature the name "F. Tumblety, M. D." as well as calling him the Indian herb doctor. Apparently he felt safe enough to claim status as a regular physician in the open atmosphere of wartime Washington or, perhaps, he had another reason to publish his name. At the same time, he began publishing testimonials from citizens of Washington. Some of these were letters but often he simply published a list of names and the diseases cured. There is no difference between these lists and the testimonials we have seen before. They include men and women, young and old, mechanics and middle class. Given the time period, there are a few soldiers listed as well.

Near the end of March, he began to publish ads reminiscent of his early Toronto messages. These call for the public to "Be Wise Before It Is Too Late."

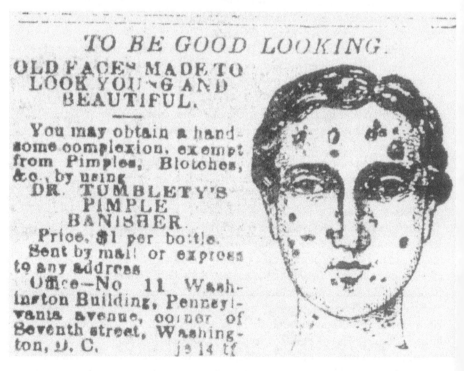

Ad for Tumblety's Pimple Banisher published in the *Washington Star* in 1863. Tumblety was a pioneer in the patent medicine business and had great success with this product.

They warn of the evils of mercury and praise Tumblety's herbal medicines. Scattered through them are pieces of poetry first used in Toronto. At the same time, his list of local testimonials grows long enough to fill an entire column in the paper. This full column of testimonials must have been very expensive but it continued through most of April and appeared sporadically in May and June.

This blizzard of advertising abruptly ceases near the end of May. On the 24, Tumblety published an ad for his Pimple Banisher that had appeared the previous year in *Harper's Weekly*, but without the illustration. It began with "To Be Good Looking," and then "Old Faces Made to Look Young and Beautiful." It goes on to extol Dr. Tumblety's Pimple Banisher and to report that for a dollar, it can be shipped anywhere. Finally, it lists the address of his office. What makes this ad different from what went before is how small it is. The ad takes up less than an inch of column space. At the same time, he published a small testimonial from E. Clay Dorsey, who is reported to have been associated with the U. S. Capitol. Tumblety cured him of consumption.[11]

There are probably several reasons why the advertising changed. Like any business, Tumblety needed to vary his pitch to keep interest high. The Indian herb doctor bit had done what it could and the Pimple Banisher was a proven success in other places. Smaller ads were certainly cheaper, although, from the descriptions of his business, financial considerations may not have been an important consideration.

After a brief lull, he began a new advertising campaign highlighting both of his products. Almost every day from June through August he had two types of ads in the Washington *Evening Star*. The first was a half-column ad which featured before and after pictures showing the effects of the Pimple Banisher. It repeats the information in the small ad and includes a large list of diseases for which it is effective. An important addition, near the bottom of the ad, under the headline "To Get Fat," reports that use of the product will cause you to gain five pounds of healthy flesh per month. This ad with its graphic images is eye-catching on the page and would have attracted much attention. It alone would have brought customers flocking to his office.

The second ad, although differing in form from time to time, trumpets the success of F. Tumblety, the Indian herb doctor. Some of these are long lists of testimonial letters while others are small and specific. One of the most frequently published testimonials was from Father C. L. Egan of St. Dominick's Church. He testifies that Tumblety's herb medicine cured him of a host of illnesses. Father Egan would later become famous as the chaplain of the Ninth Massachusetts Infantry and then of the V Corps of the Army of the Potomac, being with the army through the Battle of the Wilderness and the end of the war.[12]

In his first nine months in Washington, Tumblety had advertised exten-

sively in the newspapers. This abruptly ceased in September 1862 when he settled on a small, one-inch high ad that simply refers to the Indian herb doctor
and lists his office. From September until early December, he published only
this ad. Through the rest of December until early March 1863, he had no ad
in the *Washington Star*. Either he was so well known in Washington that he
no longer needed to advertise or his interests were elsewhere. Through
mid–March and early April, his ads appear sporadically and then cease. By
that time, he was contemplating a new move.

In fact, while he kept his office in Washington, he was personally at an
office in Frederick, Maryland. Later reports state that his office was on Court
Street and that it had a sign of a skull above the door. Why would he leave a
big city like Washington to set up in a small village like Frederick? The probable reason has to do with the timing of the move. He stopped advertising
extensively in Washington in September 1862. At that time, General Lee
crossed the Upper Potomac into Maryland and General McClellan, with the
Army of the Potomac, went to meet him. Most of Tumblety's customers went
north with the army. The two sides met at the bloody battle of Antietam near
Frederick on September 17. Huge numbers of wounded from both sides were
housed in temporary hospitals around Frederick. Many of them were ambula-
tory and easy pickings for Tumblety.[13]

Another possible reason for Tumblety's move from Washington was an
investigation begun by the Judge Advocate General's Office concerning accusations that he was selling fake discharge papers. On August 5, 1862, Major
Levi C. Turner was appointed assistant judge advocate for troops around Washington and given responsibility for all military arrests in the District of Columbia and the surrounding counties of Virginia. Included in his case papers is a
statement from Richard Render, a soldier in Company H, Second New York
Heavy Artillery, regarding the status of two other soldiers. Render reports that
Thomas Tift had received "a certificate of disability and discharge papers" that
had been made out by Tumblety in exchange for eight dollars. Tift was said
to be living in Alexandria and working as a clerk in a grocery store. Further,
George H. Torry, a soldier in Render's own company, was in the process of
getting the same thing from Tumblety for ten dollars.[14]

As this file is undated, there is no sure way to know when and why this
statement was made. A letter from Render, in the same file and dated July 9,
1863, provides some clues. Render took a leave in June 1861 which he thought
was authorized, but the military thought otherwise. He was returned to the regiment as a deserter on August 5, 1861, and was held in prison until August 25,
when he was released without charges being filed. It is likely that his statement was part of the reason he was not charged. It is interesting to note that
Thomas Tift, mentioned in Render's statement, was sent to the Mount Pleas-
ant Hospital on August 8, 1861. Perhaps the threat of being investigated for
fraudulent discharge papers was enough to make Tumblety move to Frederick.

The Judge Advocate's Office does not appear to have followed up on this case. Private Render reenlisted in Company H in January 1863, was wounded in May 1864 and received a medical discharge, presumably real, in January 1865. George Torry did not desert, as he was reported to be planning, but reenlisted in November 1863. He got sick in May 1864 and was sent to the Satterlee General Hospital in Philadelphia. The record shows that he deserted from there in October 1864, yet he is listed as being mustered out in Washington, D. C., on May 9, 1865. Thomas Tift, the other soldier mentioned in Render's statement, was sent to the Convalescent Camp at Alexandria, from which he is reported to have deserted in March 1863. However, he subsequently enlisted in Company H of the Second New York Heavy Artillery in January 1864 and died of wounds in July 1864.

By March 1863, Tumblety had decided to return to Washington. His first ad was on March 2 and included several testimonials from Frederick which were dated in February. Near the bottom, the ad reports that "the Doctor will be here again, to practice his profession, in a few days." It then goes on to say that he can be consulted at his office in the Washington Building. It is likely that while Tumblety was in Frederick he hired someone to run the Washington office, coming back periodically to check on things.[15]

While his newspaper ads are the most obvious record of his practice in Washington, we should remember that this is only what has been preserved. Several people reported that "at one time the walls were plastered with large posters advertising the virtues of the "Tumblety Pimple Destroyer." Although there is no specific information, it is likely that he used circulars and pamphlets as well. While no other record has been found of this, William Pinkerton, the famous detective, remembered that Tumblety widely advertised a cure for "a certain class of complaints," and sold "a book to soldiers which was prohibited on account of its immoralities." This might be the "Guide to the Afflicted" seen previously in Toronto. Pinkerton claimed that the book was illustrated with drawings of an "immoral character." He said that Tumblety so "flooded" the army with handbills and books that General McClellan banned the books on the ground that they would debase the army. All of his advertising was calculated to make his name, as a contemporary editorial reported, "as familiar as 'Household Words.'"[16]

Another aspect of this publicity was his own personality and lifestyle. Tumblety continued to project a flamboyant, eccentric persona for all to see. The accoutrements he collected in other cities were all on display in Washington. People remembered him riding a magnificent bay horse with white spots up and down the Avenue. It is reported that boys would run up to him with notes to make it appear that he was doing a good business. Whether the notes were real or not, we will never know, but they made an impression on the public. The only significant difference in Washington was the increasingly military nature of his costume, in keeping with the times.[17]

In addition to General McClellan, Tumblety mentioned as an acquaintance General James S. Wadsworth. He was from Geneseo, New York, just south of Rochester, and Tumblety claimed that Wadsworth knew his family. Tumblety refers to him as the military governor of Washington, a post he occupied after March 15, 1862. His headquarters were at Arlington House, the estate vacated by Robert E. Lee at the beginning of the war. The doctor reported that he was invited to dine with the general and his staff on many occasions. Although there is no way to demonstrate it, it is likely that many of the officers in Washington knew Tumblety during his stay there.[18]

As proof of his respectability and importance, Tumblety said that he was a regular at the levees held by President Lincoln at the White House. This is less impressive than it might first seem. These were public occasions, open to anyone who was "white and respectably dressed," and Tumblety could pass both tests. Once inside, the attendees were free to circulate and to shake the president's hand. However, Tumblety goes on to say that he was personally introduced to Lincoln by an officer, unnamed, whose acquaintance he made while living in Boston. When Tumblety decided to go to Europe, he said the president wrote a note of introduction to Lord John Russell, who was then the British foreign secretary. This note, as reproduced by the doctor, is dated June 12, 1863, and refers to Tumblety as "an esteemed friend of mine." The reproduction is signed and the signature appears similar to published examples of the president's own. It is the kind of note that the president probably dashed off every day for one reason or another. Even if he met the president, there is no indication it was anything more than a passing acquaintance, no matter how Tumblety might want to make it appear. There is no mention of Tumblety in any of the surviving Lincoln papers.[19]

All of these relations were later reported to demonstrate Tumblety's acceptance by respectable society but his dress and actions soon made him an object of ridicule. In December 1861, the Canterbury Music Hall, a local burlesque theater, performed a satirical skit entitled "Tumblety Outdone." While we have no specific information on the content of this skit, it is hard to believe that this was not about Dr. Tumblety.[20]

The Canterbury Music Hall, located on Louisiana Avenue behind the National Hotel, was modeled on the similarly named theater that opened in London in 1852. The London theater set the stage, literally, for music halls all over the world and just about every large city had its own "Canterbury Music Hall" by the 1860s. It was basically a saloon selling ten-cent drinks while providing entertainment for its customers. The New York example was shut down in 1862 for using "waiter girls" who peddled drinks in between other wares. In Washington, the Canterbury was

> ...nightly crowded with "soldiers and roughs, screeching, catcalling, smoking and spitting."... The entertainment was a potpourri of scantily dressed ladies, Negro comedians, acrobats and contortionists, broad jokes, farce, sentimental

songs and satires on the management of the army.... Save for a possible spree, family men did not frequent the music halls.[21]

To be ridiculed in such a place was not only embarrassing but, because much of his trade relied on his respectability, threatening to his business as well. Tumblety reported that he had asked the theater manager not to use his name in the program. According to the theater manager's later testimony, such farces were commonly performed in other places.

In March, the Canterbury again parodied Tumblety and the result was very different. When his name first showed up on an advertising bill, Tumblety asked the manager, George Percival, to remove it. However, the theater continued to mock the doctor. As a result, according to Tumblety's testimony, one of his female patients asked him to leave her house. Further, he was subjected to ridicule by others at his "boarding house." To seek redress, he filed a libel suit against the theater manager.[22]

No printed copy of this program exists and all that we have to evaluate are the ads for the Canterbury Hall in the *Washington Evening Star*. For the most part, the ads are unchanged through the beginning of March. They advertise a number of skits and near the bottom offer the following description of the regulars:

> The funny Bob Butler! The glorious eccentricities of A. J. Talbot! The comicalities of Dick Barker! The beautiful ballads of Miss Sallie Duval! The charming songs of Miss Amelia Wells! The daring gymnast James Ward! The exquisite dancing of M'lle La Folle and Emma Miles! The splendid juggling of Willie Armstrong! The old Virginny dances of Frank Wyant![23]

The only major change in the *Washington Star* ad occurred on March 5 when the theater announced a limited four-day engagement of Tony Pastor, billed as "the best comic singer of the age!" Regarded as the father of vaudeville, Pastor was a talented songwriter and comic singer. One of his later songs, "the Carte-de-Visite Album," paired Tumblety with Madam Restell, the noted abortionist, in one of the stanzas, calling him "the knight of pill and pestle."[24]

Tumblety's suit referred specifically to a performance that took place at the Canterbury Music Hall on the night of Friday, March 7, 1862. Although not listed in the newspaper advertisement, one of the farces performed that night, as listed in the program, was entitled "Dr. Tumblety's First Patient." The next afternoon, Saturday, Tumblety was in court claiming that the show caused "great injury to his reputation as a practicing and authorized Physician in the County of Washington." Justice J. H. Johnson issued a warrant for the arrest of George Percival, the theater manager. In his testimony, Tumblety exhibited the printed program showing the farce and said that it was designed to ridicule him and to question his credibility as a physician. To establish his respectability and profession, Tumblety showed the judge his diploma, a testimonial from Canada (probably the one with all the officials named) and his gold medal.

Percival was apprehended and brought to court that afternoon. In his defense, the theater manager stated that he never intended to defame Tumblety or his profession and did not even know Tumblety. He explained that in the theater, it was the practice to "introduce the most comic and unusual names in burlesques, without intending, however, to reflect upon or to injure individuals bearing the name selected." This argument might have been more successful if they had used Tumblety's name in a skit about someone other than a doctor. A more important argument for the defense, and more interesting for us, is the claim that this was not a new skit but one that had been performed many times before in other places, perhaps including the Montreal performance in 1857. Several witnesses claimed that they had seen the same farce, or a very similar one, performed by Bryant's Minstrels in New York, one of the most famous of the minstrel troupes. It is perhaps no coincidence that Tony Pastor wrote songs for Bryant's Minstrels. This is another indication that Tumblety's short stay in New York had attracted unwanted attention.

Although Tumblety had begun the case, he was not ready to prosecute it. He asked for a postponement because several important witnesses were absent. The judge set the trial for two P.M. on Tuesday, March 11, and granted Percival bail until the hearing. The last night of Tony Pastor's engagement at the Canterbury was Saturday, March 8 and it is unlikely that the Tumblety skit was performed again. If it had been, Percival would have forfeited his $500 bail. The theater was closed on Sunday night and by Monday, the *Washington Evening Star* reported a completely new program.

From the short description published the day after, the hearing on Tuesday must have been anticlimactic. The *Evening Star* reported that Tumblety brought none of the witnesses he had promised. However, Percival repeated his statement that he never intended to ridicule Tumblety and promised not to use his name in the program any more. Having reached this mutually satisfying conclusion, the judge dismissed the case. In his autobiography, Tumblety commented that his "object not being to persecute but to uphold, in my own person, the dignity of the medical profession."[25]

While Percival may have libeled Tumblety as a doctor, a far more insidious and disastrous slander was later presented about Tumblety's time in Washington. It was not published until 1888, but it applies to this period and needs to be evaluated here. A vivid description of Tumblety's life in Washington, which has been widely quoted in recent discussions about him, derives from an interview with Colonel C. A. Dunham published in 1888 by the *New York World*. More damning testimony could not have been found to blacken his character and cast suspicion on him as Jack the Ripper. Because of the importance of this testimony, we need to look at it in detail.

Colonel Dunham, so the interview begins, was a well-known lawyer who lived near Fairview, New Jersey. In 1861, he was a colonel "in the army" and met Tumblety in Washington a few days after the Battle of Bull Run (July 21,

1861). He goes on to describe him as an "arrant charlatan and quack." It is obvious from the whole tone of the report that Dunham had no love for Tumblety.[26]

Dunham reports that he accepted a dinner invitation from Tumblety. He described the location as Tumblety's rooms, saying, "he had very cozy and tastefully arranged quarters in, I believe, H street. There were three rooms on a floor, the rear one being his office, with a bedroom or two a story higher." The dinner was excellent and afterwards the guests settled in to play cards. The subject of women came up and, according to Dunham, Tumblety got almost apoplectic. He took his guests into his office and showed them a number of jars with anatomical specimens of uteri and lectured his companions on the evils of women. At a later time, Dunham reports that Tumblety was asked why he hated women and he told a story of marrying a woman who turned out to be a prostitute and that he had given up on women.

According to Dunham, soon after this, Tumblety's "real character" became known and he slipped away to St. Louis. Dunham states that Tumblety had himself arrested as Dr. Blackburn in 1865 to get publicity. Finally, he goes into a long story about Tumblety parodying himself on the stage at the Canterbury Music Hall in Washington and later suing the proprietor to make it look like he had not.

Dunham's interview makes Tumblety appear threatening, deceptive, foolish, and misogynist. At the time it was published in 1888, it colored all of the press reports about Tumblety. The idea of Tumblety's hatred of women played right into the hysteria over Jack the Ripper. Its rediscovery and publication by Evans and Gainey has set the tone for all modern discussion of Tumblety. On the face of it, the story has the look of truth and meets our expectations. But what if it is not true? Who was C. A. Dunham and does his story fit the facts? These are questions that no modern reporter would allow to remain unanswered. Nor should a modern historian accept on face value any story so conveniently appropriate without checking it.

The colonel claims to have met Tumblety in Washington a few days after the Battle of Bull Run. As the battle took place on July 21, 1861, there is a problem. At that time and probably until September, Tumblety was in New York, not Washington. He had just started a major advertising campaign in *Harper's Weekly*. This, along with other evidence from the last chapter, shows he could not have had a residence in Washington at that time. Thus Dunham could not have met Tumblety then. Dunham's biographer reports that he was in Washington for brief periods in July, August and November 1861. Beyond that, his whereabouts are unknown.[27]

In his interview, Dunham goes to elaborate lengths to describe Tumblety's office and rooms on H Street. Everyone else who knew Tumblety in Washington, as well as listings in the city directory and all of his advertising, reports that his office was at the corner of Pennsylvania Avenue and Seventh Street, nowhere near H Street. It has been suggested that Dunham's memory may have been faulty on the location, after all it was some 25 years after the fact. If Tumblety's office was located anywhere other than where we know it to have been, this could be excused. However, even after 25 years, no one would mistake Pennsylvania Avenue for H Street. The "Avenue" was the center of Washington life while H Street, in 1861, was a largely undeveloped residential neighborhood of small houses. Dunham made it appear that Tumblety had his office in one of these structures but the earlier description of the Washington Building gives lie to that account.

Even if we forgive a lapse in memory as large as that above, does Dunham's description of Tumblety's living arrangements match what we know? The colonel said that there were "three rooms on a floor, the rear one being his office, with a bedroom or two a story higher." Yet Tumblety's office was a single room in the Washington Building. There was never any residential space in that structure during the Civil War.

Further, Tumblety claims that his residence was the Willard Hotel, not the space above his office. This is supported by the 1862 city directory. The only evidence to the contrary is Tumblety's statement, in his libel case, that others had made fun of him at his "boarding-house." If this is not just a reference to the hotel, it might indicate that the doctor had moved his residence to some other location. However, his office remained at the Washington Building.

Interestingly, Dunham's description of the combined office and living quarters almost exactly matches what Tumblety is known to have rented in Brooklyn almost two years later. The Brooklyn *Daily Eagle*, on May 4, 1865, reported that Tumblety occupied a suite of three rooms which he used as an office and sleeping apartments. Dunham reports being in the doctor's office in Brooklyn after the war and obtaining a copy of Tumblety's pamphlet.

Finally, there is the question of Dunham's military title and career. As it turns out, according to his biographer, early in the war, Dunham was involved in scamming the government by claiming to raise a regiment but pocketing the funds. His title of colonel was never official in any way and he never served in the military. By November 1861, that scheme was dead and Dunham's connection with the military was over. It is reported that his whereabouts during 1862 are unknown. It would seem unlikely then that he was in Washington and pretending to be a colonel without leaving a record. Who was this person whose story is so full of holes?

While these points cast doubt on his report, it is the character of C. A. Dunham, himself, that makes it all questionable. Charles A. Dunham, otherwise known as Sanford Conover, was a notorious and convicted perjurer. A report in the Albany *Evening Journal*, dated June 23, 1865, describes an encounter with the shifty Dunham:

> The testimony of this man should be received with suspicion. We are reluctantly compelled to believe either that he is crazy or something worse. Some four weeks ago, he called upon us, pretending to be in distress and representing that he was

on his way to Washington to testify in the conspiracy case; that he was robbed at or near Rome, in this state, and that having no money to pay his fare, he had walked nearly all the way from that place here—a distance of over a hundred miles.... He told us a long story about his intercourse with the Rebel leaders in Canada—some points of which are decidedly in conflict with his testimony on the stand.[28]

Dunham, a.k.a. Conover, testified before the military commission investigating the Lincoln assassination. His testimony, and the other witnesses he brought forward, were at first considered very important in proving the complicity of the Confederate government in the assassination and various terrorist plots. It was soon evident, however, that he manufactured evidence and that his testimony was false. Further, the witnesses that he brought forward all had false names, had never been to the places they were supposed to have been and had never talked to the people they supposedly met. When he was caught at this, he manufactured evidence trying to implicate the military judges in his plot.

As early as June 1865, General Dix warned Secretary of War Stanton about Conover's reliability. Having investigated his background, he reported that Conover, who had just been released from the Confederate prison in 1863, had gone to Canada and represented himself as a secret agent of the Confederate government under the name of James W. Wallace. While there he served as the Montreal correspondent for the New York *Times, World, Tribune* and *News* under four separate aliases. Dix reported that his character was disreputable.

In July 1866, the House Judiciary Committee fully exposed his treachery. He admitted everything, and was tried and sentenced to ten years for perjury. He served two years of his sentence and was later pardoned by president Andrew Johnson. Dunham was in Brooklyn in 1868 when he reported getting a copy of Tumblety's autobiography from him. Much of his 1888 interview seems like a twisted version of the same material presented in Tumblety's own book.

Why would Dunham, in 1888, go to the lengths he did to make Tumblety appear so guilty? Several reasons suggest themselves. Dunham was known to be vindictive and hold grudges for a long time. People who he felt had injured him were likely to end up in one of his fantasies in a none too complimentary light. Perhaps the meeting with Tumblety in Brooklyn did not go well. It may just be that Tumblety spent so much time decrying the abuses of the military tribunal and Stanton, that Dunham felt he was attacking him personally. Probably the most pertinent reason was that Dunham saw a way to make money off these sensational stories. This may not be the only Tumblety story he penned in 1888. Another article quotes "Colonel James L. Sothern," a well-known lawyer of Chicago, who met Tumblety in a number of places over the years. This "well-known" lawyer does not appear to be listed in any Chicago census, city directory or newspaper. The story had the smell of Dunham all over it.[29]

Despite heavy reliance on Dunham's story about Tumblety by later historians and writers, none of it can be shown to be true. All the facts which can be verified, Dunham has either gotten wrong or misinterpreted. How much more fabrication is there in those parts not subject to verification? Dunham seems to have been a habitual and pathological liar. We are forced to agree with General Dix's statement that his testimony should not be accepted "unless corroborated by witnesses of unquestionable credibility." Such witnesses do not exist. Ironically, the most widely known account of Tumblety's life is the least true.

By the spring of 1863, Dr. Tumblety was getting restless. He contemplated taking a trip to Europe. He was traveling in Virginia and Maryland. He spent some time in Frederick, Maryland. Dunham stated that he left when his true character was known but there is no evidence that he left Washington other than voluntarily. Nevertheless, by May he was on the move. According to his own testimony, dated 1872, he left Washington on May 15, 1863, headed for New York. He soon shows up in Philadelphia and then New York, so this may be true. However, if it is, then he was not in Washington on June 12, 1863, to receive the reported note from President Lincoln for his proposed trip to Europe. While we cannot completely rule out the existence of this note, it appears very dubious.

8

---oee---

A Year in Brooklyn
(1863–1864)

Leaving Washington, the doctor headed north, first to Philadelphia. Tumblety's short and unhappy stay in Philadelphia began in May 1863. As he did in Washington, Tumblety checked into the most prestigious hotel in the city. The Girard House was described in the guides as one of the "largest and most magnificent in the country." The barroom at the Girard House was so luxurious that it was a tourist attraction of its own. A block away, he rented an office at 333 Chestnut Street. This was a six-story commercial structure in the heart of the business district. On the building, Tumblety suspended a sign, done in chrome and crimson, of an Indian brave flanked by two Indian women. His office was on the second floor and reportedly had a screen, several chairs and a table. It is important to note that there was no large, anatomical museum here, nor any indication that Tumblety had any preserved specimens. In fact, the *Philadelphia Press* said that it contained "nothing to indicate medical practice."[1]

Tumblety probably began by having handbills distributed but his ads soon started to appear in the local papers. The first of his ads appears on May 15 in the *Inquirer* and on May 21 in the *Philadelphia Press*. He would later testify that he left Washington on May 15, 1863, and the ads generally confirm this. These ads continue sporadically into the last week of June.

There are two significant changes evident in Tumblety's ads which will characterize his strategy for some time to come. First, to attract more patients, Tumblety decided on a new and aggressive advertising technique. The Philadelphia ads begin with a reward offer of ten dollars if the doctor cannot diagnose the patient's illness without any information being given. Prior to this, Tumblety had made the same diagnostic claim but it was never linked with a monetary reward. One can be sure that the reward was never paid, but it attracted attention and that was what was needed.[2]

The second innovation was the lack of any identification of Tumblety himself. Prior to this, even recently in Washington, the ads always referred to Dr.

95

Tumblety. While frequently termed the Indian herb doctor, his name was also prominently displayed. From now on, he would be known simply as the Indian herb doctor. Perhaps, as he said in his lawsuit, the connection of his name with a burlesque had caused him to lose respectability. Whatever the reason, he took care to keep his real name out of the ads.

But he was not hesitant to make himself known to the citizens of Philadelphia. Reportedly he rode through the streets on a spotted horse dressed in a cavalry outfit, including boots and spurs. Here we see a continuation of his activities in many other places. In Philadelphia, as he walked the streets, he was followed by a colored servant, rather than a valet. The parade was completed by a greyhound. This was part of who Tumblety thought himself to be and an effective bit of advertising.[3]

His stay in Philadelphia would probably have been no different from his stay in any other location had it not been for an incident that Tumblety brought on himself. On May 21, Tumblety went to the police station and filed the following affidavit:

> Dr. Tumblety, of Washington—333 Chestnut street—Stolen, this morning, a gold medal, presented to deponent by the citizens of Montreal, Canada; name on it; value $800; taken by a man named St. Clair, stopping at Girard House; was showing it to him; he ran off with it. F. Tumblety, M. D.[4]

An arrest warrant was prepared and St. Clair was taken the next day. He said his name was Joseph Aspinwall, alias St. Clair. A hearing was held on May 23 where Tumblety testified that St. Clair came to see him and asked if he had been in Montreal. The doctor said he had and proceeded to show him the medal. A patient came in and Tumblety went to deal with him. When he came back, both St. Clair and the medal were gone. Based on this evidence, St. Clair was committed to jail to await trial.

From the time he arrived in Philadelphia, Tumblety had aroused suspicions among the police and they were watching him. Because of these doubts, Benjamin Franklin, the police chief, wrote to the authorities in Montreal to find out about Tumblety. His doubts were further raised when, a few days later, Tumblety called at the station to say that he had recovered the missing medal. According to the doctor, someone had slipped it under the door of his office. St. Clair was released soon afterwards but the wheels were in motion.

As one would expect, when the reply came from Montreal it was not positive about Tumblety. It called him a quack, imposter and charlatan. The authorities flatly denied that any medal was given to Tumblety by the citizens of Montreal. Chief Franklin called Tumblety to his office and began to berate him for having an innocent man put in jail. He accused Tumblety of being an imposter and suggested that he was a rebel spy. According to the report, he gave him 24 hours to leave Philadelphia. Apparently Tumblety did not take this too seriously, as he continued to advertise until June 27. But the Philadelphia authorities were not going to let this pass and on July 1, the mayor of Philadelphia issued a warrant for Tumblety's arrest on a charge of perjury. Whether he knew about the warrant or just felt that the city was getting too hot for him, Tumblety was nowhere to be found when the police came to look for him.[5]

After the difficulties in Philadelphia, Tumblety continued to head north. He may have visited family in Rochester and he was practicing in Albany in September. He showed up in Brooklyn in early October 1863. His first ad appeared in the *Brooklyn Daily Eagle* on October 3 and for the next eight months, he was a regular advertiser. This is the first time since his departure from Washington that we can look in detail at his public persona and his practice.[6]

Unlike previous expressions, Tumblety did not make any attempt to make a big splash on his arrival. He rented three rooms on the second floor of a building at 181 Fulton Street, near Nassau, over the Arnold and Young grocery store. The building was at least four stories and had both office and residential units. It was located in a respectable but normal neighborhood and did not carry the prestige of his other office locations. One of the rooms served as his office and the other two were his living quarters. This was quite a change from staying in the most exclusive hotels. Part of this space was described in 1864 in an ad published when Tumblety was getting ready to move out:

> To Let, Fine Offices (Suitable for any business) to let in the most eligible part of Brooklyn. A large, commodious and very desirable front room, with four windows, on the second floor of the building No. 181 Fulton Street, corner of Nassau (now occupied as a herb doctor's office), to let, with possession on the first of May, at the reasonable rent of $12 per month. Also a rear room (well lighted) on the same floor. Rent $7 per month. Or both rooms let together for $18. Apply to Elisha Henshaw, 4th floor of building.

The person renting this space, Elisha Henshaw, (or Hanshew) was a 36-year-old shoemaker from England. Mr. Hanshew was married and had grown children. This was the beginning of a friendship that would last for decades. He would remain Tumblety's friend for the rest of their lives. In 1889, he was one of the character references for Tumblety and claimed to have known him for 24 years.[7]

The low profile Tumblety put forth in his office and residence was carried over into his ads as well. In all of his Brooklyn advertising, Tumblety was known simply as "The Indian Herb Doctor." As he had since leaving Washington, his public persona was tied up in this image and his real name, so prominent in previous years, is nowhere mentioned. Even his testimonials are no longer addressed to Dr. Tumblety but to the Indian herb doctor. Throughout his career, up to this point, his name was prominently displayed in all of his ads. From here on, the name Francis Tumblety is seldom seen. Perhaps the recent troubles in Philadelphia caused him to change his strategy or it could be that the title was a better seller than his name. Whatever the reason, his ads for the next few years do not mention his name.

Much of the quack medicine business depends on getting patients through the front door. Once there, they are likely to be talked into purchasing medicine. It is getting them there that is important. To accomplish this, Tumblety used the ad first seen in Philadelphia, which promised a monetary reward if he could not tell the patient what his illness was without any information being given. The new ad differed from those in Philadelphia by dropping any reference to Canada and increasing the reward from $10 to $30. When the prospective patient came seeking the reward, some way would be found to avoid paying it. As before, the ad promises no charge for consultation or advice.[8]

While the initial ad was simply the $30 reward offer, by the next day it had expanded to include a poem extolling the virtues of his natural medicine: This was the poem first seen in Boston, then in Washington and entitled, as it is here, "Our Motto." As he has before, Tumblety praises natural medicine over mercury and continues his opposition to surgery as a therapy. In the process, he invokes a pious tone, implying that the healing power comes from God.

This ad, the $30 reward associated with the motto, appears repeatedly in Brooklyn and through the next decade wherever Tumblety began his practice. It was his introduction to the public. The last sentence of the ad reports that he has 5,000 certificates from former patients that may be consulted at his office.

As we have seen, testimonials or certificates were an important part of proving legitimacy in the 19th century. Testimonials from local people were significant in attracting business and Tumblety soon began publishing a record of his remarkable cures in Brooklyn. From the sixth through the twentieth of October, the only ad he ran was the $30 reward. However, starting on the twenty-third, he began to publish testimonials from people in Brooklyn and other local places. It seems to have taken him about two weeks to start getting material for his ads. Over the next eight months, he would publish 59 testimonials and these provide insights on his evolving practice.

There is no way to tell if the testimonials accurately reflect the breadth or style of his practice. In the absence of other evidence, we must use what is provided. The first thing we can see is that his clients were overwhelmingly male, as 38 of the 59 testifiers are men. Women comprise 15 and children another 6 examples. Given Tumblety's homosexuality, the preponderance of males raises questions. In an effort to know who these men were, the 1860 and 1870 censuses for Brooklyn were consulted. Only seven of the 38 were securely identified. Most often there were too many men with the same name to positively identify the testifier. However, all seven of the identified men were married and had children. It seems likely, therefore, that the testifiers reflect his practice and not his lovers.

Much has been made of Tumblety as a provider of abortion drugs or treatment of sexual disorders but, as usual, his public ads do not support this. There is a single instance of a woman who was treated for an unspecified female complaint. The majority of his practice involved lung problems (consumption, catarrh, cough) and skin problems (scrofula, blotches, boils, pimples). Together these constitute 49 percent of the testimonials. A far third is the condition of general debility, with 15 percent of the cases. Of the total, 22 percent of the cases were represented by fewer than three examples. These included such diseases as blindness, cancer, fits, piles, rheumatism and tapeworm.

The clients who sought out the Indian herb doctor were from the middle to lower classes primarily. Of the 59 testimonials, the profession of 15 can be determined, either from the ads or from the census. The most prominent may have been the daughter of Michael Keeler, who had been the supervisor of Brooklyn. At least two had significant estates, totaling several thousand dollars. However, most were working men, including engineers, ship carpenters, laborers, a machinist and an organist. Not surprisingly, a number of testifiers listed the Brooklyn Navy Yard as their place of employment. For people such as this, the $20 charged for a course of treatment was a significant investment. Yet they came in large numbers and made Tumblety wealthy.

Over time the testimonials expand in area. In the beginning, the testifiers are all from Brooklyn, most from the area around his office. Within a month, the first testimonial from New York City appears and from then on, these form a significant number of ads. By April, there are cases from Bell Tower, Williamsburgh and South Brooklyn. Finally, in June, just before the ads stop, there are people from Newark and Morristown, New Jersey, listed.

Not all of the doctor's patients were satisfied with his treatment. One such incident, which came to involve the police, was reported in the *Daily Eagle* on May 6, 1864. Late in April or early May, a man named Fenton Scully (or Shulley) came to the doctor to be treated for asthma. Scully was 31 years old and living in New York City when he heard of the doctor's fame. Tumblety said that he could cure him for an agreed-upon price of $20. Scully put up $15 on account and took home a supply of medicine. The *Daily Eagle* facetiously reported the specified treatment: "he was directed to take it in liberal doses, a wine glass full, say every five minutes, until he was better or worse." The medicine did not have the effect Scully desired and on May 5, he came back to the doctor to complain. According to Scully, Tumblety told him that his case was hopeless and he should live with it. The patient then suggested that a refund was in order. The paper, in its own style, reported what happened next:

> The Doctor then tried a course of physical treatment on the recalcitrant patient with the most signal success. The prescription read: Patient taken vigorously by the collar; well shaken after taken; sole leather promptly applied to the base of the dorsal vertebrae; result prompt evacuation—of the premises by the patient.

Scully swore out a warrant against the doctor and he was arraigned on May 6. His attorney, Mr. Parmenter, asked that the case be postponed until the next Monday. The paper reported that, to record the case properly, the court asked the Indian doctor what his name was and he reported it as Francis Tumblety. This last part is important because it indicates he was known only as the Indian herb doctor. No other names are mentioned in the article.

The case was presented to the judge on May 10 and Scully testified that when he complained, the doctor refused to have anything to do with him. When he persisted, Tumblety kicked him twice in the ribs and knocked him down the stairs. The defense presented two witnesses who told a very different story. They claimed Tumblety never touched Scully. According to the witnesses, Scully was disruptive and drove several other patients out of the office. Finally, the doctor politely asked him to leave and eventually took him by the arm and escorted him out. Whatever the truth of the matter, the judge accepted the witnesses' testimony and dismissed the charge against Tumblety. Needless to say, Fenton Scully does not show up in the many testimonials published in the papers.[9]

The attitude of the *Daily Eagle* in this case is interesting. They pegged Tumblety as a fraud from the beginning and made every effort to ridicule him. Nowhere in his ads did Tumblety claim to be an Indian medicine man. In the 19th century, an Indian herb doctor used natural medicines, often said to be based on Indian knowledge. He himself was seldom an Indian. Yet the paper made a point of joking about this:

> The Doctor is a mystery; his presence being too awe inspiring to permit anybody to inquire into his history. He is supposed, however, to be as genuine an Indian as most of the Indians exhibited in this latitude. It is given out that he was a great medicine man of the Saltz-an-Sennah tribe, who, instead of placing himself in the Museum of the L. I. Historical Society, as a curiosity, concluded to make a living and bless his fellow men by practicing the healing art.[10]

While ridiculing him as a quack, the *Daily Eagle* provides us with the first full description of his public persona. As in other places, Tumblety's appearance and style raised considerable comment. Tumblety kept two piebald ponies which he and his valet would ride through Brooklyn, much as he had done in other places. The paper reported that while the doctor was sometimes seen on horseback, he was more familiar walking the streets with a stout yellow cane and accompanied by a big yellow dog, sometimes called a greyhound. They describe him as an unusually "elongated young man," and commented on his large mustache. Customarily he wore a pork pie hat and a butternut colored suit with wide pants and short coat tails. A "pork pie hat" is described in contemporary sources as "a hat with a flat crown and a brim turned up all the way around," and it was most popular from 1855 to 1865. His pants were described as "nankeen" which is a durable fabric made of Chinese cotton and dyed a buff to yellow color. This outfit was apparently considered to be quite fashionable and he was soon nicknamed the "nankeen swell."[11]

The clothes, horses, servants and dogs were all part of Tumblety's public image. At this same time it is reported that as he rode through Brooklyn, he would scatter change, as he had in Toronto, for the boys in the street, which also gained him great notoriety. These clothes and actions got him noticed and they demonstrated his success and therefore his legitimacy. Like his newspaper ads, they brought in customers. To put on such a show was expensive and suggests that his practice was doing very well.

While this butternut suit may have been his trademark, another description suggests that fashionable clothing was a mania for him. At the time, he was associated with two other males, a tall thin one, who served as his valet, and a short stout one, who took care of his horses. It was reported that the doctor wore new clothes each day and that the valet wore the clothes the doctor had worn the day before. From him, on the third day, the clothes would go to the third man and after, as the paper suggested, they would go to the secondhand clothes dealer. If this is true, even in part, it represents a very well-to-do lifestyle and is another indication of how well his practice was doing.[12]

Because of later events, it is important to understand who Tumblety's associates were and how they interacted with him. It is clear that the valet was more important to the doctor than the stable hand. As the doctor rode the streets of Brooklyn, the valet was often in attendance, following behind on another horse. When Tumblety decided to leave Brooklyn and head to St. Louis, he took the valet with him but left the other person in Brooklyn and now unemployed. It is likely that this created considerable animosity which would soon cause Tumblety many problems.

The valet Tumblety took to St. Louis was Mark A. Blackburn, whom the Doctor first met when he came to New York in 1861. Blackburn was a man of many names. Although his real name was Mark, he was commonly known in the 1860s as J. H. Blackburn. Apparently he was also known as B. R. Farrell. In a later article, after the Lincoln assassination, the *Brooklyn Eagle*, mistakenly identifying Blackburn with David Herold, reports that he performed a heroic deed while a building was burning. Using that information, it was possible to go back to the original and find the story.

On April 2, 1864, a large fire broke out in Brooklyn which destroyed twelve frame buildings on Doughty Street. These were old buildings and the progress of the fire was so swift that people were not able to save much of their possessions. A woman residing in one of the structures was frantic. She

informed a young gentleman named B. R. Farrell, that a trunk containing $200 was in the upper story. Mr. Farrell went to the room, secured the trunk, but found that all means of egress by the stairs had been shut off. He secured the money, however, and made his escape by jumping out of the second story window, fortunately without injuring himself, and handed the money to the woman.[13]

Blackburn was a confidant of Tumblety and while variously described as a servant, a coachman or a valet, he appears to have been a student as well. As others had before him, Blackburn was taught the medicine man business by his mentor. There is considerable confusion about Tumblety using the name Blackburn as an alias in his business in Brooklyn. There is no contemporary reference to Tumblety as Blackburn. It is known that in St. Louis, Mark A. Blackburn was known as J. H. Blackburn and practiced as a doctor. When people later referred to Tumblety using this alias in Brooklyn, they were confusing him with his student.

The third person of this trio, the stable hand, is mostly unknown. Other than the description of his being short and stout and his handling of the horses, there is no sure information about him. However, Tumblety's abandonment of him would, within months, have the most serious of consequences.

As usual, there is no indication of when Tumblety chose to move on or any reason for the move. The rental ad mentioned above indicates that as early as April he was thinking about moving. Up until June 1864, his advertising shows no change and his practice appears to be flourishing. Tumblety continued advertising in the *Daily Eagle* every day until June 15, 1864. After that date, there is one more ad on July 9 and then the ads stop. Several sources, admittedly later in time, suggested that Tumblety left Brooklyn quickly and did not tell anyone where he was going. On the other hand, he reported that he stayed in New York until December 3, 1864, when he left for St. Louis. There is no indication of what he might have been doing between the date of his last ad and his arrival in St. Louis. However, he is listed on the passenger list for the *George Cromwell* sailing from New York on December 4, 1864, for New Orleans. There is no Blackburn on the list but a few names after Tumblety is the name M. J. Farrell, similar to a name used by Blackburn while he was in Brooklyn.[14]

There have been many reasons suggested for this change. It has widely been reported that he had some dispute with the Greenwood Cemetery in Brooklyn. Some have seen in this a sinister overtone of dealing with dead bodies. The connection with the cemetery stems from a satirical notice in the New York *Sunday Mercury* that was published late in 1865. It suggested that the doctor's practice was so successful that he was cheating the Greenwood Cemetery of its customers. Because of this, the cemetery got the secretary of war to arrest him. This was never intended to be taken seriously.[15]

Other reasons which were more realistic have been suggested. The *Daily Eagle,* in discussing why Tumblety left, reported that "by and by his patients dropped off and [he] found it prudent to leave the city." They also reported that he had wooed and won the heiress of one of the richest families on Brooklyn Heights, although they did not say how this worked out. One of the St. Louis papers stated that Tumblety had to leave Brooklyn abruptly since he had been accused of practicing abortion. While there is no mention of this in the New York papers, given Tumblety's overall career, it may have some validity.

For whatever reason, Tumblety and his assistant left Brooklyn, probably late in July, for New York. In December, they left for New Orleans. Ultimately, their path would lead to St. Louis and the next crisis in the doctor's life.

9

─────── ∞ ───────

Arrest in St. Louis
(1865)

Arriving in New Orleans after a six-day trip on the steamer *George Cromwell*, our travelers quickly arranged transport up the Mississippi to St. Louis. From the short time they spent in New Orleans we can deduce that St. Louis was their ultimate destination, but why remains elusive. Tumblety and his assistant arrived in St. Louis by early January 1865. His earliest ad appears in the *Missouri Republican* on January 5. From that point until his forcible removal in May, he was a regular advertiser in both of the major dailies in St. Louis. For the first two weeks, his only ad was the $30 reward come-on that he had developed and used in Brooklyn. It included the poem which had previously been printed under the title "Our Motto" in Boston and other places. As had been the case for some time now, there was no name in the ad and he was described as "The Indian Herb Doctor from Canada."[1]

For his office, Tumblety hired space over an oyster saloon at 50 Olive Street between Third and Fourth. This was in the heart of the city's business district, an area of multistory brick office buildings. To catch the public's eye, he hired a newsboy to stand at the bottom of the stairs and distribute handbills or "dodges." These were most likely testimonials to the doctor's cures as was his normal practice. In keeping with the Indian theme, he painted the boy's face red and put feathers on his head. With this kind of show being offered, it was not long before the public knew there was a new personality in town.[2]

Tumblety stayed at the Lindell Hotel on Washington Avenue between 7th and 8th Streets. Most likely this was out of personal preference and the need for a prestigious address. The Lindell had been begun in 1856 but was not opened until 1863, when a banquet and ball attracted 3,000 people. It was huge, six stories tall, and elaborately decorated. Most descriptions comment on its 36 miles of bell wire. It cost 1.5 million dollars to build and was the largest hotel anywhere in North America at the time. High-ranking visitors to St. Louis sought the Lindell Hotel. At a minimum, it suggests that Tumblety was successful and well off.[3]

Within two weeks of his first ad, Tumblety began a two-pronged campaign to gain the public's trust. The first prong was composed of the usual assortment of testimonials from cured patients. Although the names and circumstances are different, the tenor of these ads and the diseases listed are the same as in any of the other cities where he practiced. Such banes of human existence as scurvy, rheumatism, dyspepsia, and consumption all fell before the doctor's medicines.

The second prong of his attack on the public trust consisted of ads addressed to the sick and invalids who were advised to seek the doctor without delay and be cured. These were most often accompanied by some fragment of poetry. Most of these fragments were previously published in Canada and, where they originally contained Tumblety's name, the phrase Indian herb doctor was now substituted, even if it did not fit with the meter of the poem. Often, stanzas of different poems were published together with less than poetic grace.

On February 28, Tumblety announced that he moved his office to a new location at 52 Third Street between Olive and Pine. While this was also on the second story, it was presumably a better location, being close to both the custom house and the chamber of commerce and opposite the post office. At this new location he dispensed with his little Indian helper and chose a more sedate method of advertising. At the foot of the stairs leading to his office, he placed a cedar bush in a tub. A placard with "The Indian Herb Doctor" printed on it was attached to the cedar.[4]

In St. Louis, Tumblety continued his practice of riding a beautiful horse and being followed by his valet and greyhounds. His costume continued to evolve and became more military in style. In his own words, he dressed in a "handsome robe, high patent leather boots and spurs." At the time, St. Louis was a hotbed of rebel sympathizers and potential spies which the authorities were nervously watching. It did not take long for Tumblety to catch their eye. On or about March 9, 1865, as he rode out to view a piece of property in nearby Carondelet, members of the Provost Guard arrested him for impersonating a federal officer. In a short notice, under the title "False Colors," the *Missouri Democrat* reported the affair in the tone the press often used for Tumblety:

> The "Indian Herb Doctor" as he calls himself, was arrested a day or two ago, by order of the Provost Marshall General, for wearing the insignia of a Federal Officer. His tigerish moustache was closely scrutinized but having nothing soldierly about it, was not molested.[5]

Tumblety, not mentioning any insignia, reported in his autobiography that he was arrested for "putting on foreign airs," and, as he was told by one of his captors, "You think yourself another God Almighty, and we won't stand for it." He reported he was held in jail for a couple of days and then released, presumably with the admonition to change his style of dress. However, in his memorial to the Joint High Claims Commission, Tumblety said that he had been held only for half a day. He further stated that the provost had taken away a robe and a hat, keeping them for a week. It was reported that the doctor switched to a less military style for the rest of his stay in St. Louis. In a rather candid self-assessment after this incident, Tumblety wrote:

> I have been charged with eccentricity in dress, but I presumed, as this is a free country, that as long as a person does not outrage decency or propriety, he has a perfect right to suit his own taste in the color and fashion of his own garments.[6]

During and after this incident, Tumblety made no change in his advertising. The papers continued to print his ads during the short time he was in jail. The only significant difference during this time was that on March 17, about a week later, he felt the need to publish the familiar testimonial from Canada that listed such luminaries as the governor of Canada and the mayors of Toronto, Montreal, Quebec and other cities. This testimonial was published twice in each of the St. Louis dailies. Perhaps he felt the need to rebuild his reputation after the recent incident.

This issue of respectability was vital to his practice and Tumblety took a step that he had never taken before to establish it. Previously, he had fought battles with the regular physicians in Toronto and St. John over his training and the right to call himself a doctor. On March 21, he published an ad that summarized many of his previously published testimonials but included this introductory paragraph:

> The following are a few of the many testimonials to the Indian Herb Doctor, of No. 52 Third street, St. Louis. It is with pleasure that we lay them before the public. The Doctor, who by the way has his diploma, and is a regularly educated physician, his skill as a Doctor, however, is undoubted, his practice being very extensive, and among the higher classes of society.[7]

In the less regulated atmosphere of St. Louis, no one challenged this assertion, but one wonders how much of a difference it made. Given that Tumblety blamed his arrest on the jealousy of the medical faculty of St. Louis, this may have been a way of tweaking their noses. It was only published once and the normal testimonials reappeared thereafter.

Events occurring elsewhere were soon to make a major impact on Tumblety and his business. President Lincoln was assassinated on April 14 and a massive manhunt was set in motion not only for the assassin Booth but for anyone who might have been associated with the conspiracy. Several hundred people were eventually arrested and held for a certain time; most were set free. Meanwhile, the nation mourned the loss of its president.[8]

Lincoln's funeral train left Washington on April 21 and twelve days later arrived in Springfield, Illinois. People came from all over the country to be part of this funeral. Tumblety, who claimed to have met the president on a number of occasions, reported that he went to Springfield and was there on the day of the ceremony. His advertising abruptly stops on April 29 after having been seen in both major newspapers every day up to that point, perhaps in anticipation of his absence. The *Missouri Republican* reported that a special train was sent to Springfield from St. Louis on May 3 and that it was crowded with the mayor, other dignitaries, military officers and hundreds of citizens. It probable that Tumblety went on this train like everyone else.[9]

Around this time, a boy, about 15 years old, was arrested in Brooklyn for a minor crime. He was taken to a police station where he was held overnight. While there, either for revenge or to get out of his own offense, he began to spin a tale for the authorities. He claimed to have been an errand boy for Booth while he was in New York. Further, he knew Booth's accomplice, David Herold, very well since he worked with him. The boy claimed that Herold had lived in Brooklyn under the name Blackburn and that he had been an assistant to Dr. Tumblety. This kind of accusation, at the height of the hysteria over the assassination, was dangerous. By May 4, the *Brooklyn Daily Eagle*, in a highly imaginative story, reported that a United States detective had taken charge of the boy and conveyed him to Washington. The newspapers, either out of ignorance or to make a better story, soon changed the sequence of events to show that the detective had come to Brooklyn looking for the boy. The *New York Times* reported this story in full on May 5 under the heading "An Alleged Accomplice of Booth":

> A few days since a young man, whose name has not been divulged, was arrested by Detective Frost and others on the charge of theft, and, proving to be a smart fellow, told something more than he knew to be facts, in order to exculpate himself from the actual offense of which it is alleged he is guilty. He stated that he knew the assassin Booth ... and said that Harold had been a resident of Brooklyn and an attendant of a physician who formerly resided here. The officers believing that he knew something of the assassination, and having an eye to the reward, kept him in custody for some days, and reported the case to General Superintendent Kennedy, of the Metropolitan Police. That officer examined the matter thoroughly, and, as reported, found it to be "bosh."[10]

The *Daily Eagle* reported the arrest on April 28 of Thomas Pursell for stealing a pocketbook with $200 in it. Pursell was described as being 14 years old and the paper reported that he was held for examination. There is no certain way of associating this boy with the one who made up the story of Booth and Herold, yet the timing and age are remarkably well suited.[11]

While the *Times* printed the news as false, other papers printed the story as if it were true. By the morning of May 5, the news was already published in the St. Louis papers and Tumblety, recently returned from Springfield, must have been incensed. The *Missouri Democrat*, in a report dated May 4, repeated the story about Herold's association with "the notorious Dr. Tumblety." This story makes no mention of his using the alias Blackburn.

But it was only a matter of time until this would come to haunt him. On the same day, Special Order 111 from Col. J. H. Baker, provost marshal general of St. Louis, was issued to Peter Talbot, chief of U. S. police, to "arrest

Engraving of Tumblety being arrested in St. Louis from the 1866 biography. This remarkable scene was most likely commissioned by Tumblety himself to show his valiant struggle against false arrest. The actual event was probably less dramatic.

one Dr. Tumblety, otherwise known as the 'Indian Herb Doctor.' In addition, he was to search his premises and seize all correspondence and papers. Below this order is a note indicating that it was executed by Officers Convers and Hutchins. This order does not mention the alias Blackburn either.[12]

This official notice of the arrest gives none of the dramatic impact that it had on Tumblety. He reports being in his office when the officers came to see him. They arrested him, I suspect without much trouble despite what his later illustration of the event shows. Tumblety was brought to the Provost Marshall's Office, where he was incarcerated. Meanwhile, in his words, "my office and apartments were searched, ransacked and plundered of every article of portable value, including a considerable amount of money." In his later memorial, Tumblety reported that his iron safe was forced opened and valuables and an unnamed but large amount of money seized. The illegal seizure of goods and money was a charge made by many of the people arrested by Col. Baker and the police in St. Louis. It has been suggested that a number of people were arrested simply as an opportunity for property seizure. Tumblety would seek compensation for this money well into the 1870s, filing a claim for $100,000 against the government.[13]

On May 6, both major dailies in St. Louis reported on the arrest of the "Indian Herb Doctor," and repeated various parts of the *Brooklyn Daily Eagle* story. In their reports, both papers, following the Brooklyn paper, said that he used the alias of Blackburn. Based on newspaper accounts, Tumblety's own recollections and the timing of events, it is certain that Col. Baker decided to arrest Tumblety on his own, without orders from the War Department. On May 7, the *Missouri Republican* reported that Tumblety was arrested on the strength of dispatches sent by the Associated Press, in other words based on the article in the Brooklyn paper. This is the same thing Tumblety was told by several officers, who said: "Oh they have such an amount of excitement in Washington, that Colonel Baker ... thinks that we ought to have a little sensation here." Col. Baker knew that Tumblety was in St. Louis but it is clear from newspaper accounts that no one on the East Coast, including Washington, knew where he was. The informant held by the police suggested that he was in New Orleans. The order for the arrest, coming so soon after the publication of the story in the St. Louis papers, indicates that Baker took the initiative.[14]

Having arrested Tumblety and having had his papers searched, Baker had a problem. No evidence linking Tumblety to the assassination conspiracy was found and he did not know what to do with him. A telegraph was sent to assistant secretary of war Charles Dana asking what should be done with him. The secretary ordered that he be sent to Washington for questioning. By another special order, dated May 6, Col. Baker ordered assistant chief of police A. B. Convers to take charge of the prisoner and deliver him to assistant secretary of war Charles A. Dana in Washington. Transport to Washington was to be provided by the Quartermaster's Department. How long such transport took to arrange is unknown. Tumblety said that he was held in St. Louis for a couple of days.

Through all of this uproar, both in official documents and in the papers, the prisoner is referred to as Dr. Tumblety or the Indian herb doctor. It is not until the publication in St. Louis, on May 5, of the story first appearing in the *Brooklyn Daily Eagle* that anyone begins to identify him with the alias Blackburn. Once that happens, he is forever tagged with the alias. One of the first uses of that phrase is in the letter sent with Tumblety by Col. Baker:

> I have the honor to forward herewith, in compliance with your telegram of this date, Dr. Tumblety alias Blackburn. All of his papers have been carefully examined previous to the arrival of your order, but nothing was found in them tending to implicate him with the assassination.
>
> Tumblety's papers and his own admissions show that he has tramped the continent from Quebec to New Orleans, in the character of an "Indian Herb Doctor"; has gained an extensive notoriety as an imposter and a quack; has been compelled to leave several towns and cities in Canada for his rascality and trickery, and is being continually importuned and threatened by those he has deluded and swindled.
>
> Tumblety's principle associates in St. Louis have been one J. W. Blackburn, his assistant in the "medical profession" and one Oregon Wilson, an artist. There appears to be nothing against them, except they belong to a class of adventurers that encumber and prey upon society.[15]

In addition to Col. Baker's identification of Tumblety as Blackburn, this letter presents several other insights on the situation in St. Louis. It is clear that Tumblety was a person of interest in the Lincoln assassination and no other investigation. This is important because soon, his name will be embroiled in another plot which he also had nothing to do with. Eventually, that will become the one thing he and others comment on. Col. Baker gives us an honest look at Tumblety's career, having seen documents we no longer have. Most importantly, he reports on Tumblety's associates in St. Louis.

Oregon Wilson is a minor American artist. He was born near Winchester, Virginia and his most famous painting, entitled "Angel of the Battlefield," depicts an incident after the Battle of Winchester. On July 20, 1864, Matilda Russell, a local woman, spent the night on the battlefield cradling the head of a wounded Confederate messenger so that he survived till the next day. Her actions were widely praised in the Confederacy and Wilson's painting made her even more famous.[16]

More important for our story is the other person mentioned by Col. Baker, J. W. Blackburn, who is identified as Tumblety's assistant. As we have seen, Blackburn, alias Farrell, came to St. Louis with Tumblety when he left Brooklyn. The 1865 St. Louis city directory reveals some interesting data on this connection. The doctor is listed as "Tumblety, F. (J. Blackburn & Co.)" and the directory reports that he was boarding at the Lindell Hotel. In the business section, the listing is: "Blackburn, J., & Co. (John Blackburn & F. Tumblety) physicians, 52 N 3rd." Looking for Blackburn in the residential section showed "Blackburn, J. (Blackburn & Co.), r. 52 N 3rd."

Could Tumblety have used the name John Blackburn as Dr. Reynolds used the name Lispenard, to cover his association with the less respectable aspects of his business? While it is possible that Dr. Tumblety also used the name, it seems unlikely. Tumblety's assistant was Mark A. Blackburn, then going under the name of John H. Blackburn. Listing the firm as J. H. Blackburn & Co. may have been a way of flattering or showing affection for his young friend. What is clear is that the authorities were as confused as we are about who was who.

When Tumblety was arrested, the papers took the opportunity to comment on his appearance and his style in St. Louis. The *Missouri Democrat* referred to him as a "queerly dressed individual," and commented that he attracted attention by "his jet black mustachios and box-like pantaloons." They further commented, when he was sent to Washington, that the doctor was given a few hours to "settle his worldly affairs, dispose of his "herbs" and put a new coat of dye upon his flowing mustachios." Tumblety was only 34 at the time so one wonders why he was said to dye his mustache. Nevertheless, his facial hair certainly made an impression on the reporters. His own illustration of the arrest shows a truly impressive mustache.[17]

In a strange twist, the *Brooklyn Daily Eagle* took Tumblety's arrest as a sign that they were right in the first place. The *New York Times*, as we have seen, suggested that the story was "bosh." With Tumblety's arrest, the *Daily Eagle* could crow that the *Times* was wrong. However, it was the story published in the *Daily Eagle* that led to the arrest they now pointed to as their vindication.[18]

Following his orders, Officer Convers took Tumblety by train from St. Louis to Washington. After his departure, the papers continued to pick up stories about him from New York and Philadelphia. None of them were flattering. Blackburn attempted to keep the business going in Tumblety's absence. On May 11, the *Missouri Democrat* published a notice saying the Indian herb doctor was summoned to Washington to testify at Herold's trial and not to answer any charges against himself. It noted that he was expected to return in a few days and that his office was still open. This notice must have been placed by Mark A. Blackburn. There is no way to know how long Blackburn carried on as there are no ads or other indications that he was still in business.[19]

While it remains possible that Tumblety used the alias of Blackburn, there is no sure evidence of it. J. H. Blackburn was an alias used by Mark A. Blackburn in both Brooklyn and St. Louis. Given Tumblety's penchant for self-promotion, it seems unlikely that he would use an alias except in the utmost necessity. He was much more comfortable being the anonymous "Indian Herb Doctor" than using someone else's name. However, having been painted with this brush, circumstances were about to tar him with a much worse color.

Early in May, the northern papers broke a horrifying story about an attempt to infect New York and other cities with yellow fever. This was one of the diseases that plagued the South and cities on the East Coast throughout the 19th century. There were 50 major epidemics of yellow fever in East Coast cities before the Civil War. In 1853, an epidemic in New Orleans killed 8,000 people. The public was naturally fearful of any attempt to spread the disease. This early example of bioterrorism was termed by one prosecutor an "infamous and fiendish project," and occasioned a huge public outcry.[20]

The first evidence of the plot came to light when Charles Allen, U.S. Consol in Bermuda, was told that a humanitarian mission by Dr. Luke Blackburn during the previous year, aimed at helping to contain a recent yellow fever epidemic, was in reality a plot to spread the disease to northern cities. He was told that the doctor had left several trunks with a man named Swan and that these contained clothes infected with yellow fever. The consul informed the Board of Health on May 10, 1865, and, when they investigated, they found three trunks that Swan was holding for Blackburn. On inspection the trunks were found to contain mostly new and unused clothing but also included a number of stained clothes and bed linen. The inspector suggested the yellow and black stains were of the kind produced by people sick with yellow fever. When questioned, Swan produced a tale of frightening implications. He said that Blackburn offered him $500 to take the trunks to New York City and that he knew they were infected with yellow fever. Swan was supported by several other witnesses who made a very convincing case.[21]

Blackburn was arrested in Canada on a charge of breaking the Neutrality Act. A great deal of testimony was taken in the case but much of it was unreliable. However, the testimony of W. W. Cleary, secretary of a special commission sent to Canada by the Confederate government, clearly shows that the scheme was talked about and attempts were made to put it into action. Eventually, Blackburn was acquitted for lack of evidence and he was never prosecuted in the United States. He came back to the United States and had a long and successful career. In the 1870s, Blackburn was elected governor of Kentucky.[22]

Whether or not there was any validity to the "yellow fever plot," Tumblety became inextricably linked to it by his supposed alias of Blackburn. On May 12, the *New York Tribune* published a short piece about Tumblety's arrival in Washington and his incarceration in the Old Capitol Prison. It was sent from Washington by a "special" report:

> Dr. Tumblety, alias Blackburn, Chief of the Rebel department for the importation of yellow fever, has been brought to this city and is lodged in the Old Capitol Prison. He is just as vain, gaudy, dirty, and disgusting as ever. He wears the same stunning clothes, and it is widely suspected that by collusion with others, he produced his own arrest in this singular allegation, in order to add a little to his already disreputable notoriety.[23]

Whoever wrote this report knew who Tumblety was and was familiar enough with him to comment on his habits. He must have known that this was not the Dr. Blackburn associated with the yellow fever plot. That individual was already known to be in Canada. The reporter chose to link Tumblety with the plot anyway. Just to add a little extra twist, he suggests that Tumblety had himself arrested.

There is no way to know for sure who this anonymous reporter might be. However, we know of a *Tribune* reporter who was in Washington at the time, who claimed to know Tumblety and, from his later testimony, had a strong dislike of the doctor. At just this time, Sanford Conover, also known as Charles A. Dunham, was perjuring himself in front of the military tribunal investigating the assassination and other conspiracies. The story contains two elements that Dunham would still be repeating 23 years later, that Tumblety was arrested in connection with the yellow fever plot and that he had himself arrested. Both of these are false and Dunham knew it at the time.

But the public perception of his character was the least of Tumblety's immediate worries. He was incarcerated in a federal prison with no charges and no idea of when he might get out. His plight was not unusual in the days immediately following the Lincoln assassination. Hundreds of people were swept up in a hysterical dragnet which saw conspirators in every major city. In an era when most newspapers were more concerned with getting a good story or putting forward a particular political position, settling scores with old enemies became a well-practiced game. In Tumblety's case, two false accusations, within days of each other, had mired him deeply in the morass of conspiracy.

The Old Capitol Prison, where Tumblety was jailed, was a four-story brick building that had been built in the early 19th century as a boarding house. It was located roughly where the Supreme Court building now stands and in its time was an exclusive place of lodging. When the British burned Washington in the War of 1812, Congress met in this building, hence the name Old Capitol. By the time of the Civil War, the building was abandoned. The government looked on its forty rooms as a convenient space to house political prisoners. Col. N. T. Colby, military superintendent of the prison, described the prisoners thusly:

> The character of the prisoners was a matter of wide variation, differing in this particular from any other place of confinement. Especially is this true of the Old Capitol, where were held the prisoners of State particularly, such as parties charged with active disloyalty at the North, bounty frauds, counterfeiters of United States notes and other issues, contractors who had swindled the government, and, I doubt not, men who were arrested by detectives upon trumped-up charges simply to blackmail them, and who were wholly innocent. In fact, it would be quite unfair to assume that because one had been a prisoner here, that he was, therefore, a criminal, for I met *many* gentlemen there, *as prisoners, too,* whose claims to regard as gentlemen and men of refinement and social standing is *to-day* widely honored.[24]

Photograph of the Old Capitol Prison, c. 1862. Tumblety was in prison here for three weeks and eventually let go without an explanation. This was the chief Union prison for political prisoners. (Library of Congress, Prints & Photographs Division.)

Tumblety does not say much about his time in prison except that he was there unjustly. He does mention meeting several people, including Governor Vance of South Carolina (actually North Carolina), Governor Brown of Georgia and Mr. G. B. Lamar of Georgia. Col. Colby reported that these three were housed together. Tumblety claimed to have been assigned to their room and to have been well treated by them. All of them later acknowledged being in prison with him. The other incident he mentions involves a female prisoner who leaned out a window, a violation of prison discipline, and was shot at by a guard. He placed this incident at the time of the parade of Sherman's army into Washington, which took place in May 1865. Col. Colby describes a very similar incident involving a Mrs. Baxley, but this took place in 1862. It is likely that Tumblety is repeating a story he heard while there but did not actually witness.[25]

As the trials of the assassination conspirators progressed and the hysteria died down, the government began to release those people against whom it had little evidence. Tumblety was one of these and, after three weeks in prison, he was set free. During his time in the Old Capitol he was never charged with anything nor was he interviewed about the assassination or the yellow fever plot. On his release, he took a room at the Kirkwood House and began trying to clear his name. Naturally he was indignant about the treatment he received. As it was the newspapers that caused him this trouble and spread rumors about him, he set out to have notices printed in a wide variety of papers across the country. The fact that this would be free publicity was probably not lost on the doctor as well. His letter to the *Washington Evening Star* is typical of these types of notices:

> After three weeks imprisonment in the Old Capitol Prison in this city, I have been unconditionally and honorably released from confinement by the directions of the Secretary of War, there being no evidence whatever to connect me with the yellow fever or assassination plot....
>
> While in imprisonment, I noticed in some of the New York and other Northern papers, a paragraph setting forth that the villain Herold, who now stands charged with being one of the conspirators in the atrocious assassination plot, was at one time in my employment. This too is false in every particular, and I am at a loss to see how it originated, or to trace its origin. For the past five years I have had but one man in my employment, and he is with me yet, his character being beyond reproach. I never saw Herold, to my knowledge and I have no desire to see him.
>
> I do hope the persons which so industriously circulated these reports, connecting me with these damnable deeds, to the very great injury of my name and reputation, will do me the justice to publish my release, and the facts of my having been entirely exonerated by the authorities here, who after a diligent investigation, could obtain no evidence that would in the least tarnish my reputation.[26]

In addition to the *Star*, he sent this same letter to the *New York Times* (June 10), *Brooklyn Daily Eagle* (June 19), Philadelphia *Sunday Mercury* (unknown), *Rochester Daily Union and Advertiser* (June 20) and probably others. The *Times* published it with no comment while the *Daily Eagle* added that as he was discharged, "it is fair to assume that he is innocent." The paper in Tumblety's hometown of Rochester was much more critical, saying: "Dr. Tumblety is profiting by his recent arrest.... He is making it a means of advertising himself all over the country."

Having been released, Tumblety took some time to enjoy his freedom and to bask in the glory of having been unjustly incarcerated. At this time, the press was strongly divided between those who supported the administration's war policies and those who were against them. The target of those opposed was Edwin M. Stanton, secretary of war, and cases like Tumblety's were trumpeted widely as examples of his dictatorial usurpation of power. Newspapers that opposed the secretary generally gave Tumblety and cases like his a lot of attention. A number of people who had been imprisoned in the Old Capitol soon published pamphlets and books about their experience, which further fueled interest in the institution. The most famous of these was written by Virginia Lomax and entitled "The Old Capitol and Its Inmates." Published in 1867, this volume sensationalized the arbitrary use of power by the government and its detectives as well as decried the squalid conditions of the prison. As one of the "persecuted," Tumblety received a warmer reception in many areas than he would have on his own.[27]

From Washington, the doctor went to New York and then spent some time in Saratoga Springs. Here, according to his autobiography, he became good friends with General Joseph Hooker and, through him, was introduced to General Grant. Both of these military men are known to have been in residence at Saratoga during part of the summer of 1865 but there is no indication that they met or knew Tumblety.

Next, he decided to go back to St. Louis to pick up the shattered pieces of his business. His arrival was noticed by at least one newspaper (or he advertised his arrival). The article stated that he intended to reopen his business in the city. It is not certain when Tumblety arrived back in St. Louis or how long he stayed. However, shortly thereafter, he was on his way to Cincinnati. Given all of the places Tumblety could have gone, Cincinnati seems, on the surface, an odd choice. I suspect there was a personal reason for heading to the "Queen City."[28]

On the trip out west, Tumblety reports a curious meeting in Indianapolis. While on a stopover there, he was approached by a stranger who claimed to have been impersonating Tumblety in Louisville under the title of the "Indian Herb Doctor." Having heard that Tumblety had been sent to prison, this person assumed he would never get out again so there would be no harm in using the name. In Louisville he developed a large practice but implied that he had tarnished Tumblety's image. Nevertheless, he showed Tumblety a bank draft for $8,000 which he realized in this practice. He offered this draft to Tumblety on the condition that the doctor take him under his wing and teach him the medical game. In his autobiography, Tumblety said that he was incensed by the impersonation and by the offer and dismissed the fellow.[29]

What is the purpose of this curious story? From what we know of Tumblety's career, it seems unlikely that he would turn down the offer of $8,000. As he had no problem taking students in other situations, why was it a problem now? It would seem more appropriate to his character to take the money, agree to take the impersonator as an apprentice and to say nothing of the whole incident. One of the purposes of Tumblety's autobiography was to clear his name and rebuild his practice. At the time it was published, he was in Cincinnati, not too far from Louisville. If someone had been using the title of Indian herb doctor, along with his other attributes, it would be important to distance himself from that performance.

When we review this story, it is appropriate to consider the one person who would have known the doctor's business more intimately than anyone else. When Tumblety was arrested in St. Louis, Mark A. Blackburn kept the office open for a time. How long he was able to keep things going is uncertain. Given the state of affairs, he might have thought he would never see Tumblety again. It is possible, having been left on his own in St. Louis, Blackburn began working his way back towards New York, portraying himself as a doctor. As shall become clear in the next chapter, it can be demonstrated that Mark A. Blackburn was in Cincinnati by early 1866. He may have been there earlier. Beginning on September 26, 1865, a Dr. Blackburn advertised his office at 102 East Fifth Street and described himself as "the most wonderful private disease practitioner of the age." Among other things, he claimed to specifically treat diseases of the skin and he offered consultation and advice free of charge. While there are echoes of Tumblety in this ad, it cannot be proved that this was Mark A. Blackburn. The ads appeared sporadically through October and the last one appears to have been in early November. By early December, Tumblety was advertising in Cincinnati. It does not seem so strange to think Tumblety went to Cincinnati to be with his friend. However, in the end, he may have been disappointed with the result.[30]

10

———❤❤❤———

Cincinnati, Pittsburgh
and Back to Brooklyn
(1866–1869)

Based on the appearance of his first ad, Tumblety was in Cincinnati by December 13, 1865. His arrival was heralded by the same ad which began his St. Louis practice, offering a $30 reward if he could not make a diagnosis without information from the patient. It included the poem, "Our Motto," seen in many other places. Neither the first ad nor any other in Cincinnati uses his real name. One might suggest that this is because of his recent arrest. However, this was his practice long before 1865. For the first three weeks, the $30 reward ad was the only one he published.[1]

He listed his office as "139 West Fourth Street, between Race and Elm, upstairs," and as usual, this was in the heart of Cincinnati's business district. As in Washington, his office was adjacent to an important social space for the upper levels of Cincinnati society. One observer described West Fourth Street in 1869: "In the city itself, Fourth Street is the center of attraction. There are few more brilliant scenes than it presents upon bright afternoons in the spring or fall, when it is thronged with promenaders, and glittering with the gay and costly equipages of wealth." He reports that all of the major retail stores are in this area and that it was the "fashionable promenade" of the city. Major hotels and Pike's Opera House, the city's most important theater, were located in the vicinity of Tumblety's office.[2]

Beginning with the new year, Tumblety's ads began to include the inevitable testimonials. This time, however, he seems to have striven for greater respectability. His earliest testimonials prominently mention people's church membership and include the Rev. Howell Powell, pastor of the Welsh Church. In the same vein, he has a testimonial from William Fenton, a justice of the peace in Cincinnati. The diseases treated or cured are no different than what we have already seen. Through early January, these testimonials are always associated with the $30 reward ad and are relatively small.

In mid–January, he introduces the "Be Wise Before It Is Too Late" ad with its admonition against mercury. This is a trimmed down version of the ads he first published in Toronto. It is accompanied by testimonials similar to what we have already seen. Near the end of January, this is followed by an ad trumpeting his "astonishing cures" and reporting that crowds of people are consulting him.

Early in February, the ads get much larger and normally begin with the headline "A Few of the Many Testimonials to the Indian Herb Doctor." These ads are a full column long and are a compilation of many testimonials previously published in smaller ads. The large ads are published a couple of times a week and the $30 reward ad is published on the other days.

Tumblety published ads every day from January through February and almost every day in March. However, in April, he only has one ad a week. These are all copies of the large ads. His final ad is published on May 5, 1866, and it is the $30 reward ad without any testimonials.

If Tumblety's newspaper ads were infrequent in April and May, it may be due to his working on the biggest bit of self-promotion he had yet attempted. Sometime after coming to Cincinnati, he decided to publish his autobiography. While we can't know when he began to write it, the last few pages give a reasonable idea of when it was being finished. He refers to it being "within a few days" of the date he was arrested (May 5). In the next paragraph he specifically states that it was then the month of May. That would seem to settle the issue.[3]

However, things are never so certain with the doctor's writings. After extolling the virtues of the month of May, he reports that he sat at his breakfast table, opened the paper and found a story about cholera on board a crowded passenger ship. That particular story appeared in the *Cincinnati Commercial* on April 10. He also comments on seeing, in the same paper, that Professor Fowler, the noted phrenologist, was scheduled to give a series of lectures in Cincinnati. Those lectures were scheduled on April 2 and April 5 and Professor Fowler advertised that he would be available for consultation from April 3 to 15 at the Burnet House. We should keep in mind that the doctor was not averse to modifying the facts or the sequence of events in his writings.[4]

In May 1866, Tumblety published an 82-page pamphlet on his life, practice and his recent arrest in St. Louis. It provides an invaluable source for his career, reveals how he felt about a number of things that happened to him and suggests motives for its publication. In studying this document, it is important to remember that it was written specifically as a justification of his life. Events which would cast him in a bad light are studiously avoided or manipulated. The pamphlet was published in Cincinnati under the following title:

> A few passages in the life of Dr. Francis Tumblety, The Indian Herb Doctor, including his experience in the Old Capitol Prison, to which he was consigned with a wanton disregard to justice and liberty by order of Edwin Stanton, Secre-

tary of War. Also a journalistic and documentary vindication of his name and fame, and professional testimonials, respectfully inscribed to the American public.

The document is part autobiography, part medical treatise and part testimonial. All three parts are openly self-promotional. His motives in presenting this to the public are varied but clear. First, the public was fascinated by tales of abuses during the recent war. Inmates of the Old Capitol Prison were publishing their memoirs and the public was avidly buying them. Most famous were those of Rose O'Neal Greenhow (1863), Belle Boyd (1865) and, shortly after this period, Virginia Lomax (1867). Tumblety's pamphlet played to that audience and he probably hoped to sell quite a few. Secondly, as Tumblety was actively trying to get compensation for a large amount of cash and valuables lost when his office was raided in St. Louis, the description of his unjust captivity would aid those claims. The publication could be sent to influential people who might help in that quest. Thirdly, several parts of his autobiography look as if they are recycled from his or other medical books. Continuing his practice was as important as securing the lost items. This portion, with the pages and pages of testimonials about his cures, would entice new patients for both his office and his mail orders.[5]

This last item, continuing his practice, was the overt reason Tumblety himself gives for writing the pamphlet. His arrest made national headlines and, regardless of his release, his name was still tainted by association with the assassination and the yellow fever plot. Many of the papers avidly reported his arrest but were less avid in reporting his being cleared. In the preface, Tumblety said:

> As, outside my professional pursuits, my name, for a brief period, was dragged before the public in a manner anything but agreeable to my mental or bodily comfort, I have ... concluded to publish the ensuing pages, not only in self-vindication, but to exhibit in its true light a persecution and despotism, in my case, that would hardly be tolerated under the most absolute monarchy, and which should serve as a warning to all who believe in the twin truths of Liberty and Justice.[6]

The autobiography has proved invaluable for researchers looking into Tumblety's life. Much of what has been written about the doctor's early life comes directly from this pamphlet or from research derived from it. The present work has already reported many of the specific historical points presented in the document. Rather than repeat all of that, we need to focus on two aspects of the presentation. The first is his reaction to and understanding of his arrest in 1865. This incident provides the basis for the publication and is the thread that ties it all together. The second aspect explores his feelings and perceptions about his profession. It also allows us a chance to see how his practice might have evolved over time.

No matter what we may think of Tumblety in other facets of his life, he had every right to be outraged over his treatment by the government. As we have seen, there was not an ounce of truth in the charges that were lodged against him. Yet he was arrested and imprisoned for three weeks. Never once was he asked about the charges and, in the end, he was let go without any apology. Anyone who found themselves in similar circumstances would feel bitter and vindictive. That tone certainly pervades the narrative, yet it is not the primary tone. Perhaps because he had fought for so many years for respectability, Tumblety saw these recent incidents as a continuation of his heroic struggle against the many dark forces that constantly assailed him. This is particularly evident on the cover of the pamphlet.

The cover of the book has a spectacular engraving showing a flattering rendition of Tumblety's arrest in St. Louis. In the center of the tableaux is the doctor valiantly resisting the attempt of four policemen to put him in manacles. Two of the officers hold his right arm, a third is holding his left shoulder while the fourth has Tumblety's left arm extended in the air. While this is a very dramatic illustration, there is no indication that the arrest took four policemen or even that Tumblety resisted.

Several aspects of the drawing are significant. Tumblety, in his struggling resistance, is shown with his legs wide apart yet he is still taller than all of the other men. If he were standing up straight, he would tower over the policemen. While some of this may be dramatic license, repeated descriptions refer to Tumblety as over six feet tall. That characteristic shows well in the drawing. Another feature mentioned in most descriptions is his large mustache. In the illustration, this is shown as long and full. He wears his hair at a moderate length and parts it on the right side.

Tumblety is dressed in a dark coat and light colored trousers. These may represent the butternut colored pants previously mentioned in the Brooklyn paper. On the ground are two hats, one in front of the group and one behind. The hat behind the group looks like a police hat and belongs to the man trying to manacle Tumblety. The hat in front of the group has a relatively low crown and a moderate brim. This may be the "pork pie" hat also mentioned in the *Brooklyn Daily Eagle*. Missing from the picture is any trace of a military uniform.

The cover illustration provides the focus for the nature of the struggle described inside. Tumblety depicts his arrest and imprisonment as a great conspiracy organized against him. There are a number of people who Tumblety felt were guilty of wronging him. They were responsible for his arrest, imprisonment and the loss of his reputation. All of them are the subject of considerable vituperation in the autobiography. Even with his hatred of these people, there is no suggestion that he might chose a violent means of retribution. His righteous anger should not be mistaken for any violent tendencies.

As we have seen, the man most responsible for his arrest was Col. John H. Baker, the provost marshal of St. Louis. Without orders from anyone, Col. Baker had Tumblety arrested on the strength of newspaper reports that came from New York. At times, it seems as if Tumblety understands that his troubles began with Baker but his anger at other members of the government tends to obscure this knowledge. Whether Baker was the chief instigator or just part of the conspiracy, Tumblety had little good to say about him:

> The then Colonel is now a General, but if his tyrannical proceeding toward me, and the reckless disregard he evinced to the right and liberty of a citizen, are samples of his integrity and capacity, he is as prominent a specimen of misplaced promotion as any in the service.[7]

Another group that Tumblety blamed for his troubles was the press that had reported his arrest and imprisonment. If he was aware of how his name was linked to either the assassination or the yellow fever plot, he does not make that obvious. However, he was well aware of the many newspapers that were willing not only to report his arrest and imprisonment but to publish embarrassing details of his life. Even more than the arrest itself, this public exposure was galling to Tumblety. He tried very hard to project a respectable image and these revelations virtually destroyed it.

To Tumblety, this exposure was not fair for a number of reasons. He goes into a long discussion of how important advertising is to the public and then reports that he spent $90,000 on newspaper ads over the course of his career. He felt that this should entitle him to better treatment from the press. He accuses the newspapers of knowingly twisting the facts and slandering him. As we have seen, there was some truth in this. Further, when he was released, those same newspapers ignored the fact that he was never charged with anything. An outraged Tumblety stated:

> They repudiated the old manly system of fair play; they had wantonly assailed me, and even when convinced that not the slightest taint attached to my character or fair fame, they remained silent. They had propagated and prejudged a slander which was proved to be false as the father of evil, but they persevered in their dastardly meanness by refusing the *amende*, and only to that portion of the press who had never assailed me, am I indebted for sympathizing with and placing me in my true position before the public.[8]

Curiously, while Col. Baker and the newspapers were most responsible for Tumblety's arrest and exposure, his strongest bile was reserved for Edwin M. Stanton, the secretary of war. It is likely that Stanton had nothing to do with Tumblety's arrest and may have had little knowledge of it. Col. Baker initiated the arrest and Assistant Secretary Dana, at Baker's prompting, asked for the doctor to be sent to Washington. Stanton's involvement remains uncertain.

According to Tumblety, however, Edwin Stanton was the devil himself. Stanton is said to have practiced an "iron despotism" and to have acted as a tyrant. Tumblety accused him of a "flagrant abuse of power and wanton outrage of the liberty of the citizen, as was exemplified in my case." He attributed his arrest to "a reckless and irresponsible official, wielding absolute authority, and without the pale of the fear of God or mankind."

The secretary of war, regardless of his involvement, made a good target for Tumblety. From the beginning of his term as secretary in 1862, Stanton had taken actions that might have been necessary for a nation fighting a civil war but which outraged even loyal citizens. Under his orders, over 38,000 people were arrested without benefit of trial, property was seized, newspapers were closed and strict censorship was enforced. Stanton's high-handed abuse almost led to another rebellion in the North.[9]

Even today, Stanton's actions during the Civil War continue to spark lively debates among historians. But at the time that Tumblety was writing, this debate was front page news. In the immediate postwar period, the North was polarized into two factions. One, associated with Stanton, wanted to severely punish the South for its rebellion. The other, led by president Andrew Johnson, following the policy that Lincoln had advocated, wanted to heal the wounds and bring the country back together. As Johnson had retained Lincoln's cabinet, the two came into increasing conflict. It has been suggested that Stanton passed on sensitive material to the radical Republicans in Congress to use against Johnson. Given these circumstances, it is natural that the president would want to remove this problem.

In 1866, Congress began debating the Tenure of Office Act, which would require Senate approval before any cabinet official could be removed. This was to protect Stanton and was the issue that would lead to the impeachment of Andrew Johnson. Newspapers on both sides vilified the leader of the other side. Tumblety quotes one paper with a typical diatribe against Stanton. The editor asks,

> I trust this Congress will do something to settle the question whether the Government under which we live is a republic, of which Andrew Johnson is president, with Edwin M. Stanton—to use the language of a distinguished military chieftain—"a d----d clerk," or whether it is really an absolute monarchy , under the reign of Edwin I.[10]

Congress, led by the radical Republicans, did settle the issue, but not the way the editor wanted. The Tenure of Office Act was passed over the president's veto in March 1867. As a result, relations between Johnson and his secretary of war grew progressively worse.

Why does Tumblety's pamphlet focus so specifically on Stanton as the root of all his troubles? Certainly Stanton's actions during the war created an atmosphere where the arrest and imprisonment of Tumblety could occur, but the doctor implies that the secretary ordered his arrest. When Tumblety was preparing his narrative, Democratic newspapers were roasting Stanton every day. Rather than blame his arrest on the vindictive lies of a boy left in Brooklyn or the greedy motives of a minor official in St. Louis, Tumblety decided to attach his case to a larger, more prominent target. This would increase the sympathy he got from the public and make his chances of getting compensation greater.

Seeking compensation was another of the reasons why Tumblety wrote this narrative and it was a topic being discussed in the newspapers at the time. The United States was lobbying for England to pay damages for losses caused by the Confederate Navy, whose ships were built in Great Britain and allowed to sneak out of British ports. On the other hand, Britain was claiming losses caused to its shipping by the U.S. Navy and in the name of its citizens, whose money and goods were seized by Union troops. This would eventually lead to the 1871 Treaty of Washington and the establishment of the United States–British Claims Commission. Under this commission, as a British citizen, Tumblety would claim losses totaling $100,000 for his two arrests in Missouri. By establishing his case in the pamphlet, Tumblety was setting the stage for his eventual claim. Tumblety used this pamphlet to make his case for compensation, directly stating at one point:

> But the pecuniary loss I have sustained, and the disarrangement of my business, are other matters, for which I have a clear claim upon a government by whose authority I have been so outraged and despoiled.[11]

There is no way to know how many of these items he sent out but it is likely that he sent them to anyone who might be able to influence the Claims Commission. The only evidence of this activity are references in a later autobiography where he reprints replies from prominent people. It is clear from these replies that he sent them a pamphlet specifically so that they would support his claim for compensation. Between 1868 and 1871, there are seven such replies recorded from such people as General Robert E. Lee, General William T. Sherman, former Governor Brown of Georgia, and Edward Thornton, British ambassador to Washington. He also sent copies to Earl de Grey and Lord Stanley, British members of the Joint Claims Commission.[12]

A second focus of the pamphlet is the need to reestablish his practice. Tumblety lived and died by the newspapers and the pamphlet clearly shows this aspect. Not only does he take advantage of Stanton's troubles and the discussion of the Claims Commission but other events receiving exposure in the newspapers ended up in the pamphlet. There is a four-page discussion of the poet George W. Cutter, including a copy of a long poem he wrote. Although Tumblety introduces this by saying he treated Cutter for a bronchial "affectation," the section seems out of place. Its inclusion becomes understandable when we realize that Cutter died in December 1865. Tributes to him had been published in newspapers across the country in early 1866, just as Tumblety was writing the narrative. Like many other aspects of the narrative, it serves to increase Tumblety's importance by demonstrating the people he knew. With Cutter dead, there was no one who could deny that Tumblety has so treated him.

Another example of this publicity grabbing occurs in his discussion of Captain James Anderson and the *Great Eastern*. According to Tumblety, some of his relatives in England thought he had been killed in the Civil War. Captain Anderson, who knew Tumblety from his time in Boston, and Tumblety's

relatives, who worked for his employer, the Cunard Line, served as interme-
diaries in assuring them that Tumblety was in fine health. A simple letter would
have done the same thing. This touching family drama is made more understandable when we realize that Anderson and the *Great Eastern* were then
engaged in laying the first transatlantic cable. This was a major scientific event,
akin to the moon landing in our own time, and garnered huge press attention.
Tumblety was closely associating himself with the hero of the moment, and
gaining stature by that fact.[13]

Mentioning Cutter and Anderson, along with a number of other prominent people, was necessary for Tumblety to restore his own damaged
respectability. We might look at this name dropping as pretentious but it was
vitally important for Tumblety to demonstrate that individuals with unassail-
able respectability called him friend. After his arrest, newspapers across the
country reported all of the dirt they could find on him, thoroughly destroying
his carefully crafted veneer of gentility. If he was ever to continue his practice
at a level above the normal working man, he had to do something to regain
this reputation. The pamphlet went a long way to reassuring potential patients
that he was truly wronged and had a respectable practice.

In addition to proving his respectability, Tumblety gives his potential
patients, and us, an unprecedented view of his medical ideas and practice. Up
to this point, the only information we have had on his practice was small tid-
bits included in his advertisements. In his pamphlet, Tumblety discusses, at
great length, his theories on medicine and the medical profession. There are
two lengthy expositions on medicine in the pamphlet. The transition to these
discussions is awkward and, as previously mentioned, these may be recycled
from earlier medical treatises.

The first of these discussions begins with a standard attack on the regular physicians and their mineral poisons. To illustrate his system, Tumblety tells
a story about two English physicians, John Abernethy and Astley Paston
Cooper. Both doctors were prominent surgeons in the early 19th century. The
difference between them, as Tumblety correctly observes, is that Abernethy
thought of surgery as a last resort and tried to find other ways of treating
patients. It was this trait that attracted Tumblety, but he overstates the case.
Abernethy was a leading surgeon and operated on hundreds if not thousands
of patients.[14]

Tumblety makes no secret of how he, as a physician, feels about surgery.
He calls the surgeon's knife "the source of immense mischief." He recounts
cases where seemingly healthy patients went under the knife only to die within
days or weeks, which is not surprising given early-19th-century sanitary conditions. Going even further, he accuses some surgeons of doing operations not
for the benefit of the patient but just to show off their skills. These sorts of
complaints were not specific to Tumblety but were common perceptions among
the public and a standard part of the botanic physician's advertising.

Indeed, immediately after this, Tumblety launches into a description of his purely botanic system, which he refers to as the "Reformed Practice." He states that nature provides a wealth of plants which can be used to treat illness and it is the responsibility of the physician to seek out these plants and test their properties. Interestingly, up to this point, Tumblety's narrative is in the first person singular but during this discussion of the Reformed Practice, it drops into the plural "we" and is another reason to suspect that this passage is lifted from some other publication.

In an echo of his brief flirtation with science, Dr. Tumblety praises the new insights that physiology and anatomy were producing. He agues for the development of a system of medical knowledge based on facts, not suppositions. In addition, Tumblety rails against a reliance on authorities such as Hippocrates, Galen and others. In this group, Tumblety includes Benjamin Rush, America's most famous doctor in the late 18th and early 19th centuries. It was Rush who strongly advocated the use of bleeding and mercury for treating disease. Whether his own or lifted from some other publication, Tumblety presents a remarkably perceptive understanding of the medical treatment of his time, followed by an equally remarkable claim:

> All of our systems are either false conclusions from mere imaginary whims, begged principles or mere suppositions; or even false conclusions from erroneous principles. All systematizers pretend to build upon facts; but their facts are *pressed* and *whipped* into their service. The doctor first spins his system out of the cobweb of his fancy, and afterwards squeezes some facts into forms resembling proofs of it, and very honestly shuts his eyes against all such facts as are at variance with his beloved air-castle....
>
> I offer the public a *new system of medical science*, which I have formed conscientiously clear of all those impediments, and which is confirmed in its salutatory effects by a life-time's practice.[15]

From our vantage point, one can only wonder about the juxtaposition of these two statements. Was Tumblety being incredibly self-deceptive or intentionally lying? Although he reports having a system, he does not detail it in his autobiography. In a few years, Dr. Tumblety will describe his "system" and it will be evident that it is based as much on Hippocrates and Galen as any other in the 19th century. Further, it is clear that Tumblety *pressed* and *whipped* his own facts to fit his system. In his tirade, he complains of doctors reducing disease to one source or cause and then following fashion in seeking a panacea for that cause. Yet, he will do exactly that in his exposition of his medical system.

Other than the reliance on herbal medicines, the autobiography does not detail the specifics of Dr. Tumblety's medical theory. However, some idea of his practice can be gained from the numerous testimonials contained in it. Pages 55–71 of the autobiography are filled with testimonials from patients treated by Tumblety. Some of these are detailed letters while most are just lists of names, diseases and addresses. Most all were published in newspapers that we have already looked at through his career. Taken together, they provide an excellent view of his practice and how it changed over the years. In this section, there are 196 testimonials stretching from his earliest days in Canada up to and including his residence in Cincinnati. Although he made finer divisions, we can divide them into six chronological periods: Canada (1856–1859), Boston (1859–1861), New York (1861 and 1863), Washington (1861–1863), St. Louis (1865) and Cincinnati (1866). Conspicuous by its absence is any reference to New Brunswick or Philadelphia.

The number of patients per location ranges from a low of 19 in Canada to a high of 38 in St. Louis, with an average of 33 patients per location. The ratio of male patients averages 66.6 percent of the total and is relatively constant except for his stay in Washington. Reflecting the influx of men because of the Civil War, his patient list shows 83 percent males in Washington. In the last location, Cincinnati, the percentage of females and children reaches its highest number since the small Canadian sample with 43.4 percent. It would be interesting to know if this represented a change in his practice but there is nothing later to compare it with. In any case, women and children consistently make up a third of his practice and he seems to have had no problem in attracting them or treating them.

Another aspect of his practice is the list of diseases treated by Tumblety. There are 36 different conditions listed in the testimonials. They cover a wide range of ills that "the flesh is heir to." Rather than repeat all of them, we can look at two aspects of this list: frequency and persistence. The most frequent condition listed is consumption and diseases related to congestion in the lungs. These account for 40 cases or 20 percent of the total. While a real case of consumption could be deadly, most cases were really just bad congestion. These kinds of things were easily treatable with Tumblety's medicines. Next in frequency were pimples and skin diseases. These made up 12 percent of the cases. This was followed by the amorphous conditions of debility and dyspepsia, each of which accounted for 10 percent of the cases. Together, these easily treatable conditions made up over 50 percent of his testimonials.

While frequency reveals how Tumblety's practice was structured over the entire period, persistence explores whether there was a change in the types of cases he treated. Only consumption or bronchitis is listed in all six locations. It ranges from four to seven cases except for New York, where there were 14 cases. Skin diseases are reported from five locations. There are none from Canada, which may reflect a change in emphasis after he escaped from New Brunswick and developed the Pimple Banisher. Dyspepsia and debility each occur in five locations, the former not being listed in Cincinnati while the latter was not listed in Canada. Interestingly, while only accounting for 5 percent of the total number of cases, female diseases are reported from five of the six locations. Only Cincinnati does not show this treatment.

What does all of this tell us about Tumblety's practice? It indicates that he had a stable set of conditions that he could treat and that his practice did not vary significantly over time. No matter what his personal or professional problems, patients came to see him for the same sorts of ailments. Whether he realized it or not, these were the kinds of diseases that medical researchers suggest would have cured themselves over time. They were the stock in trade of quack doctors and regular physicians alike. Tumblety made a good living in treating them.

While Tumblety's professional career, helped by his autobiography, seems to have recovered, his personal life may have been more rocky. Whether or not his friend, Mark A. Blackburn, was the "Dr. Blackburn" who advertised in the *Cincinnati Commercial* in November 1865, he was in Cincinnati with Tumblety during the early part of 1866. This is when he met and fell in love with Olivia B. Young. She was 17 years old and living with her mother. Eventually, they ran away to New York and were married on October 7, 1866.[16]

There is no certain information on why they had to be married in New York but it may be that Mrs. Young did not approve of her daughter's choice. Nor is there any indication of how Dr. Tumblety felt about this. After his last ad on May 5, there is no evidence of where he was until October. Perhaps he went to New York with the young couple or maybe he had to get out of town because of the controversy. There is simply no evidence. We can say that Mark A. Blackburn married Olivia Young in New York in the first week of October and Dr. Tumblety began advertising in Pittsburgh little more than a week later.

There was some confusion in the Indian herb doctor's introduction to the public in Pittsburgh. On the same day, October 24, 1866, two ads were placed on the front page of the *Pittsburgh Commercial*. The first was a large ad featuring the $30 reward and the poem, "Our Motto." This ad listed the doctor's office as 194 Liberty Street, which would be his office for his entire stay in the city. A smaller ad, a few inches above the other, stated that the doctor was available to see patients in room 99 of the Merchant's Hotel. Tumblety boarded at the hotel for the length of his stay. The most likely explanation for these ads is that Tumblety placed the small ad as soon as he got to town but before it was published, he found the office space.[17]

The ad campaign in Pittsburgh was the same as those we have seen since his time in Washington. It began with the $30 reward ad, soon added local testimonials and, eventually, those from further distances. The ads all focus on his persona, "Indian Herb Doctor," and do not mention his name. This represents the fully developed and financially successful formula developed in other places.

If there is anything different about this ad campaign, it is the veritable flood of testimonials produced here. Tumblety published the names of 144 individuals in the *Pittsburgh Commercial*. This is by far more patients than in any other location. The people and their ailments reveal a maturing of the doctor's practice. As usual, most of the doctor's patients are men, with women and children accounting for 30 percent of the total. This is within the range for other locations.

What has changed dramatically is the range of diseases treated by the doctor. At other locations, Tumblety published testimonials relating to 36 different conditions that he had successfully treated. Here in Pittsburgh, where so many more testimonials were published, the list of diseases is only 17 long. The emphasis on specific diseases changed as well. In Pittsburgh, conditions related to consumption and lung conditions made up 32 percent of the total, up from an average of 20 percent in other places. In a like manner, dyspepsia was up to 25 percent. The list of easily treated diseases mentioned earlier (consumption, dyspepsia, debility and skin conditions) rose from 50 percent to 80 percent of the total. This suggests that Tumblety was aware of his success with certain conditions and emphasized those in his ads.

At the same time, he was adapting his ads to the audience he felt he could get the most money from. Of the 58 individuals whose profession is listed, all are working men. Of the total, a third are transportation workers (railroad and steamboat), a third are factory workers (glass works, iron works) and the rest are miscellaneous clerks, constables and farmers. This was the class which either could not afford or did not trust regular physicians. They were attracted by Tumblety's democratic-sounding ads and his emphasis on low fees.

Dr. Tumblety spent more time in Pittsburgh than any other place since his days in Toronto, yet, except for his ads, there is little information on what he did or with whom. He left few reminiscences about his time there and few people commented on him in the papers. Later the papers would recount a story about Tumblety being thrown off his horse and being thought dead for three days. Because of his height, the undertaker had trouble fitting him in the coffin so decided to cut off his legs, causing the doctor to recover quickly. This sounds like a folktale adapted to Tumblety. There is no evidence in the Pittsburgh papers of Tumblety being involved in an accident or this miraculous tale of the dead coming back to life.[18]

The last ad of the Indian herb doctor in Pittsburg was published on January 11, 1868. As usual there is no indication that he was leaving or of where he was going. For a few weeks after his last ad, there is an ad from a grocer named John A. Best extolling the virtues of the Pimple Banisher. It may be that Tumblety sold his remaining stock to Best when he knew he was leaving.[19]

Coming back to New York, Tumblety had established himself at the Fifth Avenue Hotel, his usual stopping place in the city, by May 6, 1868. During the next two months, he sent copies of his pamphlet to several different people, hoping they could help him make a claim against the government. While the doctor republished these as examples of his extensive friendships, they clearly are anything but intimate. He continued to live at the hotel and send out these pamphlets through May 1869.

To continue his practice, Tumblety took office space across the Hudson River in Jersey City, New Jersey. His office was located at 18 Exchange Place, which was the junction of several rail lines and the ferries going across to New York and Brooklyn. This was an area of intense traffic with ferries arriving every 15 minutes from five A.M. to ten P.M. and at 30-minute intervals through the night.[20] This location would have provided him ample patients for his practice. To alert former patients in Brooklyn, he placed ads in the *Brooklyn Daily Eagle* in mid–June. He may have been advertising elsewhere but examples have not come to light. It is unknown how long he maintained an office in Jersey City but in 1869, major changes awaited Dr. Tumblety.

11

·∞∞∞·

Europe and the West
(1869–1873)

By mid–1869, a strong wanderlust seems to have seized Dr. Tumblety and would keep him moving for much of the next decade. Unlike previous times when he would stay in one place practicing until he got in trouble or he sensed a better opportunity, now he seemed almost constantly in motion. As it is always harder to hit a moving target, Tumblety's movements are less clear in the record and we have to rely more on his own words for clues. Nevertheless, he did continue to practice medicine and set up offices in several major cities during this period.

As early as 1863, Tumblety claims to have expressed an interest in going to Europe and that design he now put into effect. He later recalled that this trip "was not one of mere pleasure, but rather of research in behalf of my profession." As with many things in his life, we only have Tumblety's word for where he went and whom he met. To hear him tell it, he cut a wide swath through England, Ireland and Europe, meeting important people and being accepted into the highest levels of society. We should not completely dismiss these claims out of hand. He was a wealthy, respected physician. In Europe, the seedier aspects of his life were unknown at the time. Tumblety always had the ability to make himself seem more important than he was and to impress people. These characteristics would have opened many doors for him.[1]

In July 1869, Tumblety made arrangements to sail to Liverpool on the steamer *Nebraska*. The ship was part of the Black Star line run by Williams & Guion and was registered at 3,985 tons. She was a relatively new ship; her maiden voyage was in 1867 and she was one of the first ships owned by the line. The *Nebraska* was a hybrid ship, having both sail and steam power. It carried about 70 cabin passengers and as many as 800 steerage passengers. Tumblety paid $80 for a ticket from New York to Liverpool. Prior to his departure, he secured a line of credit from Williams & Guion drawn on the London firm of A. S. Petrie & Son.[2]

The ship sailed from New York on July 14 and arrived in Queenstown on

July 23, 1869. Tumblety went ashore and toured Ireland. One wonders if he visited the neighborhood where he grew up. His autobiography reports that he visited Cork, Dublin and Belfast. While primarily being a tourist, there are a few indications that Tumblety pursued his medical interest as well. Soon after arrival, he visited Dr. Richard Barter. Tumblety reports that he was given a picture of the doctor with the inscription, "Presented by Dr. Barter to his friend Dr. Tumblety, of the City of New York, July 27, 1869." This was shortly after his arrival in Ireland.[3]

Dr. Barter was a leader in the introduction of hydropathy in the mid 19th century. He opened his hydropathic practice, St. Anne's Hydropathic Establishment, in Blarney, County Cork, in 1843 and in 1856, introduced the first Turkish bath. Within a decade, he was associated with ten baths in different locations in Ireland. He is noted for having built the "People's Bath" in Cork, which was the first attempt to provide working-class people with access to the treatment. In theory, the sweating induced by the Turkish bath made people healthier and combated disease. If nothing else, the baths promoted cleanliness and hygiene.[4]

The association with Dr. Barter was one that Tumblety could be justly proud to report. He was a well-known and highly respected physician. Tumblety reports that he stayed with Dr. Barter as his guest for a few days. Of course, we only have Tumblety's account of this relationship but there is nothing to suggest this was other than described. Later in his life, Tumblety associated with several of the major proponents of Turkish baths and hydrotherapy in America and once donated money to provide free baths for as many as 4,000 New Yorkers. Perhaps this interest began during his visit to Dr. Barter.

From Cork, Tumblety said he traveled southwest to County Clare and visited the lakes of Killarney. Here he stayed at Aghadoe House as a guest of Lord Headley. Aghadoe house was a large, Italianate villa overlooking the lower lake of Killarney. It was set on a model farm of 100 acres within his larger holdings of 15,000 acres. In the 1872 edition of his pamphlet, Tumblety published a complimentary letter, reportedly from Lord Headley, regarding the exchange of plants. In later editions the letter was edited to keep the complimentary part but eliminate the plant exchange.[5]

The exchange of plants was important in 1872 when Tumblety was trying to show that this trip was of a scientific nature. Lord Headley was well known as a botanist and agricultural experimenter. Such an exchange would reflect well on Tumblety. By the late 1880s, when Tumblety's motives had changed, correspondence with Lord Headley served simply as a sign of respectability.

Tumblety introduced the letter by commenting on the "large and liberal philanthropy of Lord Headley." Numerous guidebooks to Ireland published in the early to mid 19th century refer to how Lord Headley took his inherited estates of bogs and fens and improved them, in the process making life much better for his tenants. An alternate view is widely reported in Ireland, however, where Lord Headley is described as a deeply unpopular and brutal landlord. An enlightening description of his estates was published by a visiting English agriculturalist:

> Lord Headley's estate of Glenbeg, situated in a wild district of Kerry, ... consisting of 15,000 acres, much of which is rocky, boggy and mountain ground, was, in 1807, inhabited by a people, to whom the bare idea of labour was offensive and work considered as slavery.[6]

Leaving Ireland, Tumblety reports that he went to London. He published a long letter describing the sights of the city which bears the heading of Langham Hotel, August 23, 1869. As he frequently did, Tumblety chose the most prestigious location to rent a room. The Langham had been built in 1864 and is said to have been England's first luxury hotel. Located on Portland Place in the fashionable West End of London, anyone staying here was automatically considered to be a gentleman. It was just the kind of place Tumblety needed to be accepted into London society. While he was in London, he claims to have met or been introduced to many prominent people. There is no way to check the truth of any of these assertions. The letter was written to an unspecified friend in New York and includes details on many of the tourist sites in London. It contains virtually no personal detail. Much of the letter seems to have been lifted from some unidentified guide book.[7]

In his autobiography, as part of this European trip, Tumblety tells of traveling to Paris, treating Louis Napoleon, then going to Berlin and being accepted into the royal household of King Wilhelm I. From these experiences, he said he gained the Cross of the Legion of Honor, which he would wear for many years, and had his picture taken in the uniform of the Prussian Imperial Guard, which provided the picture for the front of his later biographies. It is the picture by which he is most well known. If these experiences are true, we must accept that Tumblety was the truly unique and well-recognized individual he thought himself. However, like all things in his life, the doctor seems to have played fast and loose with the truth.[8]

If we look in detail at the story and its chronology, there are a few problems. Tumblety tells his readers that he went to Paris and treated an attaché of the English embassy for scrofula. The Englishman was miraculously cured and this reached the ears of Louis Napoleon, who was suffering from a similar disease. A private audience, unbeknownst to the imperial physicians, was held and, following Tumblety's course of treatment, Louis Napoleon was also miraculously cured. For this Tumblety reports that he was given the Cross of the Legion of Honor. The first American to receive the Legion of Honor, in 1854, was Thomas Wiltberger Evans, dentist of Napoleon III. While several other Americans were granted this medal in subsequent years, Tumblety is unlikely to have been one of them. However, there would be no way to question him on this point since the archives of the Legion of Honor were destroyed during the Siege of Paris in 1871. Following his interlude in Paris, Tumblety reports that he traveled to Berlin and in less than a week was formally presented to King Wilhelm. After this, he gained an appointment to the imperial medical staff, lived in the Royal Palace and had his picture taken in uniform.[9]

Unlike other parts of the autobiography, there are no specific dates provided and no letters of friendship or support from either the French or the Germans. It would seem that an American, particularly one of Tumblety's reputation, receiving the Cross of the Legion of Honor would be newsworthy. However, there seems to have been no press coverage. The same is true of his stay in Berlin. On these circumstances alone, we have to question the truth of these stories.

A more serious problem exists in the timing of these events. There was just not enough time for these things to happen given what we can prove of Tumblety's movements. Tumblety's published letter from London was dated August 23, 1869. In it, he reported that he was about to leave for Paris. On his return trip to America, Tumblety left Liverpool on the steamship *Nevada* on September 1, 1869. His whole European adventure took place in the space of eight days. With travel from London to Paris, Paris to Berlin, then Berlin to London and London to Liverpool, there was just not enough time for the sequence of events to have occurred. Tumblety himself makes them even more unlikely by publishing a letter concerning his supposed meeting with Charles Dickens. This reportedly took place after his trip to the Continent. He tells his correspondent that he was delaying his return to America by a week to ten days at the request of Dickens. Even assuming just a week, the latest this letter could date would be August 26, leaving him only three days on the Continent. Given the lack of supporting detail and the chronological problems, we can only conclude that Tumblety made it all up.[10]

These lies should not surprise anyone. Tumblety tottered on the edge of respectability all his life. In several previous episodes of his life, his respectability had been, directly or indirectly, challenged. The whole purpose of his pamphlet was to repair and enhance his image. Lacking personal knowledge of someone, the only way to judge him was the company he kept. By claiming to associate with British Lords, French emperors and Prussian kings, Tumblety could project the kind of image that wanted. While people could, and often did, doubt the truth of these assertions, there was no way to disprove them. Among certain groups of people, they made a significant impression.

Whether or not Tumblety delayed his return to America at the request of Charles Dickens, the time eventually came for his return to his adopted home. He boarded the steamer *Nevada*, in Liverpool. This was another combination ship of the Guion Line which had just made her maiden voyage in February 1869. On the passenger list, the doctor is listed as Francis Tumbleton, age 32, and his profession is listed as gentleman. He was a Salon passenger and listed himself as a citizen of the United States. Tumblety comments that on this voyage he met Rev. William H. Milburn, who had been congressional chaplain. Milburn was internationally famous as the "blind preacher," and was the author of a number of books. His name is indeed on the passenger list for the *Nevada*. The ship arrived in New York on September 13, 1869.[11]

Tumblety had not been back in New York very long before he decided to try his fortunes out West. His choice to take this trip by train was more than just a whim. The year before, on May 10, 1869, the golden spike had been driven at Promontory Point, creating the first transcontinental railroad. A trip which used to take six weeks to six months could now be made in a week. While much shorter, the trip still had the aura of a dangerous adventure. During its first year of operation, there were numerous articles and books written about the trip. It became fashionable to make the pilgrimage from New York to San Francisco. This may have been part of the reason Tumblety decided to go.

Even though the trip was only a week, it still was a major undertaking. A first class through fare, from New York to San Francisco, was $112–$150 and entitled the passenger to take 100 pounds of baggage for free. There were a choice of railroads from New York to Omaha and the trip took 62 hours according to the schedule. At Omaha, passengers boarded a westbound Union Pacific train. Leaving Omaha at nine A.M., the train reached San Francisco, if there were no delays, about 85 hours later. The whole trip took a little over 6 days.[12]

Tumblety later published a letter he sent to a friend in New York which described various places along the railroad. Several passages in this letter are lifted directly from one or more guidebooks published by the railroads to advertise the trip and spur tourism. Although the exact edition from which Tumblety took his extracts has not been reviewed, the 1871 *Nelson's Pictorial Guide Book: Scenery of the Union Pacific Railroad*, contains verbatim the story of A. D. Jones of Omaha with his improvised post office and the description of Sherman, Wyoming which Tumblety appropriated as his own.[13]

After his transcontinental rail trip, Dr. Tumblety arrived in San Francisco late in February 1870. He took a room at the Occidental Hotel on Montgomery Street. Here again, Tumblety placed himself in an exclusive and expensive hotel in the center of social activity in San Francisco. The Occidental Hotel was a four-story, Italianate building which occupied the entire block of Montgomery Street from Sutter to Bush. While the first part was built in 1861, the structure was only completed in 1869, the year before Tumblety arrived. It was one of three luxury hotels built in the same area. Over the years it hosted a number of notable visitors to San Francisco. Mark Twain, who stayed at the Occidental in the mid 1860s, called it "Heaven on the half shell."[14]

Montgomery Street, where the Occidental was located, was the social heart of the city and the financial center of the western United States. It was characterized by large, multistory brick buildings, many of which were plastered over to resemble stone. It was home to numerous large banks, businesses and the best hotels. Montgomery Street was filled with bankers, railroad magnates, lawyers and prosperous businessmen—just the kind of clients Tumblety wanted.[15]

Not surprisingly, Dr. Tumblety located his office in the heart of this district. His advertisements show his address as "No. 20 Montgomery St., opposite the Lick House." This was the location of the Odd Fellows' Savings Bank, one of those large brick structures. The upper floors of the building housed numerous professional offices and here Tumblety set up shop. The Lick House, across the street, was the second of the luxury hotels in San Francisco and it was said that its banquet hall was the most beautiful in the entire country. San Francisco's social elite went there to eat a typical heavy dinner and, when they inevitably suffered the heartburn and indigestion that accompanied the meal, they were only steps away from the Indian herb doctor's office.[16]

To attract these and other clients, Tumblety began advertising extensively almost as soon as he got to town. He published ads in at least three major newspapers during his stay in San Francisco: *Alta California, San Francisco Call*, and the *San Francisco Chronicle*. His first ad published in the *Chronicle*, on March 1, 1870, included the familiar offer of a $30 reward if the doctor could not make a diagnosis without any information from the patient. It also included the poem, "Our Motto," which he had used in many other places. As was typical of his introduction to other localities, it took about two weeks for Tumblety to acquire and publish local testimonials. The first of these appeared on March 16 and he continued to publish them, mixed with self-congratulatory notices, through April.

At the same time, beginning on March 17, Tumblety published a series of large ads that provide our best understanding of his medical theory and how he viewed himself professionally. The first ad, titled "Common Sense," explains why he is different from other doctors. He comments, quite reasonably, that many diseases produce similar symptoms and each case should be evaluated individually. Most doctors, he said, find diagnosis the most difficult phase of treating a patient. Without an explanation, Tumblety then produces the claim that he can diagnose patients just by looking at them. To reassure the doubtful, he ends this part by stating, "Our Practice is founded upon the principles of Science, Truth and Humanity." I am sure the patients were happy to know that.

This belief in his superiority over other doctors is further outlined in the same ad under the heading "The Reason Why." Here Tumblety puts forth five statements or principles of his practice. Most of these repeat the first part of the ad, such as the need to look at each case individually and to develop medicines to treat each case. Further, he states that his medicines are harmless vegetable remedies and that he has tested them in thousands of cases. But the most telling of his statements is the first one, where Tumblety described himself as "One of the few mortals to whom the divine gift of healing seems to have descended as a legitimate inheritance." Even given the accepted exaggeration of Victorian advertising, this seems a bit over the top.

Soon after, on March 31, Tumblety further elaborated on his theory of medicine in a long narrative titled "Another Address by the Indian Herb Doctor." It was supposedly set in the doctor's waiting room and adds new, interesting insights on his practice. He begins by saying it was late in the day and the number of waiting patients was too large for him to see that day. Presumably using his amazing ability to diagnose disease by sight, he tells the crowd that most of them just need some advice and he begins to explain how they can be healthy.

It all begins in the stomach where food, if not properly digested, becomes sour. As this is where blood is made, the blood soon becomes sour as well. It carries this bad nature to all parts of the body. The lungs become clogged with mucus and phlegm because the blood is too thick, the skin erupts in acne and scrofula because the blood is bad. In this view, all disease stems from bad digestion and sluggish blood. According to the Indian herb doctor, "Get up a good appetite, eat good, rich food—fat, meat, gravy—in fact nearly everything the appetite craves and the lungs begin to heal.... You can hardly stop it. It is nature to heal."

The basis of the doctor's treatment is equally simple. You begin first by cleansing the stomach and liver, using a "gentle" laxative. When the stomach is clear, the patient recovers his appetite. Tumblety helps this along with an alkali that stimulates appetite at the same time that it keeps the food from souring in the stomach. When the digestion is good, the rest of the body heals and the patient gains weight.

To assure them of the value of his treatment, Tumblety reports that he was once in the last stages of consumption. His weight had dropped to less than 100 pounds, dangerous for one as tall as he was. Through the same cure that he offered his patients, he fully recovered and now weighed 175 pounds. Remarkably, nowhere in his history has this wasting disease been reported.

Although Tumblety claimed this treatment was his own discovery, the system he described was the basis of most herbal medicine in the 19th century. The concern for cleansing the system with laxatives and stimulating the appetite was central to the Thomsonian, Botanic and Eclectic schools of medicine. While he may not have developed it on his own, Tumblety clearly understood the botanic theory involved. It is also interesting to note that he recognized the body's natural tendency to heal itself, even if he felt it needed a little nudge.[17]

Tumblety had a number of large ads published in April through June that continued to elaborate on these medical theories. He also continued to garner and publish local testimonials. There is nothing unusual about these and they reflect the same sorts of diseases we have seen him treat in other localities.

One curious aspect of his narrative is the revelation that Tumblety had acquired a piece of pseudo-medical equipment. For those people who needed a full examination, he described the process of testing the lungs. The full examination cost five dollars. Tumblety would take the patient into his private rooms and listen to his or her lungs with the "Respirometer." He could tell the patient what was wrong with their lungs and whether it was curable. It seems odd that he would publish this at the same time that his other ads repeatedly claimed that he could make a diagnosis without any information from the patient.[18]

On June 13, 1870, the U. S. Census taker caught up with Dr. Tumblety. He was no longer living at the Occidental Hotel but had moved to a boarding house in Ward Five. The census lists him as 45 years of age and states that he was born in England. His profession is listed as herb doctor and he has a personal estate valued at $1,000. Ward Five, where the boarding house was located, was a very small area bounded by Kearny, Market and California Streets. He may have moved there because he was soon to open a new office in the area.

On July 26, Tumblety published a simple ad stating that he had moved his office to 30 Kearney Street. Although it was only a block away, Kearney Street was a very different neighborhood. The 1870 census shows it to be an area of boarding houses rather than large hotels. It might be assumed that by moving his office from Montgomery Street to Kearney Street, Tumblety was losing his prestigious address, perhaps reflecting a decline in his business. Certainly the adjacent boarding houses had their share of carpenters and dressmakers. However, there were a number of other doctors who had offices on Kearney Street. Further, the 1870 census shows that Tumblety had some interesting neighbors. On one side, over one building, was Alfred Ellis, a well-known San Francisco inhabitant, who described himself as a "capitalist" and listed a personal estate of $5,000 and real estate valued at $100,000. Immediately adjacent was Walter Garloph, a bookkeeper, who had a personal estate of $10,000. On the other side of Tumblety's building, one of the boarders was Miles Sweeney, who also described himself as a capitalist with a $50,000 personal estate and real estate valued at $60,000. There were some wealthy and influential people in this neighborhood.

Following the move, the simple ad was repeated through early August. It was followed by a small testimonial that had previously been published, but this time, Tumblety inserted his new address in the ad. In September, on the third and fourth, he published two testimonials and then there are no more ads. Later testimony reported that Tumblety left San Francisco in September 1870.[19]

While in San Francisco, Tumblety left, as he always did, a mixed impression on a number of people. Several members of the police remembered him, although there was some confusion with another doctor by the name of Stanley. Captain Lees reported that he paraded around the streets in 1871 or 1872 "with a negro behind him, who led a greyhound." However, Chief Crowley stated that this was Doctor Stanley, a surgeon who had been in the British army and came to San Francisco from Australia. Dr. Stanley, said the chief, had an office on Washington Street. He further recalled that Tumblety, who was in San Francisco in 1870, owned no dogs during his time there. According to Chief Crowley, Dr. Stanley did something "contrary to the law" and while the police were looking for him, he slipped out of town. Dr. C. C. O'Donnell had the same confusion, attributing to Tumblety the servant and dogs but stating that he came in 1871 and had an office on Washington Street. He reported that "when a great row was being made about unlicensed physicians," Tumblety was brought to court and required to leave town. There was nothing in the San Francisco papers in September 1870 that indicated a "great row" about unlicensed physicians and it may very well be that Lees and O'Donnell were recalling someone other than Tumblety. Mostly what this shows is how bad people's memories are and how newspaper stories need to be taken with a grain of salt.[20]

The man who seems to have known Tumblety best during his stay in San Francisco was Charles F. Smyth, who was a bookkeeper at the Hibernia Savings and Loan Association. Smyth reportedly first met Tumblety in Toronto in July 1858. He described Tumblety as he knew him in Toronto:

> As usual he was then accompanied by his greyhound, and, to my judgment, was the finest specimen of physical manhood I ever looked upon. He stood about six feet two inches in height, was of faultless physique, had coal black hair and mustache, florid complexion, dressed in a semi-military style and wore a large gold medal on his breast.[21]

Smyth next saw Tumblety when the doctor came to San Francisco. He correctly reports where he stayed and where his office was located. Smyth commented that Tumblety deposited a large sum of money in the Hibernia Savings and Loan Association and that the money had never been withdrawn. Over the years, Tumblety had conducted a correspondence with the bank concerning this money and these letters would later become evidence sent to London. Smyth simply said Tumblety left San Francisco in September and did not give a reason.

Tumblety's reason for leaving San Francisco may have something to do with a curious fact that the 1870 census reveals. Olivia Blackburn was living back in Cincinnati with her mother while Mark A. Blackburn is not listed in the census. This marriage, if it was not already dissolved, would be soon. With his old friend once again single, Tumblety may have come east to be with him.

By November 18, 1870, Tumblety had returned to Brooklyn and opened an office at 284 Fulton Street. His first ad was a reprise of an ad published in October 1863. It offered the same $30 reward and repeated the poem entitled "Our Motto." This ad was only published for two days and was replaced with a smaller ad, dropping "Our Motto," which ran until early December. On January 18, 1871, the *Brooklyn Daily Eagle* published the same ad but the doctor's office was now located in New York City at 850 Broadway. Tumblety later published four letters addressed to himself at the Fifth Avenue Hotel during this time, early 1871. That move to New York City does not seem to have worked out because by May 4, 1871, the same ad now has his office at 263 Fulton Street in Brooklyn. The 1871 and 1873 Brooklyn directories list both Francis Tumblety and M. A. Blackburn as physicians at this address. This time with Blackburn in Brooklyn represents a stability on par with the time he spent in Pittsburgh.[22]

Early in 1871, Tumblety began to see an opportunity to seek redress for his perceived persecution by the government during the Civil War. Even before the war ended, the American government began to make claims against Great Britain for shipping captured or destroyed by Confederate raiders built in British shipyards. While the most famous of these was the *Alabama*, there were a number of others and they caused havoc with American shipping. At

Photograph of Tumblety in uniform from the 1871 biography (collection of the New-York Historical Society). While this uniform was supposed to represent a Prussian Hussar's uniform, it looks more like a stage costume. The helmet plate matches nothing used by any European army in the nineteenth century. In the 1871 biography, this photograph was pasted on the front cover.

the same time, the British government had a large number of claims made by its citizens against the United States for losses sustained during the war. To arbitrate these claims, in 1869, the two governments had agreed on terms in the Clarendon-Johnson treaty.[23]

However, they did not count on the determined opposition of the Senate Republicans led by Charles Sumner. In his opposition to the treaty, Sumner stated that the Confederates had been beaten at Gettysburg and, had it not been for the ships Great Britain built and failed to stop from going to sea, the war would have been over. In his view, Britain was responsible for all of the costs of the war after the Battle of Gettysburg. Sumner demanded that they pay two billion dollars in reparations and/or cede Canada to the United States. The defeat of the Clarendon-Johnson treaty and Sumner's hostility led to a freeze in the relations between the two countries and the real possibility of war. This cold war began to change with the election of President

Grant and his appointment of Hamilton Fish as secretary of state. Quiet negotiations were begun which led to the creation of the Joint High Commission in 1871.

The "Alabama Claims" and the topic of reparations were all over the newspapers and Tumblety, with legitimate grievances, was well aware of them. His first autobiography, published in 1866, was written, in part, with an eye to recovering some of the property he lost in St. Louis. If his later publications are to be believed, Tumblety began sending his pamphlet to anyone who would listen. By the responses that he printed, they do not seem to have been greatly impressed.

The Treaty of Washington was signed on May 8, 1871, and approved by the Senate on May 24, officially setting up the process for making claims. Tumblety hired Alvin Burt, a lawyer with an office at 11 Wall Street in New York, to prepare a memorial to the commission stating his claims. On January 15, 1872, the memorial was ready and Tumblety signed it in front of a notary public. In the memorial, Tumblety recounted his two arrests in St. Louis and made an outrageous claim for $100,000 in lost goods and damages. Unfortunately for him, the second arrest was made in May 1865, after the cessation of hostilities, and was therefore not allowed under the treaty. A much smaller claim for his brief arrest in March of the same year was processed but it was eventually dismissed as well.[24]

Naturally, Tumblety was not satisfied with this result. The Joint Commission had dismissed his claim on a technicality. It did not say that it had no merit but that it did not fall within the treaty's specified time. They left him free to pursue this case with the United States government. In fact, as late as 1876, Tumblety's claim is mentioned in the *Journal of the House of Representatives*.

As he had done earlier, Tumblety published his life story to boost his claims against the government. The first of his new editions was published in 1871 and bore the title "Dr. Tumblety's Narrative, How He Was Kidnapped by Order of the Infamous Baker, His Incarceration and Discharge, an Exciting Life Sketch...." It is important to note that as Stanton was already out of office, the cause of Tumblety's arrest has now shifted. More importantly, this edition replaced the cover sketch showing his arrest with a photograph of Tumblety dressed in what was supposed to be a Prussian Hussar's uniform. This is the only photograph known to exist of Dr. Tumblety and it was pasted directly onto the front cover of the pamphlet. The uniform looks more like a stage costume. Tumblety can be seen wearing two medals; one is a cross that is correct for the Legion of Honor while the other is a large, round medal. In very high resolution, one can read on this medal "Awarded to Francis Tumblety..." and it represents the medal he claimed was awarded to him by the citizens of Montreal.[25]

Perhaps because the photographs were too expensive or the uniform was so laughable, Tumblety published another pamphlet in 1872. This one was published in New York by Russell's American Steam Printing House. This was a large establishment with many titles and, perhaps importantly, it published the *American Eclectic Medical Review*. There are several differences between this edition and the 1866 one. The most noticeable is the lack of testimonials. The entire section detailing his many patients has been removed. To the end of the original, he added a supplement that covers his life from 1866 to 1872. This details his first trip to Europe and his trip to California and reproduces many letters from famous people. These events have already been discussed in their chronological order and need no further comment.[26]

Probably the most significant item from this edition of the autobiography is the picture on the cover. Tumblety reports that it is an engraving done from a photograph taken while he was in Berlin. It shows him dressed in the uniform of the Imperial Guard with a large walrus-type moustache. His hair is cut much shorter than in 1866 and he looks older and heavier. On his chest are five medals which can be identified from the picture and later descriptions.

On the lower left is a large cross topped with a crown. This is an accurate depiction of the Legion of Honor given out during the Second Empire Period when Tumblety is supposed to have received it from Napoleon III. The crown had been part of the original cross but had been removed during the Second Republic (1848–1852) and brought back by Napoleon III during the Second Empire Period (1852–1870). Wherever he got it, Tumblety had a good copy. Three of the other medals are not pictured well enough to distinguish but Tumblety would later claim they were the Iron Cross of Prussia, a cross from the Austrian Emperor and a medal from the Prince of Wales. The final medal, which is round and located on the far right, is the medal he claimed to be from the citizens of Montreal. This picture would be reproduced as late as 1893 without change and it is certain that he still had the medals as late as 1881 in New Orleans. As the "Indian Herb Doctor" was his persona in the early part of his career, this picture and his medals were part of it in the later years of his career.[27]

Aside from the publication of the second edition of his autobiography, there is little information on Tumblety's activities at this time. He stopped advertising in the *Brooklyn Daily Eagle* in mid 1871. Both he and Blackburn were still listed at the 263 Fulton Street address in the 1873 directory. Several important events took place which must have had an impact on his life. On May 27, 1873, Margaret Tumblety, his mother, passed away in Rochester. Around the same time, his friend, Mark A. Blackburn, married a second wife, named Elizabeth, with whom he would spend the rest of his life. These events may have led to Tumblety making a major change in his life over the next year.[28]

12

—◇◇◇—

English Interlude
(1873–1880)

Whether it was his mother's death or the marriage of his friend, Mark Blackburn, Tumblety determined that he needed a change of scenery. In July 1873, he set sail for Liverpool with the intention of carrying on his medical business in England. As this was a business trip and not a "scientific" trip, Dr. Tumblety immediately set about establishing his practice in Liverpool. However, he faced a problem in the presentation of his public persona which was unique to that country. In North America, he was known far and wide as the "Indian Herb Doctor," which played on the public's belief in the power of Native American medicines. Had he used that title in England, people would have assumed he was a doctor from India and it would not have the same effect. In Liverpool, he seems to have become the "Great American Doctor," which he used in all of his advertisements.[1]

Tumblety arrived in Liverpool on July 21 on the Guion line steamship *Idaho*. He may have been met by his Liverpool relatives, but little is known of his first days in England. While it is likely that he quickly set up practice in Liverpool, no ads from this period have been found. It was reported that Tumblety visited London during October, probably staying at the Langham Hotel. He was cruising the streets looking for a companion when he found Henry Carr, a likely 17-year-old boy. They struck up a conversation and Tumblety offered him a job as his secretary. It seems Carr accepted and, like others before and after him, would live to regret the choice.[2]

At the time, Henry Carr was a carpenter and this looked like a rare opportunity to him. His father, Charles Carr, was butler to Lt. General Sir Henry J. W. Bentinck, K.C.B., and therefore knew something about the gentry. Charles Carr was very leery of Dr. Tumblety. At some point, Henry gave his father a copy of the 1872 biography to demonstrate the doctor's respectability. The father was not too impressed and advised his son to steer clear of the man.

After an unspecified time in London, Tumblety announced that he was going back to Liverpool and asked Carr to go back with him. Over the objections of his parents, Carr decided to accompany his employer. Tumblety gave Carr a gold chain to take care of for him. Giving expensive jewelry or a checkbook to his "secretary" was something that Tumblety often did to prove how much he trusted them or to have a potential hold on them. Frequently this ploy turned out badly. There is no way to know the actual relationship between the doctor and Carr. For whatever reason, Carr, "not liking the gentleman's manner," decided to return to London, bringing the chain with him. Either Carr intended to steal the chain or, more likely, thought it was a present to him. Tumblety traveled with a lot more cash and jewelry. If Carr was intent on robbing him, he could have taken so much more.

Back in London by December and unemployed, Carr took the chain to a pawnshop to get what he could for it. When the pawnbroker questioned him about the chain, Carr was evasive about how he got it. The pawnbroker contacted the police and Carr was arrested. On December 1, 1873, at Marylebone Police Court, Carr told his story to the magistrate. In the end, the magistrate discharged Carr but held on to the gold, saying he clearly had "no right to the chain." It is important to point out that Tumblety took no part in this proceeding. The article does not even mention if he was notified at the time of the hearing.

In a much later reminiscence, William Pinkerton, the detective, recalled that he was in London when this case was heard. In his 1888 description, he managed to get all of the details wrong. He also said that as a result of Carr's testimony, the police issued a warrant for Tumblety on unspecified but implied charges. Based on Pinkerton's description, we can assume it was because of his homosexual activity. Supposedly, Tumblety never called for his property and the police eventually discovered that he had fled to Paris. Despite this newspaper article, Tumblety went from London back to Liverpool, where he soon met one of his most interesting partners.[3]

Sometime in 1874, Tumblety began to treat a small, nervous young man by the name of Thomas Henry Hall Caine, who was trained as an architectural draftsman but had pretensions of being a writer. Much later in time, he would be world-renowned as a novelist and today, he is mostly remembered for his relationship with Dante Gabriel Rossetti, who is reported to have died in his arms. Caine was a hypochondriac and daily worried about his health. Tumblety was just the kind of doctor he needed and he prescribed medicines for the young man on a regular basis.[4]

As he so often did with young men, Tumblety served as a model of a worldly and wealthy gentleman to Caine. At the time Caine was 21 years old, having spent almost all of his life in Liverpool, while Tumblety, at 43 years old, had traveled widely. They must have made quite a pair as Tumblety was over six feet tall while Caine was only a little over five feet. Tumblety's highly embroidered tales of adventure, which he helped edit, appealed to Caine. Perhaps some of that wore off on him, as his biographer described Caine as a "consummate self publicist and not always entirely truthful." What better description could there be of Tumblety? The two men shared a friendship for almost three years. We know about this because, unlike that of all of Tumblety's other acquaintances, Caine's correspondence has been preserved. In the Archives of the Manx Museum are a series of letters written by Tumblety to Caine in 1875 and 1876 which provide much of the information on his whereabouts during this sojourn in England.[5]

Caine was also a reporter for the *Liverpool Mercury*, and on September 1, 1874, Tumblety began publishing ads in the paper. His first ad begins with the familiar title "Good News for the Afflicted" and includes the poem "Our Motto," which he had used for years. In addition to the usual fluff, the ad states that the doctor "has arrived from British America," despite his residence in Liverpool for the past year. It listed his office at 177 Duke Street.[6]

Duke Street had been, in the late 18th century, one of the most exclusive neighborhoods in Liverpool and a number of large mansions were built here. Through the 19th century, as the neighborhood became more commercial, these mansions were let out for shops and offices. In early 1874, a doctor named Martin had an office here treating corns, bunions and other foot problems. Dr. Martin's ads stop that summer and Tumblety's begin in September. A later ad, from 1897, describes 177 Duke Street as having "several large rooms to be let as offices, workshops or storerooms."[7]

Very quickly, Tumblety's ads change from general information to testimonials. He published a huge number of testimonials from September through January 1875. Almost every day, Tumblety had one or more testimonials in the *Liverpool Mercury*. The diseases mentioned are no different than previously reported. The leading diseases are consumption (a bad cough), blood disease (indigestion) and scrofula (acne) with a few miracle cures thrown in.

He later quoted an example of the type of ad he published, stating that a reporter for the *Liverpool Mercury* (Caine?) had written about him:

> Dr. Tumblety is not an easy man to interview. He is utterly free, both in private and public, from effusiveness that longs to overflow into confidence. He is far from an ungenial man; indeed, having traveled with him under all kinds of circumstances—and travel is a great test of man's amiability—I can say truly that I never found a fellow traveler more agreeable and more unselfish. He carries into the smallest details of his life a high-bred curiosity which is a far higher proof of his good birth and breeding than his descent from so many of the statesmen of Ireland and his relationship to many of the best families in England. But he is distinctly not an effusive man, and of all subjects that of which he least likes to speak is himself. It is doubtful if he ever spent a moment of his whole life in self-analysis, and if he ever did so, he has certainly never communicated the result to anybody.[8]

Despite extensive searching, this particular ad could not be located in the digitized archive of the newspaper.

The large number of testimonials was an effective advertising technique but it came with a potential problem. These were supposed to be letters sent to the doctor but it is obvious that Tumblety often used people's names without asking them. Some people did not want their names used or their disease publicized. Others sensed a chance to make some money. On November 2, 1874, the *Liverpool Mercury* published the following ad for Dr. Tumblety:

> My face was covered with pimples and blotches and my blood was very impure. The Great American Doctor, of 177, Duke-street, has cured me—William Carroll, 2, George's-road, West Derby-road, Liverpool.

Some time after this ad was published, Carroll hired a lawyer and sued Tumblety for libel, charging that he suffered £200 damages. Tumblety hired a barrister named Devey and prepared to fight the allegation. In the Manx Museum is a poster calling a public meeting where Tumblety would "tell the whole truth of the matter." The case was scheduled for a hearing in late January 1875.[9]

While preparing to meet this challenge, a far more serious problem confronted the doctor. On January 11, 1875, a couple, Edward and Ann Hanratty, came to his office seeking his help. Hanratty was 45 years old and worked for the Lancashire and Northwestern Railway. Tumblety had published a number of testimonials from other employees of the railway and this may have been what prompted Hanratty to seek him out. For two years, Hanratty had been under the care of a Dr. Bligh, who was associated with the London and Manchester Insurance Company. Dr. Bligh described his condition as congestion of the lungs and heart disease. He also added that Hanratty drank too much. Initially, the patient seemed to get better under Dr. Bligh's treatment and even went back to work. However, he suffered a relapse and Dr. Bligh told Ann Hanratty that his condition was now critical.[10]

It was at this juncture that the couple decided to see Tumblety. On examining the patient, the doctor tapped Hanratty on the chest and told him that a cure would cost £2 10s but when Mrs. Hanratty complained, he lowered it to £2. Tumblety told them he would have their medicine on Wednesday, two days later. Mrs. Hanratty stopped by to pick up the medicine and was given "a bottle of medicine, a box of pills and some herbs." Attached to the herbs was a set of directions on how to take the medicine. It seems to be the same set of medicines that he had been giving out since the early days in Toronto. On receipt of the medicines, she gave the doctor the fee of £2 but he gave her back 10s, saying that her husband would need nourishment.

That evening, around five, Mrs. Hanratty gave her husband a tablespoon of the liquid but none of the herbs or pills and by nine, he was dead. Next morning, she went to ask Dr. Tumblety to sign the death certificate. According to her testimony, he pretended not to know who she was and eventually left the office for 20 minutes. When he came back, he did recognize her and he refunded the rest of her fee. He did not sign the death certificate as this could cause him even greater problems.

To apply for the insurance, Mrs. Hanratty needed a signed death certificate. She applied to Dr. Bligh, under whose care her husband had originally been. However, he refused to sign it because he heard that Hanratty had been under the care of another medical professional, through he did not know whom. When he found out the man was Tumblety, he went to see him and reported a very interesting and revealing conversation:

> When he first saw Tumility, he asked him if he had examined the deceased, and his reply was that he sold him medicine. — Witness then asked him if he knew what was the matter with the man, and he said that he did not. — Tumblety said he only sold medicine and he did not know anything about disease, adding that he had come to Liverpool to make money for the purpose of bringing an action for the recovery of some property he had in Canada.[11]

If this was a true statement, and it might be, it casts Tumblety in a very bad light. However, it does seem strange that Tumblety would open up to a member of the regular medical fraternity, his lifelong enemies. Dr. Bligh invited Tumblety to attend the post-mortem he was to perform on Hanratty to determine the cause of death. At this point it gets a little muddy, with Bligh claiming Tumblety never showed up and with Tumblety's lawyer claiming that Bligh intentionally misled Tumblety about where it was to be held. Dr. Bligh testified that Hanratty had died from natural causes but implied that Tumblety's medicine had hastened the issue. The inquest was adjourned for a week so that the brain and stomach contents could be examined.

The coroner's jury reconvened on January 27, with Dr. Bligh testifying that the brain showed no evidence of drugs and that he would list the cause of death as disease of the heart and lungs. Dr. J. Campbell Brown, who examined the stomach, said there was no evidence of inflammation and no evidence of a drug. Mr. Murphy, representing Tumblety in this hearing, cross-examined Dr. Bligh about the timing and location of the post-mortem. This led to a heated exchange with the coroner, who told Murphy that if he was implying that Tumblety had been kept from the post-mortem, then the coroner would subpoena him to find out the reason. He objected to Murphy's continued use of the term "the American Doctor," suggesting that his nationality was not an issue, only whether he was a doctor. In the end, the jury found that Hanratty died from natural causes, but "the jury strongly censured the conduct of Mr. Tumilty in administering medicine, he being in total ignorance of the condition of the patient."[12]

On January 26, the case of Carroll v. Tumblety came before the County Court. Because of the publicity surrounding the inquest, Tumblety's lawyer, Mr. Devey, asked that the hearing be postponed for a month. When the case came to be called on February 23, no one on either side showed up and the case was dropped.[13]

Tumblety reacted to these legal problems in his usual way — he ran away. His last ad was published in the *Liverpool Mercury* on January 15, two days after the death of Hanratty, and by the twenty-eighth he was living in London. The move to London would seem to have been a reaction to problems in Liverpool rather than an opening of new territory. Despite being cleared of all charges, Tumblety would not have a regular practice in Liverpool again.

On moving to London, Tumblety probably could not afford to permanently stay at the Langham Hotel, but he wanted to stay in the same fashionable area. He took a room in a lodging house run by Mrs. Annie Higgins at 58 Margaret Street, close to Regent Street and a few blocks south of Portland Place, where the Langham was located. Mrs. Higgins usually had four lodgers, most of whom were clerks. He was at this address by late January 1875. The exact location of his office in London is yet unknown. However, later reports state that he practiced at Charring Cross. If true, this was an area of intense foot traffic located near the main hub of railroad activity in London. As a supplement to business generated by his ads, the foot traffic would have added considerably to his practice.[14]

While he was now in London, numerous aspects of his life in Liverpool, as reported in a January 28 letter, were still important. He was actively preparing for the publication of his biography and he requested that Caine get a price for printing 10,000 copies in Liverpool because it was cheaper than London.

In the letter, Tumblety complained about a supposed friend who had betrayed him in Liverpool. He went on to praise Caine and said, "you have proved yourself feminine and I feel under a great obligation and hope some time to be able to make a recompense." This is how the letter was transcribed and many have seen Tumblety's use of the word "feminine" as some type of homosexual reference. However, I suspect, not having been able to review the original, that the word is actually "genuine," and this would much better fit the context. Whatever the actual word, Tumblety had strong feelings for his small friend and missed him greatly.

On February 1, Tumblety was again writing to Caine. He thanked him for forwarding some letters from Liverpool and discussed matters relating to the upcoming publication which Caine was editing. He enclosed the letter supposedly written by Napoleon III from the Isle of Wight. Presumably, this was added to the pamphlet and it was a part of each edition afterwards. The first ad for Tumblety's new pamphlet, which claimed it was in press, was published in the *Liverpool Mercury* on February 2, 1875.[15]

For unknown reasons, Tumblety soon changed his lodgings. A week after he answered Caine's letter, he wrote from 5 Glasshouse Street. This was another lodging house located south and west of his first location. The lodging house was run by Louisa Willcox, who had between three and six lodgers. She had a wide range of boarders, including a gentleman, a stockbroker, and a professor of languages. On the other end, a number of young, foreign men, who all listed their occupation as waiter, lived here. This location was no less prestigious than the one he left but it may have been more convenient. Glasshouse

Street was much closer to his office at Charring Cross and just outside of Piccadilly Circus. The proximity to Piccadilly may have been important because of its known association as a meeting place for homosexuals.[16]

An urgent telegram from Caine eventually caught up with Tumblety at his new address. There was some problem with the printing or content of the pamphlet and the doctor told Caine to stop working on it until he could see the proofs. Tumblety offered to pay for Caine to come to London for a visit. Apparently this offer was accepted because Tumblety's next letter, on February 16, indicates that Caine had been there and gone back to Liverpool. Near the end of February, there was a flurry of letters mostly dealing with the publication of the pamphlet. Tumblety complained that he was sicker than he had been in 20 years and too ill to even think about things. Still, he told Caine to warn "the printers" that if they continued to print a certain pamphlet, he would sue them for libel—apparently Tumblety had made enemies in Liverpool. He was conveniently too ill to send Caine any money and he sent him a printer's bill to be paid. The letters also reveal that Tumblety had hired another "secretary" and, as the doctor was too ill to get out of bed, the young man read parts of the proofs to him.

The pamphlet was published around March 15, when an ad in the *Liverpool Mercury* reported that it was available at the office of the *Liverpool Lantern* for the price of 3d. It was entitled "Passages in the Life of the Great American Doctor," and was 46 pages long. Apparently it was similar to the 1872 version but with a Liverpool imprint. There would probably have been some specifically English testimonials in it. This was the fourth of Tumblety's autobiographies published.[17]

During March, Tumblety wrote to Caine six times, mostly with praise for Caine's writing and expressing a desire to see him again. Near the end of the month, Tumblety wrote a letter full of praise to his young friend. He reported that he was coming to Liverpool to treat patients. Based on the sequence of letters, he never made it to Liverpool, and in April, he suggested that he could teach Caine which medicines to dispense and offered to bring him into the business. This is the same thing he did with Mark Blackburn but Caine was reluctant to give up his profession.

Still trying to get his young friend into the medical business, Tumblety proposed to manufacture pills to compete with those made by Thomas Holloway. These pills had been around since 1839 and they were the world's most well-known patent medicine and one of the most heavily advertised. Holloway's Pills were originally an aid to digestion and contained a powerful purgative. Through the years, the claims evolved and the pills became a "blood purifier," and a cure-all. Ironically, soldiers in the American Civil War took these pills as a cure for dysentery with often fatal results. His strategy for getting the pills known included giving away ten pounds worth of them for free.[18]

In the same letter, Tumblety comments on the eating habits of the British and, with a mixture of medicine and greed, comments on why his pills will do well: "There is no place in the world like England for good pills.... The English people all indulge in eating late suppers which produces costiveness and they must have cathartic pills." He wanted Caine to discuss the idea with some druggists in Liverpool. The pills that Tumblety wanted to sell were no different than those he had offered since his time in Toronto. What was different was that he wanted to begin a large ad campaign just for the pills. There is no evidence that this ever became more than an idea.

Through April, Tumblety was in touch with Caine possibly as many as seven times, although a couple of the letters are undated. Apparently, they had recently talked about Caine going to America with Tumblety, as the doctor mentions it twice. He also suggests that Caine come to London and said that he would guarantee him a living in the medicine business. On April 9, Tumblety sent a desperate telegram to Caine which said, "Come here tomorrow evening. I must see you." But Caine was ill and Tumblety sent several packets of medicine for him. He recommended that it be taken with "three or four glasses of ale per day" until Caine felt better.

At the end of that letter, Tumblety told Caine that he would be gone from London for a while and would not be able to keep in touch as he had. For a couple of weeks, Caine heard nothing from Tumblety, in sharp contrast to the constant letters in April. He may have thought that Tumblety had left for America without him. Disturbed by this seeming slight, Caine apparently wrote to Tumblety's nephew-in-law, Thomas Brady, and asked if he had seen the doctor. Brady replied, on May 7, that he had not heard from him since late April and, when he went to check at his London boarding house, he found he was gone. Finally, on May 15, Tumblety was back at Glasshouse Street and wrote to Caine. He reminded him that in his last letter, he said he would be gone for awhile and assured him that he would never leave for America without him. He wrote of how important Caine was to him:

> Though I have been long silent you have not been absent from my remembrance. The ultimate friendship which has subsisted between us for so long a period has prompted me to feel lively interest in all that concerns your welfare and happiness. It is not therefore in the mere observance of a cold and formal custom that I at present write but in obedience to the dictates of the trust and friendship.[19]

While relations between Tumblety and Caine were restored, we are left to wonder where the doctor had been and what he was doing. There is one piece of evidence that might provide some insight on this question. On May 2, 1875, Caine received a telegram from a W. J. Morgan, at 5 Frear Street, that said, "Wire at once to Eames your spark only just received wire forty wire wire wire wire wire wire." It has been assumed that W. J. Morgan was an alias that Tumblety was using. The problem with this assumption is that if Caine knew where Tumblety was, having sent him a telegram, why was he concerned about not hearing from him?

Tumblety remained in London through the summer and moved to a new boarding house at 16 Devereux Court. This was a very fashionable address located in the Strand near the Inns of Court. In the 1871 and 1881 census returns, other boarders included an architect, a surveyor, a professor of languages and several gentlemen. His first letter from this address was on August 4 in reply to something that Caine sent to him.

For unspecified reasons, Tumblety traveled to Birmingham on August 6 and was at the Midland Hotel when he wrote an angry letter to Caine complaining that he was expecting two pounds but instead got an excuse. He told Caine that the Liverpool printers had been paid and they had no claim on him. This whole incident is curious and unexplained. Tumblety went on to say, "Nobody else knows anything about it, there is no fraud being committed on you as I am not in the habit of telling people my private affairs." Within days, he wrote again to Caine apologizing for his tone and saying that because all his money was in an investment, he had really needed the money. Soon thereafter, there was a wire from the doctor enclosing the two pounds that he owed Caine.

Whatever the meaning of the previous incident, it is clear that tensions were beginning to come between the two men. During that spring, Tumblety had disappeared, leaving Caine apprehensive that he had been abandoned. People had suggested to him that Tumblety was taking advantage of him and the minor point of two pounds stands symbolic of these difficulties.

On August 31, Tumblety wrote to Caine in haste to report that he had to leave for America. There was a growing wave of bank failures in California and Tumblety still had a large sum of money in the Hibernia Savings and Loan in San Francisco. He said that he had received a dispatch that required his immediate departure and had booked passage on the steamship *Greece* which would leave the next day. He had not given up hope that Caine would come to America and asked him to write to him at the National Hotel.[20]

The financial situation in California was indeed uncertain in late August. The panic began on the twenty-sixth when the Bank of California closed its doors because it could no longer pay its depositors. The president of the bank, William C. Ralston, had overextended the bank's credit by speculating in gold stocks and for several weeks, it was having trouble meeting its obligations. Eventually, this uncertainty reached the public and they began a run on the bank. Conditions were not helped when Ralston committed suicide. The failure of this bank caused a chain reaction which closed all the banks and the San Francisco Exchange. A number of articles stated that private banks were generally sound and their depositors did not have to worry. However, in September, it was stated that large amounts of gold were being sent from New York specifically for the Bank of California and the Hibernia Bank, perhaps indicating that Tumblety's concern was justified.[21]

The passenger list of the *Greece* lists Tumblety as a physician and states that he is a citizen of the United States. It lists his age as 40, slightly younger than his real age. The ship arrived in New York on September 17 and Tumblety took up residence on Cortlandt Street at the National Hotel. This establishment was close to both Castle Garden, where the ship docked, and the ferries leading to Jersey City, from which the western railroad trip would begin. On September 24, he wrote to Caine and apologized for not answering his letter sooner. He claimed to have been too tired from his recent ocean trip.

As the financial panic in California passed, the urgency of Tumblety's trip to the West was lessened and it became more of a tour of his old haunts. He stayed in New York as late as September 29 and by October 12, he is mentioned in Montreal. By late 1875, Tumblety was in California. He visited his nephew in Vallejo and spent time in San Francisco. On December 30, he wrote an affectionate letter to Caine in England. On the return trip to New York, he spent some time in Chicago and St. Louis. In a letter dated March 31, 1876, Tumblety was still expecting Caine to join him in America.

That hope was never realized, as this was the last of Tumblety's letters preserved in Caine's correspondence. It may be the last time they were in contact with each other. There is no indication that on any of his frequent trips to England in the 1880s Tumblety had any contact with Caine. By that time, Caine had moved to London, been accepted into rarified literary circles and was well on his way to world fame as a novelist. What the cause of the their final estrangement was remains unknown but it is interesting that in all of the later versions of his biography, where he cited even passing acquaintance with important people, he never mentioned Caine.

Tumblety had been traveling for most of a year and there is no indication that he was practicing medicine at this time. His investments must have been sufficient for him to live comfortably without worrying about an office. It is reported that he had $100,000 in bonds in a New York bank and a large sum in a San Francisco bank. While it is possible that on his return to New York, he opened an office, no advertisements or specific recollections have been found.

Whether it was because he knew that Caine was not coming to America or simply because he needed company, Tumblety went looking for another young man. While walking along the Battery in New York, Tumblety began a conversation with a young man named Lyons. The young man had just come from college and was unemployed. Tumblety offered him a job as his secretary. The exact date and outline of this relationship remains sketchy. It had to have begun in 1877 and Tumblety was as infatuated with this young man as he had been with all the others before him. As was his usual experience, Tumblety began trusting Lyons with more and more valuable assets.[22]

By early 1878, Tumblety had decided to take an extended trip to Europe. Whether this was for business or pleasure has not been revealed. Most of his bonds and investments were secure but a portion needed periodic attention so that the interest could be collected. Since Lyons was his secretary and friend, he gave the $7,000 worth of bonds to the young man before he left.

Tumblety was off to Liverpool on the steamer *Montana*, sailing on April 23, 1878. The ship reached Queenstown on May 2 and Liverpool soon thereafter. The doctor's activities during this trip are mostly unknown. How long he spent in England, whether he practiced medicine and who he was with are not recorded. In a later published biography, Tumblety reports on the time he spent in Rome during this trip. It is the only place in his travelogues that he provides any personal information that can be verified. In fact, enough information is available to pin down fairly tightly when he was in Rome. He reports meeting Rev. Hostelot, whom he calls the rector of the American University at Rome. Rev. Hostelot held that position from 1878 until his death in 1884. Tumblety claims to have met Pope Leo XIII, who became pope on February 20, 1878. More importantly, Tumblety refers to meeting, in Rome, Archbishop McQuade of Rochester and Father Curran of St. Andrews Church of New York City. It is not known when these two churchmen went to Rome but they returned from Liverpool on the steamer *Gallia* on April 15, 1879. It seems unlikely, given the narrow range of times and the details involved, that Tumblety could have made this up. Based on this information, Tumblety was in Rome sometime between April 1878 and April 1879.[23]

During this trip, Tumblety kept up a correspondence with Lyons in New York. These letters were more than just directions for his financial affairs. Later, in an adversarial context, they were described as "the most amusing farrago of illiterate nonsense." While we might wonder what the actual contents were, it is clear that Tumblety wrote them to a friend, not an employee. The same source reports that the letters were from all the major cities of Europe, which shows that Tumblety did travel widely on this trip. Eventually, Tumblety began to think about coming back to the States. There is no way to know why he decided to come back when he did. It may be that he sensed all was not well between Lyons and himself.[24]

He sailed from Liverpool for New York on April 3, 1880, aboard the steamer *Arizona*. The passenger list describes him as Dr. Tumilty, age 40, whose occupation is gentleman. As usual, he lists his citizenship as United States. The *Arizona* made a stop at Queenstown on the fourth and arrived in New York on April 13, 1888. As he got off the ship at Castle Garden, he could not know the storm that would engulf him in the next few months.

13

⊶⊷

New York City Years
(1880–1888)

During his absence in Europe, Tumblety kept up a voluminous correspondence with his friend Lyons. He probably intended to pick up with the young man when he came back and wrote to tell him of his intention to return. If he was expecting Lyons to meet him, he was sadly disappointed.

As he soon found out, Lyons was missing and a considerable quantity of the doctor's bonds were missing with him. Tumblety went to the house of Mrs. Lyons, the young man's widowed mother. She had no help to give and may not have approved of her son's relationship with the doctor. Not getting any satisfaction from either the son or the mother, Tumblety sued Mrs. Lyons for the $7,000 represented by the missing South Carolina railroad bonds. She was arrested and a trial date was set up.[1]

William P. Burr, whose recollections are the source for most of what is known of this affair, was the attorney for Mrs. Lyons. Tumblety hired James D. McClelland to prosecute his case. Both of these lawyers were on their way to becoming leaders in their profession. As was often the case, testimony revolved less on the facts of the case and more on the respectability of Dr. Tumblety. Burr seems to relish his recollection of asking Tumblety, "what institution had the honor of graduating so precious a pupil." He reported that Tumblety was livid at this line of questioning.[2]

While he may have enjoyed taunting Tumblety, Burr was aware that the case was more complex than that. Before he left for Europe, Tumblety had brought a power of attorney and the bonds over to Mrs. Lyons' house for her son. The bonds were bearer bonds, which means they had no name on them and could be cashed by anyone. The bonds were issued with coupons which needed to be presented to the bank every six months for the interest to be paid. If the coupon was not presented within a specified time, no interest was due to the owner. Since Tumblety would be away in Europe for an extended period, he needed someone to clip the coupons and present them for payment. The prosecution claimed that this was why Tumblety gave the bonds to Lyons and that he never thought the young man would sell them. The defense counted that the bonds were given to Lyons as compensation for taking care of Tumblety's affairs while he was away.

The only record of this case is Burr's memory that "the case fell though and the old lady was not held." In the end, the charges against Mrs. Lyons could not be sustained because it was her son, not she, who had cashed the bonds. If we look at the few facts, it looks like Lyons was guilty of stealing the bonds. The idea that the $7,000 was compensation seems ridiculous when we consider that the average yearly wage in 1880 was about $400. When he learned Tumblety was coming back, he simply disappeared, suggesting that he knew he was wrong. Perhaps Tumblety decided to await the return of the son to further prosecute, but he was in for a surprise.[3]

When young Lyons did return to New York, he filed a suit against Tumblety for "atrocious assault" which in legal terms is a specific kind of assault. It involves a cruel and malicious attack intended to do bodily harm and is punished more severely than simple assault. The report stated that the evidence was "of the most disgusting sort," perhaps implying that Tumblety had a homosexual relationship with Lyons. Conviction for atrocious assault could carry a maximum sentence of seven years in the penitentiary.

Because of the charge, Tumblety went into hiding until the trial. In June 1880, the census takers spread out across the United States but did not record Francis Tumblety as a resident. Like he would do in a later crisis, the doctor left his residence and moved to a boarding house under an assumed name. When the census taker called at 77 East Tenth Street in New York, he found it was a boarding house run by Edward McNamara and his wife Mary which had 19 boarders. One of these was James Dombletee, a 45-year-old medical doctor who had been born in Ireland. While he began staying with the McNamaras as a way of avoiding detection, he would soon make this his permanent New York residence.

The case of "Lyons vs. Sumblety, " as the *New York Times* recorded it, was heard in the Supreme Court in front of Judge Donohue on July 24, 1880. Little is know about this case but it is reported that Lyon's attorney used the article about Tumblety from the 1861 *Police Gazette* in court to discredit him. If Tumblety sued Lyons, no record has surfaced. He really would have few grounds for the suit. Tumblety voluntarily gave the bearer bonds to the young man. It was only his trust that made him think Lyons would not cash them. The whole idea of bearer bonds is that they belong to the person who cashes them. Apparently neither side pushed this suit and it was eventually dropped.[4]

Shortly thereafter, Tumblety sued William P. O'Connor, the banker who took the bonds from Lyons. It was Tumblety's contention that Lyons sold the bonds without authority and that O'Connor should not have accepted them. Again the defense, this time lead by the firm of Boardman & Boardman, attacked Tumblety's character. They called two detectives from Brooklyn, Frost and Chambers, to report on his time in that city. The court reiterated that bearer bonds were just that and denied his claim. As late as 1885, Tumblety prosecuted this case in the appellate court with the same result. It was an expensive lesson, both financially and socially, for Tumblety to learn.[5]

Losing the money was bad enough, but the doctor's reputation, which was always shaky, suffered from this incident. Stories related to the assault charges were current in New York. In a later recollection, James Pryor, the house detective for the Fifth Avenue Hotel, reported that he was requested to eject Tumblety from the hotel because the "gentlemen ... didn't care to have him near them." Pryor remembered that this occurred about April 1881 because he, on the same day, ejected Charles Guiteau, the assassin of President Garfield. His recollection was that it was three months before the assassination.[6]

Pryor's memory was somewhat confused about the date. Guiteau was in Washington in the spring of 1881 and is not reported to have been in New York. Also, Pryor states that Guiteau was writing a speech at the time of his ejection. This was for the election campaign of 1880 and would have been between August and November 1880. A Mr. Fox, who was the chief clerk for the Republican State Committee, which met at the hotel, reported that Guiteau was such an annoyance that he had to have him ejected. This was during the campaign of 1880 and Pryor was remembering this incident.[7]

Much of Pryor's description of Tumblety relates to the doctor's earlier appearances in New York, but he did comment on his character. He said, "But I never had that trouble with the 'doctor.' He was very quiet, and as soon as he humbled to the fact that I knew him he went right out.... Why, he hasn't the nerve of a chicken. He just had enough nerve to put some molasses and water together and label it as medicine—the biggest words being in the latin—and sell it." Thus ended Tumblety's longtime association with the Fifth Avenue Hotel.

Perhaps finding New York a little confining, Tumblety went to Toronto, where, on October 1, he checked into the Rossin House. As he usually did, Tumblety picked one of the largest and most prestigious hotels in the city as his abode. Rossin House was a modern, five-story hotel located on King Street at the corner of York Street, and only a few blocks from the site of his old office. The beginning of his stay in Toronto was uneventful and we do not know what he was doing. He has no ads in the Toronto papers during this period so it is unlikely he was practicing medicine.[8]

On the night of October 14, Tumblety was out for a walk, probably along the Esplanade. This area was a tree-lined walkway along the shore of Lake Ontario and, during the day, was the fashionable promenade for Toronto. Like many such places, as the sun went down, its nature changed to a place where assignations of all kinds might occur. Tumblety made the acquaintance of a boy whose name was Bulger. Whether he was just unlucky or was set up, Tumblety was soon arrested by Policeman Clark and taken to the Court Street Station, about five blocks north of the Esplanade. He was charged with making an indecent assault on Bulger and held for trial. The case came before the police court on Friday but was postponed until Monday, with Tumblety spending the weekend in jail. When the case came up on Monday, the court heard the testimony of Bulger and the judge determined that it could only be proved as a case of common assault. A fine of one dollar plus costs was assigned to Tumblety. It is interesting to note that other cases of common assault around the same time were given fines of ten dollars and as much as 20 days in jail. The light sentence may indicate that the judge was convinced this was more of a setup than an actual arrest.[9]

The year 1880 had been particularly bad for Tumblety. With his legal troubles and social problems, it was a bleak period. One light in the darkness may have been the birth of his friend's first son. Early in 1880, Mark A. Blackburn and his wife Elizabeth had a baby boy whom they named Frank, in honor of Tumblety. Perhaps the doctor was the boy's godfather. But the doctor's troubles were not over yet and another encounter was soon to make headlines.

As part of his winter traveling, Tumblety went to New Orleans for the Mardi Gras celebrations. No stranger to New Orleans, he seems to have been well known. He may have been going there every year but raised little note in the newspapers. Unfortunately this year would be different and provides us a significant view of him and his lifestyle.

Dr. Tumblety arrived in New Orleans on February 25, 1881, and engaged a room in a boarding house. His landlady had only praise for him. She commented that he was very educated and a perfect gentleman. Of importance to the landlady, he paid his rent promptly. She would also say that he had a large number of visitors to his room, describing them as "young men between the ages of sixteen and twenty years." Further, he was said to be on intimate terms with them, even having some stay overnight. This was as explicit as the newspaper was going to be about Tumblety's homosexuality.[10]

Meeting these young men required Tumblety to cruise the streets of New Orleans. On March 22, he was on Canal Street when he approached a young man and struck up a conversation. His name was Henry Govan and he was an employee of the custom house. Tumblety invited the young man to a nearby saloon where they drank and talked for about an hour. As they parted, Govan agreed to meet Tumblety the next morning. Apparently, Govan had second thoughts about the meeting and the next morning chose a different route to work. However, he was not to escape Tumblety's clutches because the doctor hailed him at the corner of Decatur and Custom House Streets. They shared a couple of the doctor's cigars and again parted amiably.[11]

Upon reaching his office, Govan noticed that he was missing his pocketbook, which had been in the top inside pocket of his coat, and the coat had been buttoned up. The pocketbook had between $50 and $70 in it. Immediately he suspected Tumblety of stealing it and went to the police. At the station, he was told to find the man and point him out to the nearest policeman to have the pickpocket arrested.

Instead, Govan chose to hire a private detective named Dominick O'Malley. They both lived on Bienville Street and may have known each other. O'Malley was just beginning a long and eventful career in New Orleans. Most of what is known about O'Malley comes from later in his life. He was described in 1891 as having served a ten-month sentence in the Workhouse and having been in court nine times for carrying a concealed weapon, jury tampering and witness intimidation. It was reported that he was a crack shot with a pistol and he was missing two fingers from his right hand. According to the story, these fingers were shot off in a gun battle and O'Malley calmly shifted the gun to his left hand and continued shooting. The O'Malley Detective Agency was widely reported to be in the service of the Mafia. Govan had gotten himself some serious muscle.[12]

It did not take O'Malley long to find Tumblety, tracing him to his rented room. Arresting the doctor, O'Malley took him to the Third Police Station. While in custody, Tumblety proved who he was and the police listed his possessions, which were reported as "two extremely valuable solitaire diamond rings, two cluster diamond rings, a large amount of money, stocks and bonds and a magnificent gold chain and a small gold watch." Not the usual belongings for a pickpocket.

Meanwhile, O'Malley had met with the judge and told him that Tumblety had confessed to the crime. He further stated that he had seen a number of burglar's tools in Tumblety's room and that the doctor had used underworld language indicating that he was a criminal. O'Malley sought and was granted a search warrant to look for Govan's pocketbook in the suspect's room. What a surprise it must have been when O'Malley found incriminating evidence in Tumblety's room. He did not find the pocketbook but he found $35.55 suspiciously wrapped in newspaper lying on the bureau. The "burglarious implements" were no longer there.

Because the whole indictment was beginning to look suspicious, the judge ordered two New Orleans aldermen to search Tumblety's room again. They interviewed his landlady, who had only good things to say about the doctor. The searchers found nothing pertaining to the case but provided a description valuable to anyone interested in the doctor's life. According to the report, they found the room littered with letters from correspondents from all over the world. Whether these were testimonials or personal letters, current or old, they did not state. They reported finding a number of medals in the room. Without claiming they were real, they described them as:

> a gold medal alleged to have been presented by the citizens of Montreal, Canada for services rendered and for skill and science, presented March 4, 1858, on the obverse side of which was the inscription, "To give light to those that sit in darkness," what purported to be a cross of the Legion of Honor, the Iron Cross of

Prussia, a cross from the Emperor of Austria and one presented by His Royal Highness the Prince of Wales.[13]

To see these medals, one only needs to look at the cover of Tumblety's 1872 autobiography or later editions. In the famous picture of him dressed in the German Hussar's uniform, he wears all five of these decorations. From what we know of his imaginary European travels, it is obvious that the four crosses are bogus. The gold medal he had with him since his time in Canada and the verse on the medal comes from the first chapter of Luke. The date is interesting because he had been in Toronto in February and was in Rochester, New York, by March 11, 1858. It seems unlikely that he traveled to Montreal and then to Rochester in that time. More significantly, the Montreal authorities denied he had been given a medal during his legal troubles in 1861. All of these decorations seem to be part of his public persona rather than actual awards.

The same newspaper report that detailed the medals also gives a description of the man and his clothes. In its details, it almost sounds like it may have been copied from the police blotter. Whatever its source, it provides a good portrait of Tumblety, except for his age, at this time:

> Dr. Tumblety is a man apparently 65 years of age, with grey hair and moustache which he dyes black. He stands 6 feet 2 inches in his stockings and usually dresses in an undress naval uniform, with a white or blue naval cap.... All persons with whom he was thrown in contact unite in pronouncing him a highly educated man, one who has seen a great deal of the world.[14]

Based on the evidence he collected, O'Malley swore out an affidavit against Tumblety on the charge of being a pickpocket. A hearing was held the same day and the only recorded witness was Henry Govan. He was considerably less certain at the hearing as to whether Tumblety had stolen his pocketbook or he had simply lost it. This case was continued until the next Tuesday. However, the fireworks were not quite over. The police arrested D. C. O'Malley as a "dangerous and suspicious character." The judge was not willing to have him charged for such a vague offense. Instead, a charge of carrying a concealed weapon was lodged against him. Both defendants were remanded to their own custody until the next week.

The hearing was held on March 30 before Judge Mittenberger, who heard testimony from both Govan and O'Malley. Govan repeated the same story, adding only that he had gone back to his room to look for the money because he was not certain he had brought it with him. This was not very convincing testimony. O'Malley got on the stand and told how he had arrested Tumblety. When he had finished, the judge asked him if that was all he was going to say. Judge Mittenberger reminded O'Malley that while in the judge's private office, seeking the warrant, he had said that Tumblety had confessed and used "thieves slang." The detective said nothing to this. The court ruled that the arrest had been improper and Tumblety was released. O'Malley, on the other hand, was sent to the criminal district court to face the charges against him. Perhaps this is where he served his first count for carrying a concealed weapon.

When we look at this case, we have to wonder why it happened at all. It could be that this was a simple mistake by Govan that got out of hand when he brought the felonious O'Malley into it. After the trial, Tumblety told the press that it was an attempt to blackmail him. It seems to have been well known that he was both rich and homosexual. Perhaps they threatened to expose him if he did not pay up. The truth may never be known. As in many things, perception is more important than reality and the news of his arrest, conviction and sentencing was reported in the press. Few papers actually got the full story and as much as a year later, some papers were still claiming he had been convicted of the charge.

After the incident in New Orleans, Tumblety managed to stay out of trouble and out of the papers for quite a while. He returned quietly to New York and there he found a new secretary to replace the young Lyons. Martin H. McGarry was a 17-year-old who listed his occupation in the census as barber. In 1882, he was looking for work and decided to apply at 7 University Place. This had been the address for Dr. Ricord's Essence of Life for many years. The doctor had moved on by 1882 and the lower floor was rented as a shop. As he was ascending the stairs, McGarry met a "big, fine-looking man standing on the stoop. He had on a braided English smoking jacket, black-striped trousers, Oxford ties and a peaked cap." The man told him there was no work inside but he could offer him employment. He told the young man that he needed a traveling companion. They went up to Tumblety's room and the doctor told McGarry all about his adventurous life.[15]

The story that Tumblety spun for McGarry and which the young man repeated to the newspapers six years later is an amazingly bold lie. Tumblety claimed to have been born the son of a wealthy Irish gentleman, to have graduated from the University of Dublin, from which he had a diploma, and to have come to the United Sates in 1853. Once here, he studied surgery and, during the war, was an army surgeon. When his father died, he left Tumblety a large amount of money, which was why Tumblety no longer needed to practice medicine. McGarry might have believed this story when he was first hired but he cannot have still believed after having spent time with Tumblety. He reports that he accompanied the doctor on many travels, including to Rochester, where Tumblety's family still resided.

McGarry describes Tumblety living a life of ease and specifically not practicing medicine. This is the first indication that he had given up treating patients. His decision to move away from an active medical career probably had to do with legal changes that were instituted in New York at this time. We saw earlier how Tumblety touted his recognition by the New York City Board of Health in 1861. Despite his claims, he was never a registered physician in the city. Through the 1870s registration was voluntary and Tumblety was not listed in any of the directories. In 1880, because of increasing complaints about "quacks," New York passed a new registry law for physicians. It required every doctor to register with the county where he practiced, listing his name and address as well as the date and university from which his diploma was granted. Originally, the process of registration was to be complete by late 1880 but the period was extended to October 1881. Even before the end of the registration period, the New York County Medical Society, which for years had impotently raged against non-traditional practitioners, began to actively prosecute cases under the law. All over the country, similar laws were being passed and the battle between the regular physicians and the alternative practitioners, from which Tumblety had derived a considerable fortune, was drawing to a close.[16]

While he provides no dates or other ways of tracking their travels, McGarry reeled off a long list of places the two visited: Niagara Falls, Rochester, Saratoga, Boston, New Haven, and Philadelphia. In between, they wintered in New York. When the spring came, Tumblety offered to take him to Glasgow but McGarry decided not to go. Then they went together to Ireland and traveled around the country. They managed to make these cross–Atlantic trips without showing up on any passenger list.

Upon their return from overseas, McGarry's uncle, Michael O'Brien, told him that he had to settle down and take care of his sisters. In the 1870s both of his parents had died, leaving the large family in the care of McGarry's oldest sister, Catherine. By 1880, the family was made up of Martin, his brother William and three sisters, the youngest of whom was 11 years old. Catherine McGarry was getting married and someone had to step in and take care of the family. One might also suppose that O'Brien wanted to get McGarry away from the influence of Tumblety.

They parted amicably and McGarry became a shipping clerk for his uncle. He reported that while he was with Tumblety, he was able to save $1,250 and with a gift of $750 from Tumblety, he was able to buy an electrician's business specializing in electric bells, burglar alarms and speaking tubes. McGarry remembered his time with Tumblety fondly and had only good, if somewhat deluded, things to say about him. When asked about Tumblety's feelings toward women, however, he said that he disliked them very much and thought that "all the trouble in the world was caused by women."

For the next few years there is little known about the doctor's life. If McGarry truthfully reported their activities, Tumblety seems to have retired and lived off his investments. He is reported to have been a frequent visitor to White Sulfur Springs and other resorts. No specific information on these trips has come to light and he seems to have stayed out of trouble. Although he is said to have made frequent trips to Europe, he does not show up in any of the passenger lists for ships arriving in New York.

On May 25, 1887, Tumblety sailed for Liverpool on the steamship *City of Rome*. This voyage was mentioned by the Rev. William H. De Puy in a letter of support which Tumblety published in 1889. Rev. De Puy wrote, "I well remember the incident connected with our first acquaintance on board the City of Rome, on a trip a couple of years since, to the Old World." De Puy, and possibly Tumblety, sailed on May 19, on the steamship *Britannic*, but two days out of New York, it was hit by the incoming steamship *Celtic*. While both ships made it back to New York, the *Britannic* was in no condition to make the rest of her voyage. De Puy booked passage on the *City of Rome* and this was the trip to which he referred. They arrived in Liverpool in early June.[17]

Soon after his arrival in Liverpool, Tumblety had a chance encounter which provides one of the few unbiased descriptions of the doctor. Frederick Douglass, the abolitionist and newspaperman, had been traveling in Europe for several months and came to Liverpool to see off his wife Helen on her way back to America. In a letter, dated June 10, to his friend, Amy Kirby Post of Rochester, Douglass reports that he met a man named Dr. Tomblety who knew her and her family. Douglass wrote:

> He told me much about himself in a very brief space, for he seemed to have more tongues than ears. I could not get a word in anywhere and you know I am too much in love with my own voice to like being suppressed and overtalked in that way, but enough of Dr. Tomblety. He seemed a good fellow after all.[18]

Where Tumblety went in England or on the Continent during this trip has not been discovered. He spent all of the summer and a portion of the fall overseas. Eventually he decided to return to the United States and sailed for New York on September 30, 1887, again on the *City of Rome*. On the passenger list, he listed his occupation as gentleman and stated that he was a citizen of the United States. The voyage was without incident and Tumblety arrived in New York on October 7 at Castle Garden.

Once again, Tumblety faded into the background after he came back to New York. While he was not as flamboyant as he once was, Tumblety was still looking for young men. Apparently, he was in Washington, D. C., in 1887–1888 and had some relationship with Isaac Golliday. It was reported that Golliday often spoke of Dr. Tumblety and that the young man's father did not approve of the association. Golliday was older than the men Tumblety usually chose, being 30 in 1888. One night, Isaac Golliday left his father's boarding house in Washington and was not heard from again, at least as of late 1888. The family hoped that he had gone to Europe with Dr. Tumblety but really had no idea. There is no further information about what happened to Isaac Golliday. He could have come home soon after the 1888 article or he may never have come home.[19]

Tumblety was back in New York in the spring of 1888. He prepared to take yet another trip to England. It is not certain when Tumblety sailed for Liverpool but he was there sometime in June. Perhaps after visiting with relatives, he moved to London and began his usual habits, but this was to be anything but a usual trip to London.

14

———∞∞∞———

Whitechapel Murders
(1888)

During the summer and fall of 1888, a number of prostitutes were murdered and mutilated in the slums of London, in an area known as Whitechapel. At the time, these murders created an international sensation and sparked an intensive manhunt for the culprit. Nicknamed "Jack the Ripper," the murderer escaped capture and began a mystery that even after more than 100 years shows no sign of abating. As the investigation developed, the police swept up hundreds of suspects, only to let them go for lack of evidence. Through the years, the list of suspects has been winnowed down to a few dozen, each with their fervent supporters. Interest in the case, among the public, continues with numerous books, television shows and movies dealing with the topic. One measure of the lure of this topic is that the murder of five outcast women in an obscure section of London over a hundred years ago can produce over 2,000,000 hits on a recent internet search.

Tumblety's connection with these murders, widely trumpeted in the American press, represents a major crisis in his life. Much of his business and his acceptance in polite society depended on maintaining a façade of respectability. When that façade was pierced in one location, he could always go somewhere else and begin again. This time, however, there was no escaping the publicity. Not only was his name associated with the most sensational murder case of the century but the papers dug deep into his past and placed all of his transgressions before an international audience. The newspapers were not satisfied with the truth of his life, bad enough as it was, but published outright lies about him in cities all across America. Even if he could prove his innocence in this particular case, he could never resume the life he had led up to that point.

When we come to consider the effect of this episode on Tumblety's life and career, we need to look at three distinct aspects: the few facts available, the contemporary press reaction and the modern gloss put on this by Evans and Gainey in their publications. Each of these aspects tells us something about

Tumblety and the perception of him. The first aspect is woefully inadequate, yet both of the other aspects are built on this. If the "large dossier" on Tumblety that was supposedly maintained by the police were to turn up, we might know a great deal more about his time in London. The press reports, which form the second aspect, both amplify and obscure what we know. Sorting the truth from the suppositions, rumors, hypotheses and lies is a big challenge. Finally, Evans and Gainey attempted to prove that Tumblety was, in fact, Jack the Ripper. This bias colors all of their writings. There is no way to discuss the effect of these events on Tumblety without assessing the validity of their arguments.

As to the facts of Tumblety's stay in London in 1888, they are few enough. The doctor later reported that he was familiar with Whitechapel and had wandered around the district, as thousands of others had, to see what all the excitement was about. He was present in the city at least as early as July 27, 1888. On this date, he was accused of committing an act of gross indecency on a male named Albert Fisher. Other such acts were charged with different men on August 31, October 14 and November 2. While the events extended over a long period, Tumblety was arrested only once, on November 7, 1888, on the charges of gross indecency for all four of these incidents.[1]

It is at this point that things become more obscure. Tumblety was not granted bail by a magistrate until November 16. If he were in jail during this time, he would have an alibi for November 9, the date of the last Ripper killing, that of Mary Kelly. Is it likely that he was held in jail for over two weeks for the charged offenses? Evans and Gainey make a good case for his being given "police bail," a procedure that allowed suspects to be set free for seven days while the police finished their investigation, and Tumblety himself stated that he was only held for "two or three days." The decision to grant police bail was made by a police inspector and was not mandatory. It could only be granted if the inspector believed that the charge was not of a serious nature. If Tumblety were a serious suspect for the Whitechapel murders, would he have been granted bail? It appears that he was granted police bail and on November 14, seven days after his first arrest, a warrant was issued for his arrest on the indecency charges. According to procedure, when he gave up his police bail, he had to be rearrested. He was charged on November 16 in the Marlborough Street Police Court. Magistrate J. L. Hannay set bail at £300 or about $1,500. The trial was scheduled for November 20 in the Old Bailey but was postponed until December 10.[2]

Based on the above facts, there are two serious problems for those who would see Tumblety as the Whitechapel murderer. If he was let out on police bail on November 7 or 8, and was therefore free to commit the murder of Mary Kelly on November 9, where were the police? We are asked to believe that Tumblety was so well known to the police that there was a "large dossier" on him and they had sufficient suspicions to trump up charges against him. Yet, they let him out and did not follow or investigate him? Then Tumblety went voluntarily back into their hands on November 14 and they allowed him out on bail again! The police may have been aware of Tumblety but it was not for the Whitechapel murders.

The bail of £300 has been seen by some as excessive and an attempt to keep Tumblety in the country while the police continued to search for evidence against him. Other published cases of gross indecency reveal that there was nothing unusual about the size of this bail. Most cases listed in the *London Times* do not report the amount of bail but there are two examples that have come to light. In 1886, just after the law was passed, Edward B. Hedge was charged with gross indecency and forced to post bail of £200 while in 1891, Hamilton De Tatum was released after paying £500 and securing two sureties of £250 each. Tumblety's bail fits between these two examples both in time and size and it was in no way unusual for the time.[3]

Tumblety would not be there for the trial. By November 24, he was in France and booked on the steamship *La Bretagne* under the name of Frank Townsend. The voyage took eight days and it was reported that "Townsend" kept to his stateroom, claiming sickness. Arriving in New York on December 2, Tumblety quickly went to his boarding house at 79 East Tenth Street. His movements were observed by two detectives sent to watch his arrival by Chief Inspector Byrnes of the New York Police. We will leave the doctor safely in his familiar surroundings for now while we consider other aspects of these events.[4]

The observant reader will note that I have not mentioned any charges against Tumblety related to the Whitechapel murders. The earliest evidence that he is connected with that case is a cable dispatch from London, dated November 17 by the *New York World* Cable Service, which was the day after he was released on bail. He is reported to be "Dr. Kumblety" from New York and is mentioned in one small paragraph of a much larger report. It adds: "The police could not hold him on suspicion of the Whitechapel crimes, but he will be committed for trial at the Central Criminal Court under the special law passed soon after the Modern Babylon exposures."[5]

The exposures referred to were a series of articles by W. T. Stead in the *Pall Mall Gazette* under the title "Maiden Tribute of Modern Babylon" in 1885. Stead reported on the child prostitution of very young girls. At the time, the age of consent for girls in England was 13 and the reformers were trying to raise it to at least 16. As a result of a massive public outcry, the government quickly introduced the Criminal Law Amendment Act. The night before this act was to be passed by Parliament, MP Henry Du Pré Labouchère introduced an amendment making any homosexual act between men, defined as "gross indecency," a misdemeanor subject to two years hard labor. Unlike the crime of sodomy, which required proof of penetration, gross indecency only required testimony about the events and made the prosecution of homosexuals much easier.[6]

There are two distinct parts of the doctor's arrest, the charges of gross indecency and his implication in the murders. By far, the latter part was much more sensational than the first and, if it had not been for that implication, Tumblety would remain unknown today. Yet it was the gross indecency charges that he actually had to face. We will deal with those first.

As stated above, gross indecency was a new crime, first defined in 1885. Between 1886 and 1889, it led to an average of 14 arrests per year in London and an average of 5 convictions were obtained per year. The government had a conviction rate of over a third based on single instances or multiple instances with a single individual. Tumblety was charged with four separate instances with four different men. Given the supposed evidence, a conviction seemed a likely possibility.[7]

If convicted, Tumblety could face two years imprisonment with hard labor. However, if the Crown proved he was a repeat offender, as the four charges would imply, his punishment, already hard, could increase substantially. An example of this escalation is the case of Burleigh and Widdows, which began in April 1888 with simple charges of gross indecency. Both were Anglican ministers, part of whose duties included serving at Christ Hospital. They were accused of repeated acts of gross indecency with two boys at the hospital and one of the boys further accused Burleigh of "molesting" him, a euphemism for sodomy. The prosecution demonstrated that Burleigh had been convicted of gross indecency in 1886 and sentenced to 18 months imprisonment while Widdows had been convicted of indecency in Toronto and served five months. The verdict in this case was guilty and Widdows was sentenced to ten years in prison while Burleigh was given penal servitude for life. Given what we know of Tumblety's previous history, the police would not have to search far for other evidence to help convict him.[8]

In addition to these troubling developments, there was something odd about the charges against Tumblety. Most often, when charges of gross indecency were brought, it was because the subject was caught in the act. Of the seven cases reported in the *London Times* between 1886 and 1888, all were the result of one or more of the principles being caught in the act. Yet Tumblety was arrested five days after the last incident was supposed to have occurred and the earliest was four months before his arrest. Part of the evidence in any of these cases would be the eyewitness testimony of the act itself so the police would have had to rely on the testimony of Tumblety's partners or someone who had been observing Tumblety.

There are two possible explanations for this oddity: blackmail or a longstanding police investigation. The Criminal Law Amendment Act was quickly nicknamed the Blackmailer's Law as it fostered the ability to extort money from homosexuals fearing public exposure. On October 26, 1886, the *London Times* reported the case of a man who was frequenting parks at night, representing himself as a detective and extorting money with the threat of charges of gross indecency. Other sources speak of organized groups which would lure subjects into committing such acts and then have one of their number arrive at the last moment to threaten arrest. A healthy bribe often made the case go away. While this might be the case with Tumblety, the length of time involved makes this unlikely. These blackmailers would not wait for four months for their payoff.[9]

The most likely explanation is that the police were investigating Tumblety and were able to find four "renters" that would admit to having sex with him. Police observation of Tumblety may have begun as early as 1873 according to William Pinkerton, the detective, and this was probably the extensive file the police were reported to have on Tumblety. That they chose this particular time to pull the noose tight suggests that they thought him guilty of more than gross indecency.[10]

The November 17 cable implies that Tumblety was a suspect in the Whitechapel investigation and that, failing to find the needed evidence, the police held him on other charges. There is no evidence that Tumblety was ever charged with the Whitechapel murders. His arrest, or the warrant issued, on the twelfth or fourteenth represents his return to custody on the original charge and not a new one. The bail given on the sixteenth was in relation to the first charge as well. This says nothing about his guilt or innocence in regard to the murders. The oft-quoted *New York Times* article of November 19, 1888, which stated he "was proved innocent of that charge" was itself based on the cable of November 17, which said nothing of the kind. On the other hand, the same cable states that as many as 20 other men were arrested that same week on suspicion of being the murderer. The net was being widely cast and a roundup of the "usual suspects" was in progress.[11]

Given Tumblety's unusual lifestyle, he was clearly a "person of interest" to the police, to use a modern euphemism. Like many others investigated at the time, the police were unable to establish a link between him and the victims. Tumblety would later claim that he was arrested because of his slouch hat. In answer to the question of why he was arrested, Tumblety replied,

> Someone had said that Jack the Ripper was an American, and everybody believed that statement. Then it is the universal belief among the lower classes that all Americans wear slouch hats; therefore, Jack the Ripper, must wear a slouch hat. Now, I happened to have on a slouch hat, and this, together with the fact that I was an American, was enough for the police. It established my guilt beyond any question.[12]

From the present view, based on the facts, there is no way to demonstrate Tumblety's guilt or innocence in relation to the Whitechapel murders. However, it is likely that the police did suspect him at the time. That he was not considered a suspect for long is evident from the lack of any mention of him by those close to the case in the years after the events.[13]

Beginning with the initial publication of the *New York World* cable dispatch on November 18, word of Tumblety's arrest as the Whitechapel murderer spread across the United States like the proverbial wildfire. Consistently, the articles begin with something like "a cable from London states..." and it is possible to trace the language of the original report, distorted and changed, through all of these stories. Researchers have found copies of this story in newspapers all over the United States and Canada.

Curiously, not one reference to Tumblety's association with the Whitechapel murders has been found in English papers. Given that these newspapers devoted huge amounts of space to cover the murders, inquests, arrests of suspects, even rumors about the case, why did Tumblety slip through without a mention? Some researchers have suggested that the police were convinced of Tumblety's guilt and therefore kept their information secret from the press. If that were true, how did a reporter for an American news service scoop all of the English reporters who must have had much better sources? Several London papers made up things about the Whitechapel murders in order to keep interest alive. Would they have passed up the opportunity to skewer someone like Tumblety? The lack of any mention of Tumblety in the English papers might suggest that he was not a serious suspect in the case.

It is significant to see how the original report in the American papers changed through time. In the original cable, dated November 17, Tumblety was arrested on unspecified charges. Then the reporter said he could not be held on suspicion of murder but would be charged with another crime. By November 19, a day after the initial publication, the *New York Times*, *New York Herald* and *Washington Evening Star* had all changed this to an arrest in connection with the Whitechapel murders. By November 20, the *San Francisco Chronicle* went further, saying he was arrested as "the" Whitechapel murderer, and both the *Herald* and the *Evening Star* named him "Jack-the-Ripper." In a very few days, without any other information, Tumblety went from a possible suspect in the case to the murderer himself.[14]

Why was there such a difference between the American press and their English colleagues? Up to this point, the American press had been bystanders on the hottest story of the century. They followed the crimes and the investigation avidly but had little to add on their own. Now, with an American involved, they had press-stopping possibilities. As Tumblety had been an interesting character in cities all over the country, reporters had a chance to find many people who knew him or claimed to know him. Hundreds of interviews were conducted in New York, Philadelphia, Washington, San Francisco and other places. As would be expected, there were good and bad things said about Tumblety by a variety of people.

These interviews form the basis of most of what is known about the doctor, but they are full of pitfalls for the unwary. They point out places where he lived and people he knew. This kind of information is invaluable for doing in-depth research. Without this start, finding information on Tumblety would be incredibly difficult and spotty. However, uncritical acceptance of these reports leads to gross errors. Even the best of the press reports got things wrong. Tumblety's first name is listed as Francis, Thomas, or John. Interviewees were convinced that Tumblety was not his real name but rather it was Sullivan, Sternberg or Blackburn. With such basic facts being obscure, we have to wonder how accurate the rest of the reporting might be. Add to this the tendency of newspapers to copy each other's stories, changing them slightly each time. A unique example of this occurred on November 21, when the *New York Herald* quoted the Washington papers quoting the *New York Herald*, an incredible piece of circular reporting.[15]

But these minor factual errors pale in comparison to those individuals who, for their own fame or from vindictiveness or simply to sell newspapers, made up stories about Tumblety. The story of Tumblety's life, as related by C. A. Dunham, was cited in the discussion of the doctor's stay in Washington during the Civil War. It was first published in the *New York World* early in December 1888 and, from there, was printed, in whole or in part, in many papers across the country. I have already pointed out that Dunham was likely not even in Washington at the same time as Tumblety, that there are several outright lies in his account and that there was nothing factual in it that could not have been garnered from Tumblety's own publications. Ordinarily there would be no reason to bring it up again except that one part of this story had, and continues to have, a major impact on how Tumblety is perceived.[16]

After a short section that shows he was familiar with Tumblety, Dunham went on to talk extensively about Tumblety's hatred of women and prostitutes. It is not by coincidence that Dunham spent so much time on this topic. To paint Tumblety as the Whitechapel murderer requires that he have a deep hatred of women and of prostitutes in particular. Dunham got his message across in two ways. In one part of the story he reports that Tumblety, when young, married a woman who was older than he was, only to find out she was a prostitute. This, according to Dunham, turned Tumblety off to women. Secondly, he described Tumblety's anatomical museum containing the uteri of numerous women. As it was generally thought that the murderer was cutting out the uterus of his victims, Tumblety's possession of such items made him suspect. The significance of this story is that it depicted Tumblety as a well-known misogynist capable of butchering women.

Tumblety's marriage to a woman who deceived him might be enough to cause him to hate all women. However, the only person who repeats this story is Dunham. If Tumblety was so vehement about this particular woman that he lectured a group of relative strangers about her, it would seem to be something he was not shy about expressing. As this would certainly make Tumblety suspicious, why is it that none of the other dozens of people interviewed mention it?

The question of Tumblety's marriage is not easily settled. He reports in his 1872 pamphlet that he had never been married and no evidence of his supposed marriage has ever come to light. Each census where Tumblety is listed (1850, 1870, 1880, 1900) shows him as single, not married or widowed. In the 1870s, he told one of his young male companions "no women for me." However, his landlady in the 1880s, Mrs. McNamara, said that when she questioned him about going out one night, he told her that he was going to the monastery to pray for his dead wife. Finally, his death certificate lists him as a widower. It is likely that Tumblety used the idea of being a widower as a way to mask his true orientation.

As to his possession of "the matrices of every class of women," again we only have Dunham's word for it. There is a report that in Washington, Tumblety had a model of the circulatory system. This is a far cry from the anatomical museum described by Dunham. If such specimens existed, it was the only time in his entire career that anyone ever mentioned them. Soon thereafter, in Philadelphia, the press reported that there was nothing medical in nature in his office.

If Tumblety had a virulent hatred of women, he hid it well. As previously stated, a good portion of his practice was treating female diseases. If he showed or intimated his hatred, those clients would not have come to him as they consistently did. Further, throughout his career, Tumblety was described as attractive to women and whether true or not, was romantically linked to at least one woman. If he were such a renowned hater of women, who would have believed the rumors? None of the early reports in November 1888 mention anything about Tumblety's hatred of women. In fact, one of the interviewees, in talking about Tumblety's stay in Brooklyn in 1863, reported that he cut "a wide swath in the hearts of certain susceptible women." This was in an article that was not supportive of Tumblety in tone and seems a strange thing to attribute to him. It does not sound like the description of a man with a "well-known hatred of women."[17]

After Dunham's story was published, Tumblety's "well-known hatred of women" becomes a standard part of his description. Like everything else in Dunham's story, this aspect seems exaggerated in order to put Tumblety in the worst light and to bolster Dunham's credibility. While Tumblety's orientation might not have been towards women, this is a long way from the murderous rage shown by the Whitechapel murderer. Uncritical acceptance of the Dunham story almost automatically makes Tumblety a prime suspect. Yet the evidence is just not there.

The reporters who interviewed people who knew Tumblety inevitably asked the question of whether he was capable of committing the Whitechapel crimes. Like all opinions on his life, these were split with no middle ground. Dunham, of course, said he had "long connected" Tumblety to the murders. Many others could easily see him as committing these crimes. However, just as many were convinced that he could not have done so. Mrs. McNamara, his New York landlady, was convinced he "would not harm a child."

The massive press coverage of Tumblety's arrest and his flight from London caused a major shift in his life. Prior to this episode, Tumblety figured prominently both through his newspaper ads and through his own self promotion. Even if he had to be outrageous to do so, he put himself in front of the public and sought their approval. From this point on he appears less frequently in the public record. The last 15 years of his life seem reclusive by comparison to his earlier existence. The glare of the public spotlight, which he had so avidly sought, forever ended the kind of lifestyle he had led. It was a different Dr. Tumblety that emerged when the public eye turned elsewhere.

Before we continue with the story of his life, we have to deal with the third aspect of Tumblety's association with the Whitechapel murders—his modern fame. Beginning in 1993, a whole new perspective on Dr. Tumblety was developed as a result of the research of Stewart Evans. With his discovery of the Littlechild letter and his publications (written with Paul Gainey), Evans gave Tumblety a kind of notoriety that makes the contemporary press coverage seem meager. The idea of an "unknown suspect" in the most studied murder investigation in history was the kind of news guaranteed to spur public interest.

The Littlechild letter was a legitimate discovery that added a significant new dimension to the study of the Whitechapel murders. However, the subsequent publications by Evans and Gainey suffer from an all too common problem with books in this field. They chose to advocate Tumblety's guilt rather than objectively assess the evidence. This allows them to pick only those facts that support their case while denying the validity of any facts that do not fit their preconceived idea. With such an approach, one can make a very convincing case against even the most innocent of men—which Tumblety was not. Before we can continue, we have to evaluate the strength of the argument that Tumblety was the fiend known as Jack the Ripper.

If Tumblety is known to modern audiences at all, it is due entirely to the discovery and publication by Stewart Evans of the Littlechild letter. Written in 1913 by John G. Littlechild, a former chief inspector at Scotland Yard, to the journalist G. R. Sims, Stewart Evans acquired it from a collector in 1993. This remarkably short letter caused an incredible uproar as it not only named an entirely unknown suspect but suggested that at least some of the police considered him likely to be Jack the Ripper. Since the letter was the first indication of Tumblety as a suspect, it is the best place to start the discussion of Tumblety's involvement in the Whitechapel murders.[18]

Although no one doubts the authenticity of the Littlechild letter, there has been considerable debate about its significance. One researcher has cautioned that "no more weight should be attached to it than to any of the other police memoirs." There has been considerable debate in print and on the internet over which police official knew what and who was the source for which suspect. While this may be important for those who wish to "solve" the mystery of Jack the Ripper, for the purposes of this biography, all we need to assess is what Littlechild himself knew when he wrote the letter. Evans and Gainey rely heavily on the theory that while Littlechild was not directly involved in the investigation, he was kept informed by those who were. Thus it becomes significant to know what the police were thinking and how much of that is reflected in Littlechild's letter. The relevant passage from the letter is as follows:

> I never heard of a Dr D. in connection with the Whitechapel murders but amongst the suspects, and to my mind a very likely one, was a Dr. T. (which sounds much like D.) He was an American quack named Tumblety and was at one time a frequent visitor to London and on these occasions constantly brought under the notice of police, there being a large dossier concerning him at Scotland Yard. Although a 'Sycopathia Sexualis' subject he was not known as a 'Sadist' (which the murderer unquestionably was) but his feelings toward women were remarkable and bitter in the extreme, a fact on record. Tumblety was arrested at the time of the murders in connection with unnatural offences and charged at Marlborough Street, remanded on bail, jumped his bail, and got away to Boulogne. He shortly left Boulogne and was never heard of afterwards. It was believed he committed suicide but certain it is that from this time the 'Ripper' murders came to an end.[19]

From this, it is clear that Littlechild knew who Tumblety was and remembered the basic facts of his case. Although no one has yet found the "large dossier" on Tumblety, we can assume that he was well known to the police. Littlechild refers to him as a "Sycopathia Sexualis" which is a reference to Krafft-Ebing's monumental study of sexual deviance called *Psychopathia Sexualis*, first published in 1886. An important part of this book was devoted to the study of homosexuals, who, he concluded, had a mental illness due to degenerate heredity. It is this context that Littlechild is using when he discusses Tumblety's sexual life. This passage reflects considerable knowledge of Tumblety's life and history but nothing that could not have been obtained from the newspapers at the time.[20]

There are several problems with Littlechild's recollection of the Tumblety case. It was, after all, 25 years after the events. He reported that Tumblety fled to Boulogne and was never heard from again. In fact, Tumblety's arrival in America made a big splash in the papers. Scotland Yard knew he was on the ship and knew his destination was New York. Inspector Byrnes of the New York police was aware of his presence, assigning two of his own detectives to watch Tumblety. Surely he cabled London in case they did not get the American newspapers. Tumblety certainly did not disappear, never to be heard from again. As we shall see, throughout the 1890s, Tumblety was frequently mentioned in the New York papers. Nor did he commit suicide as Littlechild suggests in the last line. If Tumblety was such an important suspect, would Scotland Yard have simply abandoned any interest in him? If they did maintain such an interest, why did Littlechild not know about it? Given these problems, one has to wonder how much "inside information" Littlechild had on the Tumblety case.

Another obvious problem is Littlechild's ignorance of "Dr. D." Who was this and what did the police know about him? The "Dr. D." whom Sims asked about, and Littlechild was unaware of, has been generally identified as Montague J. Druitt. Sims was aware that Druitt was the favorite suspect of Chief Constable Melville Macnaghten (and of Sims). In his biography, published in 1914, Macnaghten stated that certain facts, "not in possession of the police till some years after I became a detective officer," pointed to Druitt. He did not become a police officer until 1889, the year after Druitt committed suicide and the murders stopped. As early as 1894, Macnaghten had named three suspects in a famous memorandum about the murders, including Druitt. The memorandum was written the year after Littlechild resigned from Scotland Yard.[21]

The question becomes when did the police settle on these three suspects and how early was Druitt a suspect? If he was a suspect during the time Littlechild was at Scotland Yard, his lack of knowledge would be an indication that his information was secondhand and not the result of direct communication. It would mean that his choice of Tumblety as a "likely" suspect, when no one else mentions him, was his theory, perhaps his personal bias, and not that of the police involved in the investigation.

Several pieces of evidence indicate that the three suspects list was well known before it was codified in the 1894 memorandum. Major Arthur Griffiths, who talked to both Robert Anderson, assistant commissioner of the Criminal Investigation Division, and Melville Macnaghten, chief constable in the same division, wrote in 1898:

> But the police, after the last murder, had brought their investigations to the point of strongly suspecting several persons, all of them known to be homicidal lunatics, and against three of these they held very plausible and reasonable grounds of suspicion.[22]

This suggests but does not prove that the list of three was developed soon after the last murder. Similarly, there is an unsubstantiated report that the police told Albert Backert, a member of the Whitechapel Vigilance Committee, that the murderer had committed suicide by drowning in the Thames after the last murder. This would be Druitt, whose body was recovered from the river on December 31, 1888. The extra manpower used by the police in Whitechapel began to decline after December, but it was not a precipitous drop, rather a gradual decline based on the lack of any further murders and the worry about the large expenses involved. If anything, the manpower expended in January and February 1889 suggesting that the police were still worried that another murder could happen. So far, there is no definite proof that the list existed before Macnaghten's 1894 memorandum. Yet these suspects did not suddenly appear seven years after the events. All of them, including Druitt, must have been discussed in police circles. That Littlechild did not know of Druitt suggests that his information was faulty.

An equally important, logical point concerns the fact that none of those directly involved in the investigation considered Tumblety a suspect worth mentioning. Most all of the police officials involved with the case made some kind of statement about suspects. None of them mentioned Tumblety or anyone like him. Only Littlechild, 25 years after the fact, mentioned him. Evans and Gainey make a valiant attempt to suggest that Scotland Yard was embarrassed to admit that the murderer slipped through their fingers and, apparently because of this, engaged in a huge cover-up. Why then was Littlechild not part of the cover-up?

A final point in relation to the letter: Littlechild's reference to the "large dossier" on Tumblety has been taken to suggest political implications. As Littlechild was head of the Special Branch, whose job was to keep an eye on Irish rebels and anarchists, it has been suggested that the dossier related to Tumblety's Fenian activities. This is not what Littlechild said but rather what people have read into it. Littlechild said the police had an eye on Tumblety; he did not say the Special Branch did. Had Tumblety been under investigation by the Special Branch, we could have expected Littlechild to be better informed about his life.

The idea that Tumblety was connected to the Fenian movement is based on several slender threads, including an assumption that the dossier was held by the Special Branch. Another thread is the *New York Times* article of November 19, 1888, which states that while Tumblety was in New York in 1880, "he became a member of several questionable clubs." Some have suggested these were Irish Republican Clubs. More likely, the reporter was referring to Tumblety's homosexual associations. In the *Brooklyn Daily Eagle*, on April, 27, 1890, the reporter suggested that two years before "he was under suspicion on account of his supposed connection with the advanced branch of the Irish national party." As discussed in the next chapter, this has to do with the visit of Walter Andrews of Scotland Yard to Canada soon after Tumblety fled to New York. Andrews was seeking information on Irish nationalists and his trip got mixed up with Tumblety's flight. There is no direct evidence that Scotland Yard thought of Tumblety as a Fenian and no evidence in his life that he ever had any connection with them.[23]

A key element of Evans and Gainey's argument linking Tumblety to the Whitechapel murders is the story of the "Batty Street lodger." In an article published in the *Daily News* on October 16, 1888, a German landlady is said to have given to the police a blood-stained shirt left in her possession by a lodger in her house. As the story was reported, the lodger returned to the house at 22 Batty Street early in the morning of October 1, 1888. This was the morning after the double murder of Elizabeth Stride and Catherine Eddowes. His movements woke the landlady and, when she got up to see what was going on, he told her he was going away for a while. Before he left, he gave her a shirt to wash. Later, when she looked at the shirt, she found the wristbands and part of the sleeves stained with blood. Such a report and evidence were sure to excite police interest and it was widely reported that they were watching the house, waiting for the lodger to return. The reporter managed to get all of this despite the fact that he said the landlady was uncommunicative.[24]

This story would be more convincing if there were not a strange postscript. In 1911, G. R. Sims, the journalist whose interest caused Littlechild to write his letter, published an article concerning an interview he had with the same landlady in 1907 or 1908. At that time, she said her husband had discovered a black bag in the lodger's room. Inside was a long knife and a pair of blood-stained cuffs. The next day, the lodger returned, paid his bill and left. At this time, she told Sims that the lodger was an American medical man, clinching the argument for Evans and Gainey.[25]

However, as the authors admit, the landlady went on to say that she had recently seen the lodger again. He was still practicing in northwest London. This was four years after Tumblety had died. Evans and Gainey suggest that she was wrong in her identification despite her having two other witnesses to back up her story. Sims reports that the police made some inquiries but did not disturb the doctor. The authors use this to demonstrate that the landlady was wrong in her identification. In fact, all this proves is that the police were not interested in reopening a case that had lain dormant for 20 years.

There are some major differences between the story published in the *Daily News* and that reported by Sims in 1911. In the first, the lodger gives the shirt to the landlady, while in the second it is the husband who discovers the blood-stained cuffs. More importantly, did the lodger mysteriously disappear, one step ahead of the police? Or did he return, pay his bill, collect his effects and go away normally? Ultimately do we believe the reporter in 1888, who admits that the landlady was uncommunicative, or Sims, to whom she talked openly? It seems more likely that Sims got the correct information.

The story of the "Batty Street lodger" clearly shows the advocacy inherent in the publications of Evans and Gainey. Having decided that the published report refers to the murderer, they go through all of the subsequent articles with twin biases. As more papers picked up the story, adding real or imagined details, they see this as continued interest by the police. At the same time, police assertions that there was nothing to the story and they were not watching the house are seen as lies designed to put the suspect off guard. All it really proves is that the press, at the height of the hysteria, were doing all they could to sell newspapers. The police statements, in light of Sims' later interview, seem like they should be accepted at face value.

Another press report cited by Evans and Gainey as evidence of police interest in an American suspect was published in the *Globe* on October 10. It states that an American had rented rooms in a first-class hotel in the West End of London. He disappeared, leaving a small unpaid bill. The hotel seized some of his possessions, including a black bag (another black bag!). In the bag, they found "prints of an obscene description," along with checkbooks and other personal documents. The hotel took out an ad in the *Times*, listing the man's name and saying that the bag would be sold at auction under the Innkeepers' Act. The sale of the bag reportedly took place in September. The obscene prints were enough to get the police interested. Members of the Criminal Investigation Department (CID) soon discovered that the man had landed in Liverpool from America (where all Americans entered the country) and that he had been known to be slumming in the East End. The police had the man's name, knew about his movements and had a physical description of him. In the article, it stated that the police had determined the height of the suspect.[26]

For anyone looking for police interest in Tumblety, this report, although it does not list his name, is ideal. The emphasis on the height of the suspect suggests a tall man, which would fit Tumblety. He is known to have arrived in Liverpool from America. Staying in a first-class hotel would certainly fit his pattern. None of this, however, would get the police interested in the individual. We come back to the "obscene prints" found in his bag. If this article does refer to Tumblety, we can suggest that the prints had nothing to do with women. They might have been enough for the police to begin an investigation under the Labouchère amendment. When the officers discovered him "slumming" in the East End, they had the grounds to arrest him for gross indecency. Still, there is no proof that the article refers to Tumblety.

At this date, the only part of the story that can be checked is the report of the notices published in the *Times*. For the entire year of 1888, there are only two references to the Innkeepers' Act—September 22 and September 24. On both dates, there is an ad from the auction house of Debenham, Storr and Sons which lists goods to be sold under the act. Although general in nature, the ad does mention "bags, portmanteaux and miscellaneous items." The date and description of items to be sold fits well with the story published in the *Globe*. However, there is no similar ad listing the man's name and the hotel. Tumblety's name does not appear in the *Times* nor is the Innkeepers' Act further mentioned. There is no evidence to connect him with this report.

If the article did refer to Tumblety, it indicates that the police were interested in him possibly as early as the beginning of October. Evans and Gainey seized on a *New York Times* article dated November 23, which stated that as early as October 29, Scotland Yard had been in touch with the police in San Francisco, seeking examples of Tumblety's handwriting. The problem is that the *Times* report was a garbled reprint of articles in the San Francisco papers which indicated that Chief Crowley, of the San Francisco police, got in touch with Scotland Yard *after* reports of Tumblety's arrest were widely circulated.[27]

Evans and Gainey make Tumblety into a likely suspect with a few facts, a lot of unrelated evidence and positive assertions about his guilt. At the end of their book, they list 15 factors that point to Tumblety as Jack the Ripper. Of the 15 factors, 9 are either wrong or irrelevant. For example, number two states that Tumblety was in London at the right time. Without this he obviously would not be a suspect, but it hardly points to him as being the killer. He is referred to as "eccentric but shrewd" (no. 12). These personality traits hardly make him a serial killer. Factor no. 13 accuses him of crimes in other places without any evidence. This assertion probably refers to "Ripper-like" murders that supposedly took place in Managua, Nicaragua, in January 1889. In the first place, there is no evidence that these murders had any connection or similarity to those in Whitechapel. The authors are able to pin them on Tumblety because they are under the false assumption that he disappeared in December 1888. As we shall see, Tumblety was still in New York at this time. Accusing him of these little-understood murders is another example of how the truth is secondary to creating an impression of evidence against Tumblety. Not one of these factors relates Tumblety to the murders. The simple fact is, as for any suspect in this case, there is no direct evidence. Tumblety could fit the profile of a serial killer, but only because he was an unusual personality.[28]

If we want to critically assess Tumblety's relation to the Whitechapel murders, we have to look at the few pieces of evidence the police had to work with. These consisted of the bodies of the victims and the testimony of witnesses. A majority of the evidence, while important to the case, cannot be related to any particular suspect (otherwise the case would have been solved long ago). There are, I believe, two aspects of the evidence that make Tumblety unlikely to be the murderer.

The first of these is the supposed anatomical knowledge displayed by the murderer. Although there is some dispute, it is generally acknowledged that the removal of certain organs (e.g., Chapman's uterus, Eddowes' kidney) required some surgical or butchery experience. For Evans and Gainey, this aspect was "particularly important when we look at the Littlechild Suspect: he was a qualified doctor with surgical knowledge." If the present study has demonstrated anything, it has shown this statement to be false.[29]

No matter what he might have pretended or wanted, Tumblety was never a "regular" physician and he never studied medicine in any organized fashion. From the beginning of his career, he was an herb doctor and was constantly at war with the surgically trained physicians. His literature made a point of arguing against surgery, calling the scalpel the "source of immense mischief to the human family." There is absolutely no evidence that he cut open a body at any time. Dunham's story, describing his anatomical museum, is of dubious validity. Even if true, it is unlikely that he collected the specimens himself. A naval officer who did meet him in Washington in 1861 reported that after listening to him, "I soon saw he knew almost nothing about anatomy." Over the years, Tumblety's medicine never required surgical or even anatomical knowledge. If the Whitechapel murderer displayed such knowledge, he was not "Dr." Tumblety.[30]

The second aspect of the evidence that can be assessed is the testimony of witnesses who claim to have seen the murderer. Some researchers have suggested that no one actually saw the killer. Yet the police were convinced that they had several good witnesses. As is normal with eyewitness testimony, there are considerable differences between descriptions. Do any of these fit what we know about Tumblety?

Throughout his career, there are two physical things people remembered about Dr. Tumblety. First, he was very tall for his time period. Various descriptions put his height in the range of five feet ten inches to six feet four inches. Evans and Gainey describe his height as five feet ten inches based on the account of W. C. Streeter, who saw him once as an adult 20 years before his interview. This hardly seems a reliable estimate. Contemporary accounts refer to Tumblety as "very tall." Of the nine accounts that actually mention a number, eight place him at six feet or more in height.

These figures become important when we consider the height of the murderer and the average height of Londoners at this time. None of the witnesses described the murderer as tall. They set his height between a little over five feet and a maximum of five feet eight inches. Two studies have shown that the average height of men in London during this period was five feet six inches. Anyone who stood over six feet tall would be recognizable even if he were slouching. On the basis of height, the descriptions of the murderer do not fit Tumblety.[31]

Secondly, from early in his career, Tumblety sported a huge black mustache. It was part of who he was and people always commented on it. Drawings of Tumblety show this large mass of facial hair prominently. None of the witnesses saw a man with such a large or memorable mustache. Again, witness testimony does not fit Tumblety. Finally, many of the witnesses made an estimate of the age of the man they saw. This is perhaps the least certain of these characteristics, being based on a subjective opinion. Estimates of the murderer's age, based on witness testimony, range from 28 to 40 years old with most being around 35 years of age. In 1888, Tumblety was 57 years old. It stretches the imagination to think they were describing Tumblety.

The foregoing review suggests that Tumblety had nothing to do with the Whitechapel murders. There is no evidence that directly implicates him and several lines of evidence seem to exonerate him. Like other times in his career, his eccentricity and lifestyle attracted unwanted attention at just the wrong time. It is an open question whether his homosexual activities were being investigated before the police suspected him in the murders or if their suspicions brought his other activities to light. Either way, Tumblety was a suspect for a brief time. As such, he was one of several hundred men who were investigated, questioned and/or held for the Whitechapel murders. Like all of the others, there was no evidence on which to hold him or charge him.

Tumblety's flight from London might be seen as an admission of guilt except for the other charges he was facing. The sentence for gross indecency was two years in prison with the possibility of hard labor. There is little doubt that the government would be able to prove its case. The fact that they were charging him with four separate acts with four different men demonstrates they went to a lot of trouble to look into his liaisons. Under very similar circumstances, in the same court, the government convicted and sentenced Oscar Wilde seven years later. If Tumblety stayed in England, he was going to prison. The risks of flight were more appealing than the certainty of incarceration.

It is at this point Evans and Gainey present the most ludicrous argument of the book. They contend that Tumblety disappeared and could not be caught. The police, knowing he was Jack the Ripper and realizing how it would look that they let him escape, engaged in a truly massive cover-up. This argument is stunningly self-delusional or intentionally misleading.[32]

First, let us look at the disappearance of their prime suspect. Tumblety may have managed to slip out of London undetected but the newspapers (and probably the police) soon knew he was in France and what ship he was booked on. His arrival in New York was closely watched by the New York police. If he was such a fugitive, he could have been arrested as he stepped off the boat. A few days later, having been under intense public scrutiny since his arrival, Tumblety disappeared again. Less than a month later, he was discovered living in a rooming house in Brooklyn. For the rest of his life, Tumblety was in plain sight and could have been picked up at any time. That he was not, indicates Scotland Yard had no interest in him. When Littlechild, writing in 1913, states that he "was never heard of afterwards," he is again revealing his flawed information.

Evans and Gainey themselves raise the question about a seeming lack of interest in Tumblety by Scotland Yard. In *First American Serial Killer* they ask, "Why was he not mentioned by any of the senior investigating police officers, particularly by Macnaghten in his report? Nor was he referred to in the progress reports by the police to the Home Office." The obvious answer to this question is that those directly involved in the investigation did not think Tumblety was an important suspect. That, however, was not the conclusion the authors came to.

Instead, they believe that senior officers conspired to hide the truth that they had let the Ripper escape to America. If we follow the logic of this to its ultimate conclusion, we can see how unlikely it is. This implies that men like Robert Anderson, Donald Swanson and Melville Macnaghten, all directly involved in the investigation or having access to it, not only kept the secret for the rest of their lives but in their memoirs and private notes sought to mislead future historians. For example, Anderson published his memoirs, entitled *The Lighter Side of My Official Life*, in 1910. In this book, he discusses the Ripper case and states that the police knew the murderer was a poor Polish Jew living in the area. Was this an outright lie on his part? In the margins of his personal copy of this book, Donald Swanson explained and expanded these comments, naming Kosminski as the suspect Anderson was talking about. One can argue whether Anderson and Swanson were correct in their belief, but it seems irrational to believe that they really knew Tumblety was the Ripper. This was the most detailed and faithfully kept conspiracy in human history! Except, of course, for Inspector Littlechild, who let the cat out of the black bag.

Francis Tumblety was, for a brief time, considered to be a suspect in the Whitechapel murder case. Like many other suspects, the police quickly lost interest in him either because he provided an alibi or because there was no direct evidence against him. When he fled England, it was because of the charges of gross indecency, not murder. Scotland Yard did not try to extradite him because they had already decided he was not their man. In England, he was quickly forgotten. But for Tumblety, in America, life would never be the same.

15

---⊶∞⊷---

The Aftermath in New York
(1888–1890)

When we last saw Doctor Tumblety, he was arriving in New York, under an assumed name. During the voyage of *La Bretagne,* one passenger, "Frank Townsend," reportedly stayed in his cabin, pleading sickness. The ship docked at 1:30 P.M. on Sunday, December 2, 1888. Tumblety's arrival was not unexpected. There seems to have been two detectives from the New York police, as well as reporters from the *New York Herald* and the *New York World,* waiting for him. Sergeants Hickey and Crowley were at the bottom of the gangplank when the ship's passengers began to disembark. The detectives looked over each passenger as they descended, having no doubt been furnished with a description of Tumblety beforehand. They waited impatiently until they spied a "big, fine-looking man" coming down the gangway. The *New York World* described Tumblety's appearance as he arrived back in America:

> He had a heavy, fierce-looking mustache, waxed at the ends; his face was pale and he looked hurried and excited. He wore a dark blue ulster, with belt buttoned. He carried under his arm two canes and an umbrella fastened together with a strap.... He hurriedly engaged a cab, gave the directions in a low voice and was driven away.[1]

It is clear that despite his assumed name, Scotland Yard knew exactly where Tumblety had gone. They alerted the New York police to his arrival but do not appear to have asked them to do anything about it. A reporter asked Inspector Byrnes about Tumblety and his reply was: "Of course he can not be arrested, for there is no proof in his complicity in the Whitechapel murders, and the crime for which he was under bond in London is not extraditable."[2]

Had Scotland Yard been truly interested in Tumblety, they would have had no trouble having him arrested. All it would have taken was a telegram to Inspector Byrnes. In fact, just before Tumblety arrived in New York, Scotland Yard had done just that for a supposed murderer. A James Pennock had murdered his wife in Pickering, Yorkshire. Scotland Yard had information that he was traveling under the name James Shaw on the streamer *Wyoming*. At their request, James Shaw was arrested by the New York police on November 21, 1888, as he got off the ship. In the end, Scotland Yard admitted he was the wrong man, but the incident does show what could have happened to Tumblety if the London police really wanted him.[3]

After Tumblety got his cab, the detectives got another and were in pursuit. They followed the doctor to the corner of Fourth Avenue and Tenth Street. According to the *New York World*, Tumblety showed some confusion at this point. Reportedly he first went to 75 E. Tenth Street, which was a hotel known as the Arnold House. When no one answered the door, he went to 81 E. Tenth Street, a boarding house run by Matilda Gebhardt. As no one answered the door there either, Tumblety went to 79 E. Tenth Street. Here his ring was answered and at 2:20 P.M., he was taken in.

What makes this most unusual is that 79 E. Tenth Street was a boarding house run by Mrs. McNamara and Tumblety had been lodging with her for at least eight years during the times that he was in New York. One wonders why he would be wandering around the neighborhood if he already had a room? Other papers simply reported that he went directly to Mrs. McNamara's and did not mention any other stops, which makes the *New York World* story somewhat doubtful.

It is instructive, at this point, to consider the differences in press coverage between the *New York World* and other New York papers. The cable that first reported Tumblety's arrest was from the *New York World*'s London reporter. It was this paper that published the particularly damning interview with C. A. Dunham and the equally damaging one with "Col. Sothern," who appears not to exist. While the other papers covered the developing story in simple language, the *New York World* made it much more lurid. The *New York Herald*, for example, simple reported Tumblety's arrival and how he was shadowed by the detectives. In contrast, the *World* talked about his "fierce-looking mustache" and reported that he had a "hurried and excited" look. McKenna's saloon, 73 Fourth Avenue, figures in both the *Herald* and *World* stories. The *Herald* simply said the bartenders knew Tumblety well, while the *World* commented that he was "spoken of with loathing and contempt." We could ascribe the *New York World*'s vituperation to a different literary style, but how much of the rest of their reporting is colored by this style? Was Dunham making more money from this story? Whatever the reason, the *New York World*, from the beginning, took a very adversarial stand on Tumblety.

On Monday, with Tumblety holed up in his room, things became hectic around 79 E. Tenth Street. Reporters, friends and others were all looking to see the doctor. Mrs. McNamara, at first open about her celebrity guest, soon became exasperated by all the attention. She told the reporters that he was a gentleman and would not harm anyone. As part of this character reference, she told a story about how he had followed her up three flights of stairs to return a dollar he owed her. As far as she was concerned, the doctor was wrongly accused. As the incessant questions kept coming and the doorbell kept ringing, Mrs. McNamara began to resent the reporters and to fend them off. Originally she told them Tumblety was there, then that he had not been there for two months and, finally, that she had no idea who Tumblety was. Whatever her story, she would not admit anyone to the house.[4]

Mrs. McNamara's vigilance included not just reporters but old friends as well. Martin H. McGarry, who had worked for and known Tumblety for six years, was one of those denied admission. He told a reporter from the *New York World* his deluded but supportive story about Tumblety being the son of a wealthy Irish gentleman. Despite supposedly not being admitted to the house, McGarry told the reporter that Tumblety had not left his room since he arrived.

A most curious person made his appearance outside Mrs. McNamara's house on Monday. The *New York World* described the appearance of:

> ...a little man with enormous side whiskers ... he was dressed in an English Tweed suit and wore an enormous pair of boots with soles an inch thick.... There was an elaborate attempt at concealment and mystery which could not be possibly misunderstood. Everything about him told of his business. From his little billy-cock hat, alternately set jauntily on the side of his head and pulled lowering over his eyes, down to the very bottom of his thick boots, he was a typical English detective. If he had been put on a stage just as he paraded up and down Fourth Avenue and Tenth Street yesterday he would have been called a caricature.[5]

The report went on to describe the comic antics of this person as he watched the house or hung out with the bartenders in McKenna's saloon. He let them know that he was an English detective who had come to America to get the person who committed the Whitechapel murders. As he was asking questions about Tumblety, the implication was that he was the person. If the *New York World* were the only paper to mention this person, we could dismiss it as a reporter's fancy. However, an article in the *New York Herald*, on the same day, briefly mentions the detective as well. The story in the *Herald* is slightly different. Although the paper calls him a detective, the individual never told the bartenders much about himself. If this was a detective, he was a particularly inept one and not what we would expect from Scotland Yard. Nor does he seem to have stayed around very long.

A bigger question is whether Scotland Yard sent anyone looking for Tumblety after he fled England? In December 1888, Inspector Walter Andrews escorted Israel Barnett, who committed bank fraud, from London to Toronto. This was unusual as it was the responsibility of the Canadian authorities to go get Barnett and from the beginning people had suspicions about this trip. Earlier studies suggested that Andrews came to America in pursuit of Tumblety. He supposedly made several statements about the Whitechapel investigation while he was in Canada. However, his true purpose was soon evident. The British government was trying to collect as much incriminating evidence as it could against the Irish leader Charles Parnell and his National League. Andrews revealed that there was a network of detectives, including the Pinkertons, in America keeping an eye on the Irish-American wing of this group. Andrews went to Niagara Falls to meet with the head of this network. Despite reports to the contrary, Andrews never went to New York but sailed home from Halifax. Apparently Scotland Yard really did not care where Tumblety was. If Scotland Yard was not interested, who was the fellow with the big whiskers? It is likely that there were certain people in England who might still have an interest in him. His bail arrangements are unknown but it is likely that someone was stuck with a bill of $1,500. Such a sum might be enough to hire a bounty hunter to trail Tumblety.[6]

Whether it was Mrs. McNamara's distress over all the commotion at her door or just a need for peace and quiet, Tumblety determined to slip away from the limelight for awhile. The *New York World* reported that early in the morning of December 5, a nervous-looking man matching Tumblety's description left Mrs. McNamara's, walked to Fourth Avenue and took an uptown car. Later that night, the reporter slipped by Mrs. McNamara and entered Tumblety's room only to find it empty.

Doctor Tumblety was gone and no one knew where—not the reporters who seemed to be beating down the door of 79 E. Tenth Street, not the New York police who supposedly had him under surveillance and not the strange little man with the whiskers. This sudden disappearance led to all kinds of speculation. When Tumblety was first discussed as a Ripper suspect, his sudden disappearance seemed ominous and dark. It was suggested that he may have left the country and was responsible for Ripper-like murders in South America and Jamaica. Where Tumblety first went is still a mystery but by January 18, 1889, he had ended up in the exotic location of Brooklyn, where under the very creative name of "Smith," he took a room in the boarding house run by Mrs. Lamb.[7]

While he may have gone underground, Tumblety did not give up the fight. As he had done in 1866, he began soliciting friends for character references which he could publish to repair his reputation. One of the earliest of these is dated January 2, 1889, and is from Rev. W. H. De Puy, of 58 Bible House, New York City. What better reference could he get than one from a Bible publisher? Bible House was a large, brick building which occupied the block bounded by Third and Fourth Avenues and Eighth and Ninth Streets. It was built be the American Bible Society in 1853 to house its staff and printing facilities. De Puy was a Methodist minister and had worked at Bible House as an editor for over ten years. He reports meeting Tumblety on the steamer *City of Rome* a few years earlier and that he was a good friend.[8]

If the De Puy letter carried the moral authority of a stack of Bibles, the letter from Graeme M. Hammond did the same with the medical community. Dated January 23, 1889, the letter stated that he had been friends with Tumblety for several years. He wrote "[I] have always found you to be an honorable and straightforward gentleman. You have my sympathy in the foul attack made on your honorable character." Hammond was a widely known and respected regular doctor, the son of the founder of neurology in America. He was an officer of the American Neurological Association for 30 years and its president in 1898.[9]

While Tumblety was in hiding, some people knew he was in New York and were in touch with him. At least these two letters were written after his escape from Mrs. McNamara's and before his discovery in Brooklyn. While he apparently did not get to Mrs. Lamb's house until January 18, the letters indicate that he was still in the New York area. This is, of course, assuming that these letters are real. Some of his friends were not as discreet as others and the hideout was soon made public.

A report reprinted in the *Brooklyn Daily Eagle* described how Tumblety was found out. On January 27, a young man called at Mrs. Lamb's asking for Dr. Twombley. Another boarder in the house told him that there was no one there of that name. At just the wrong time, Mr. "Smith" showed up and was greeted by the young man by his real name. Following a hurried discussion with his young friend, Tumblety paid his landlady, packed his trunks and, accompanied by his friend, headed out to parts unknown.[10]

It would be interesting to know who this young man was and how he came to know where Tumblety was hiding. Was it Martin McGarry, who came looking for him at Mrs. McNamara's, or Mark Blackburn, his longtime friend? Whoever it was, he must have heard it from another friend who forgot to tell him about the alias. It indicates that word was spreading among his network of friends.

Once Tumblety was flushed from his hiding spot, an amazing thing happened—no one cared. Except for brief mentions in the *New York Sun* and the *Brooklyn Daily Eagle*, he was not pursued by the police, by reporters, or by anyone else. The press storm had passed on to other people and Tumblety was left to his own resources. Now that the frenzy had died down, Tumblety was ready to try to repair his reputation. With Tumblety's "discovery" quickly followed by a carefully planned advertising campaign, one wonders if the whole episode was Tumblety's own creation.

The day after Tumblety was discovered, articles began to appear in the New York papers which praised Tumblety and called the charges against him malicious and false. Although they appear to be editorials, Tumblety certainly paid to have them published. One of the first of these appeared in the *New York World*, of all places, on January 29. This article purports to be an interview with the doctor where he discusses the reasons for his arrest. Not surprisingly, Tumblety does not mention the charges of gross indecency but states that he was arrested on suspicion of being Jack the Ripper. Flashing his diamonds to the reporter, he claimed the real reason for his arrest was that the detectives wanted to extort them from him. The interview is extremely self-serving with little or no serious questioning from the reporter. Near the end of the interview, Tumblety lists many of the letters he would later publish and the reporter comments that they testify to "Dr. Tumblety's character and integrity." On the same day, the *New York Sun* commented, "Dr. Tumblety is not what slanders say he is, but a very much abused gentleman." A few days later, on February 3, the *World* informed its readers that Tumblety was soon to publish a pamphlet that would "silence his traducers."[11]

That pamphlet was described in greater detail in a very laudatory article published a day earlier in the *Brooklyn Daily Eagle*. It outlines the story of Tumblety's life and praises his remarkable career. His many friends in New York are said to be "aggrieved" by the charges against him. It is perhaps not so surprising that the *Daily Eagle* would give so much space to this pamphlet, as they were the ones printing it. Both this and the *World* article suggest that the publication of the pamphlet was to take place within days. The *Olean Democrat*, on February 7, refers to it as if it were already published.[12]

In updating his pamphlet, Tumblety had to make considerable changes to the text to suit his present needs. The title reflects these changed circumstances: "Dr. Francis Tumblety: A Sketch of the Life of the Gifted, Eccentric and World-Famed Physician." Gone is any hint of his arrest in 1865 or the invective against Secretary Stanton. It is intended to present him as a well-traveled, cultured gentleman. To support this, he mentions his extensive correspondence with prominent people and his world travels. Unlike earlier editions, he does not directly address the charges against him but depends on associations to prove his respectability.

It is possible that this pamphlet went through three press runs in 1889. The first would be the original referred to in the *Olean Democrat* published early in February. One existing copy has testimonials dated as late as April 1889. The copy that I reviewed had testimonials dated as late as November 1889. Tumblety probably sent these out to many people over the course of the year.[13]

In the copy of his pamphlet published later in the year, Tumblety had 26 testimonials from New York City residents to support his character, most of which were solicited at this time. Of the total, 14 were dated, with 12 of these occurring between January and March 1889. All but three of these people could be identified in the 1890 New York City Directory. They represented a diverse group of people but could be divided by occupation into four groups. The largest group was physicians and druggists which related to Tumblety's profession. There were nine people in this category, representing 40 percent of the sample. Next were two groups with five people each. What might be called the service group was clothiers and liquor dealers who dealt with Tumblety's needs. The other group was hotel and restaurant owners and Tumblety presumably used their facilities. The final group might be called professional and was the most diverse. There were four people assigned to this group: a minister, a civil engineer, a sculptor and a shipping line clerk. For many of these people, Tumblety could be considered a customer whose trade they wanted to keep. Cynically, we could say that a favorable testimonial was a small price to pay.

However, what is striking about many of these letters are the long-standing relationships that they indicate. Of the 26 names listed, 12 have some statement about how long they have known Tumblety. Only two of these indicated a short-term relationship, specifically saying they have known Tumblety for "several years." The rest indicate long-term familiarity, with spans ranging from 15 years to 30 years, and an average of 24 years. They indicate that Tumblety was able to create long-term friendships with diverse people.

It may be significant that of the small number of Tumblety's testimonials, three of them were from the proprietors of New York's most famous Turkish bathhouses. Dr. M. L. Holebrook ran the New York Hygienic Institute at 13 Laight Street, which was the first Turkish bath in New York. Dr. E. P. Miller, who began by working with Holebrook, ran Dr. Miller's Turkish Baths on W. Twenty-Sixth Street. Finally, Dr. C. T. Ryan operated the Lafayette Baths on Lafayette Place, which would become the most well-known homosexual bathhouse in the early 20th century. Tumblety had been interested in Turkish baths as early as his 1869 visit to Dr. Barter in Ireland. It seems likely that his interest was more than simply cleanliness. Bathhouses would become one of the few safe places for homosexual men to meet partners and it is likely that Tumblety patronized them for this reason.[14]

In his 1889 biography, we can see Tumblety's intentional twisting of history to suit his needs. If one compares the earlier (1872) edition with any of the later editions, a significant problem is immediately evident. In the earlier edition, Tumblety reports going to Europe and then traveling out West. This sequence is supported by much other evidence. However, in his 1889 edition, this sequence is reversed. This was necessary to accommodate one of Tumblety's bigger lies. On page five, he shows a "military diploma" issued to him in connection with the presentation of the Brittany Cross for service in a field hospital, known as an ambulance, during the Siege of Paris by the Prussian army.

Late in 1870, Napoleon III declared war on Prussia and France suffered several quick military disasters. By September 19, 1870, the Prussians had surrounded Paris and the city was under siege. The Prussians attempted to starve Paris into submission, rejecting Chancellor Bismarck's suggestion that the city be shelled. As the siege wore on, it became apparent that Paris could hold out for a long time. Emperor Wilhelm I ordered the city bombarded on January 25, 1871, and the city surrendered three days later. To many, the defense of Paris was heroic and worthy of praise. Had Tumblety served in a hospital during this conflict, he would have shared in this heroism.[15]

In French, the term ambulance did not mean the vehicle that carried wounded but rather the field hospital where they were treated. Dr. Evans, who was both the dentist for Napoleon III and the first American to be awarded the Legion of Honor, had brought a complete American field hospital to France in 1867 to exhibit at the Paris Fair. As a result of the Civil War, American doctors had made great strides in the treatment and care of the wounded. When war broke out, several American doctors, who were neutrals, used these materials to treat the wounded during the Siege of Paris and were awarded the Legion of Honor for their efforts. Known as the American Ambulance, it was well known to give the best care and have the lowest death rate of any of the field hospitals. Back home, Americans were rightly proud of this institution. Tumblety did not claim to be part of this unit but rather the Ambulance of Brittany.[16]

However, Tumblety was in San Francisco until sometime in September 1870. By that time the Prussians had already surrounded Paris. He advertises in Brooklyn by mid November 1870 and is well documented in New York from then until well after the siege was lifted. It seems unlikely that Tumblety broke through the Prussian lines, stayed in Paris for a month, then broke through the lines a second time to get back to Brooklyn. Nevertheless, Tumblety appropriated the heroism of the defenders for himself. In order to do this, he had to hide the embarrassing fact that he was in San Francisco at the time. Thus, the reversal of his trips in his later biographies.

Much of the rest of the pamphlet is a travelogue of places Tumblety is supposed to have visited. These include England, France, Italy, Spain, Germany, Bavaria, Belgium, Switzerland, Greece, Turkey, Malta, and Egypt. While not in the April edition, by November, Tumblety had added a section on Winter Resorts with details on Cuba and Mexico. These descriptions read like they were lifted directly from a travel guide. Unlike earlier parts of the narrative, they contain no personal detail at all and are therefore not verifiable. The only exception is the discussion of his time in Italy c. 1878 which includes specific information on people and places. The inclusion of all this travel information was to show Tumblety as a wealthy, urbane man of the world.

However, there is one section which describes Yosemite, Yellowstone and the Grand Canyon which is traceable because of its strong biblical language. It refers to God as the architect of worlds and praises the beauty of his works. The descriptions use language from the book of Revelations to relate the natural with the divine. The language is florid and unlike anything Tumblety had used before. For example, the following passage describes the walls of the Grand Canyon:

> See all this carnage of color up and down the cliffs; it must have been the battlefield of the war of the elements. Here are all the colors of the wall of heaven, neither the sapphire, nor the chrysolite, nor the topaz, nor the jacinth, nor the amethyst, nor the jasper, nor the twelve gates of twelve pearls wanting.[17]

This section is so different from any other part of Tumblety's travel narrative and the language is so vivid that identifying for its source was not difficult. Rev. T. Dewitt Talmage was a Presbyterian minister and pastor of the Brooklyn Tabernacle. His sermons were so popular that they were reprinted in newspapers all over the country. On September 22, 1889, Talmage gave a sermon whose theme was why America was a Christian country and he used his 1880 trip across the country for examples of God's handiwork in America. The descriptions that Tumblety published of Yosemite, Yellowstone and the Grand Canyon come directly from this sermon. The only changes Tumblety made were to delete Talmage's personal references.[18]

In this same regard, the later editions contain small sections on paralysis and Bright's disease. These appear to be discussions between Tumblety and an unnamed patient or reporter. They may have formed part of his ads at some point, although the source has not yet been identified. Their inclusion here adds to the perception of Tumblety's professionalism. As the purpose of the pamphlet was to restore his reputation, they were an important part of this process. Later evidence indicates that Tumblety carried around copies of this pamphlet and gave it out freely to anyone he met. Given what he had been through, he needed a somewhat larger calling card than most people.

The article in the *Daily Eagle* that reported the publication of the 1889 pamphlet also stated that Tumblety intended to settle in Brooklyn and to resume the practice of medicine. Neither of these things can be demonstrated in the surviving records. As previously mentioned, when Dr. Tumblety stopped advertising in the newspapers, we lost a great way of keeping track of his whereabouts. We can say that Tumblety is not listed in either the Brooklyn or New York City directories during this period. The loss of the 1890 census also leaves a huge gap in the record. Because of this, Tumblety's life is somewhat sketchy from now on.

As Tumblety got older he seems not to have formed relationships with young men as he had with Mark Blackburn, Hall Caine and Martin McGarry. Rather, he sought partners on the street, which inevitably led to problems. Tumblety's brush with the law in England did not make enough of an impression on him to get him to change his ways. He had been charged with four counts of sexual assault on men while in London. It is likely that these were male prostitutes that he hired off the street. Given the public's hostile attitude to homosexuals, finding a partner on the street became a difficult and dangerous task. Criminals often hung around places where homosexuals gathered because they were easy to rob and often did not report it. We hear of Tumblety twice during this period because of failed attempts at assignations.

The first of these incidents occurred on the night of June 4, 1889. Tumblety was on Clinton Place (now East and West Eighth Street), north of Washington Square Park in Manhattan. Washington Square Park was an early and well-known location for picking up male prostitutes. Tumblety saw a young man by the name of George Davis and struck up a conversation about the weather. According to Davis, Tumblety soon "used most insulting language." When Davis objected to this, Tumblety hit him across the face with his cane, reportedly laying his cheek open almost to the bone. As this was happening, a policeman showed up and Tumblety and Davis took off in different directions. Both were soon caught and taken to the Mercer Street Police Station.[19]

At the station, Davis told his story and filed a charge of assault against Tumblety. Apparently the policeman who came on the scene offered support to this charge. Tumblety either said nothing or claimed that Davis tried to steal his watch. He was held overnight and taken to the Jefferson Market Police Court the next morning. In a hearing before Justice Ford, Tumblety was given bail of $300 paid for by Henry Clews & Co., Tumblety's bankers. The case was scheduled to be heard on June 24. When the day came, the doctor was nowhere to be seen. However, the next day he showed up in court and provided an excuse for his absence. He pleaded not guilty to the charge and was remanded. Eventually the case was dismissed and the assistant district attorney that tried the case wrote that Davis "is shiftless and untruthful. I would not believe him under oath." Clearly Tumblety's choice of partners was risky at best.[20]

Even before the last case was dismissed, we soon hear of Tumblety "discussing weather" with another young man. Sometime late in July, E. H. Eaton, an editor, met Tumblety on a trolley car crossing the Brooklyn Bridge. Eaton recognized the doctor and asked his name. Tumblety admitted who he was and said that he had been greatly wronged by the press. As proof, he gave Eaton a copy of the pamphlet. Unlike the previous encounter, Eaton left the trolley at the Brooklyn end without any problems.[21]

In November 1890, Tumblety was in Washington staying at Meyer's Hotel. On the night of November 17, he decided to take a walk. This would soon get him in trouble with the police. According to newspaper accounts, he was standing in the shadows near Ninth Street and Pennsylvania Avenue. One source describes this as a "popular stretch for male cruising" in Washington during the early 20th century, and presumable the late 19th century as well. Not a word was said about what Tumblety was doing but Detective Ned Horne thought Tumblety's actions so suspicious that he immediately arrested him. It is perhaps significant that a "boy" was also held as a witness. They were taken to the station and further questioned.[22]

The police were surprised, when they searched Tumblety, to find a wealth of money and jewels on his person. It was reported that he had $250 dollars, a check for $160, two diamond rings, each worth $2,500, a ring of rubies, set with small diamonds, worth $200, and a gold watch. We can guess what the large amount of money was for. He also carried a copy of the 1889 pamphlet, which seems to have become his way of introducing himself, and he had a letter from a prominent but unnamed congressman.

The reporter from the *Washington Post* gave a concise but telling description of Tumblety at this stage of his life:

> Dr. Tumblety is an enormous man, over six feet in height, with broad shoulders. His hair is black, tinged with gray, and his skin is red and coarse. His moustache is a rather large affair, evidently dyed black, and extends around the corners of his mouth. His eyes are steely blue, and he gazed steadily at nothing, as he spoke in a weak, effeminate voice. He was dressed in a big black overcoat and wore a German cap, and had on rubber boots.[23]

The doctor was held in a cell briefly but then given bail. He was told to show up at the police court the next morning. In the brief description given by the newspapers, no charge against Tumblety is specifically mentioned. The *Brooklyn Daily Eagle*, in recapping the story, said the charge against him was that of being a suspicious character. While this may certainly describe Dr. Tumblety, it has no legal basis. It is likely that the charge had something to do with the "boy" but the papers chose not to publish it.

In any case, Tumblety is said to have presented testimony of his past good behavior—probably the pamphlet's testimonials again. Judge Miller, who heard the case, reluctantly dismissed the charges against him because of a lack of evidence but "commented strongly" on Tumblety's reputation. The police vowed to keep him under surveillance while he stayed in Washington. There is no information on how long he stayed in town or where he went.

From this point, Tumblety's life changes dramatically. When he makes the papers now, it will be for donations to charity or as a curious character at various resorts. His niece, Mary Fitzsimmons, claimed, after he died, that he used her house as his base of operations, but there is little evidence of that. Having made a large amount of money, he seems to have taken the time to enjoy it. Much as retirees do today, he seems to have followed the sun, wintering in the south and summering in the north.

16

⊶∞⊷

Retirement
(1891–1903)

During the last decade of the 19th century, Tumblety seems to have retired from active life, not surprising for a man who was 60 years old. When we hear of him, it is most often in connection with his presence at a resort. During this time Tumblety can be shown to have been at resorts or spas in Maine, New York, New Jersey and Arkansas. Another new aspect of his life is the very public donation of money to various charities and causes. Previously, he had donated flour to the poor as a way of advertising his practice. He later claimed that most of his charitable donations were done privately and, of course, there is no way to trace those. Now, his donations regularly are reported in the papers. Perhaps he was using his fortune to regain some of the reputation he had lost in 1888.

One of the places to which Tumblety frequently went was the resort town of Hot Springs, Arkansas. Later reports state that the doctor frequently spent winters in Hot Springs. This may have been his ultimate destination when he got in trouble in Washington for lurking in the shadows. Being 60 years old, Tumblety certainly could have come to Hot Springs for the healing waters or even for the warmer climate. The presence of a number of bathhouses and the possible liaisons they represented should not be discounted either.

While people had been going to Hot Springs for the medical effects of the hot waters since before the Civil War, it was only in the 1880s that the area became a fashionable resort. A large number of impressive bathhouses were built over the springs, a railroad was constructed to bring in people and modern hotels were built along Central Avenue, the main street through town. One of these, the Plateau Hotel, became Tumblety's usual stopping place. Built c. 1885, the Plateau was located on the highest point of Central Avenue with good views of the valley and the surrounding mountains. Not the largest of the hotels, it still had rooms for a hundred guests and an elevator, electric bells, a fire alarm system and a renowned dining room. It was located in the center of Hot Springs with street car lines outside the front door. Rates at the hotel varied from $15 to $20 per week, which was the second most expensive choice in the city.[1]

Like most resorts where the wealthy congregate, Hot Springs attracted its share of criminals, particularly a specialist group known as hotel thieves. Those who practiced this trade were often cultured and well-spoken. They dressed in good clothes and stayed in the best hotels. Resorts like Hot Springs were ideal for these thieves because people came from all over the country and were generally unknown to each other. This anonymity was essential for a successful "tour."[2]

This was not a random crime but rather the victim was carefully selected to ensure a good take. Thieves looked for wealthy guests who showed ready cash or jewels. They would follow them to learn their habits and, when they were sure the victim would be otherwise occupied, they broke into the room and took what they had already observed. More daring thieves waited until the guests were asleep and, using skeleton keys, slipped into the occupied rooms to gather their loot. Hotel thieves were working in Hot Springs in early 1891 and on April 14 it was reported that guests at the Eastman and Park Hotels were robbed of diamonds.[3]

A man like Tumblety, who flashed his diamonds freely, was a natural target for these men and it was not long before they got around to him. He was staying at the Plateau Hotel when, on the night of April 17, thieves broke into his room and stole cash and jewelry worth as much as $7,000. He claimed that they took $2,000 in cash and diamonds worth $5,000–$7,000. At first, it is tempting to suggest that Tumblety exaggerated the total of his loss, given his problem with the truth. However, when stopped in Washington, six months before, he had on him two rings that were valued at $2,500 each. He was a flashy dresser and had the money to support that habit. Given Tumblety's frequent stays in hotels and his habit of showing off his jewels, it is surprising that this had not happened to him before. Once the actual robbery was over, there was little chance the thieves would be caught and it is likely that the doctor never recovered what was lost.[4]

At the end of the season, if not before, Tumblety left Hot Springs to return to New York. In 1891, he was living at 109 E. Ninth Street which was a multistory building with book and shoe stores on the ground floor. He may have been living here earlier, as this was only a block north of where the confrontation with George Davis took place in 1889. By July, the Doctor was making the rounds of the summer resorts. He was in Richfield Springs, otherwise known as the "Great White Sulfur Springs," in upstate New York early in July and at the ocean in Long Branch, New Jersey, later in the month.[5]

It was on his return from Long Branch that Tumblety read in the *New York Herald* of the plight of Frank Sherman, a penniless American who stowed away on a ship coming to America. Sherman had been a clerk in Chicago when, "wishing to better his fortunes," he went to New York. Finding no work there, he signed on a cattle boat, the *Nederland*, sailing on June 10 to London. Once in London, he had no better luck and decided he needed to come home. Sherman did not have the money for a return trip so chose another course. When the steamship *England*, also a cattle boat, was two days out of London, five stowaways were found on board. Of these, three were English and two claimed to be Americans. The two Americans were Richard Richards, 24, a printer from New York, and Sherman, whose age was listed as 19. As was normal in such a situation, all of the stowaways were put to work to pay for their passage.[6]

When they arrived in New York, the five stowaways were brought to the Barge Office and interviewed. Richards, being from New York, was able to prove he was an American and, having worked off his voyage, was free to go. Sherman and the three English stowaways were locked up in the wheelhouse of the ship in anticipation of their being sent back to England. Sherman began to beg people passing by for a postage stamp so he could contact his relatives and prove he was an American. One of the strangers telegraphed Sherman's mother in Chicago, who replied that he was an American. The port authorities would still not believe him. At this point, Tumblety read about Sherman's plight and wrote a letter to the *New York Herald*. Enclosed in the letter was a check for $325.75 to cover Sherman's passage and his expenses back to his widowed mother in Chicago. This would have been an interesting story if it stopped here, but there was more to come.

On July 22, it was determined that Sherman was actually Samuel Sykerman, a resident of Chicago and an American. The port authorities released him. But Sherman's troubles were not over yet. The authorities in Chicago had read of his arrival and they were interested in him. Based on a telegram from the Chicago chief of police, Sherman was arrested on the charge of stealing $100 from the Chicago Brush Company. Perhaps this was where he got the money to come to New York and the impetus for his long sojourn. Eventually he was let go when a jury failed to indict him. While in the end, Tumblety's charity was probably misplaced, the exposure in the press was good for his reputation.[7]

After his brief visit to New York, Tumblety was off to Bar Harbor, Maine, another summer resort. Bar Harbor came to prominence in the 1880s as the wealthy and powerful built their "cottages" there. It was while in Bar Harbor that Tumblety launched the second of his public charities to provide free baths to poor New Yorkers. This was most likely in response to articles published in the *New York Herald* in early August.

The Board of Health reported that there was a major increase in the amount of sewage in the East River and it was concerned that an epidemic would result. By July 26, it was reported that the East River was covered with a "thick scum of oil and refuse" from the Battery to Harlem. Water from the East River was used in the free baths that the city had provided for the poor since 1873. Boys who used the baths were reported to be suffering from an eye inflammation that threatened to blind them and there was an outbreak of fever that health officials feared would lead to a typhoid epidemic. In the second week of August, the city closed down all of the free baths on the East River. The alternatives were to go to one of the commercial bathhouses or walk across town to the Hudson River where other free baths existed. Neither of these solutions was a real option for the poor in the nearby tenements.[8]

In response to this environmental disaster, Dr. Tumblety wrote to the *New York Herald* and enclosed a check for $200 to provide bath tickets so the boys could get free baths at commercial bathhouses. The *Herald* announced the program on August 28 and the actual ticket distribution took place on September 6. In total, 4,000 tickets were given out to boys, girls and 50 men in desperate need. Tumblety later quoted several complimentary notices from Joseph Howard, Jr., including this notice published in the *New York Recorder*, September 5, 1891:

> Dr. Francis Tumblety comes periodically before his fellow citizens with a sensation of some sort. His last is a check for $200, sent to the *Herald*, for the purchase of bath tickets to be distributed free among New York news boys. Dr. Tumblety's generous action speaks for itself yet there can be no harm done in echoing his praise. Giving two hundred dollars of your own money is a very different thing from inducing other people to give a thousand dollars of their money.[9]

Howard was one of the first syndicated columnists with a nationwide audience and Tumblety would have cherished such a notice. He had almost as interesting a background as Tumblety and the two may have been friends. Howard was the city editor of the *Brooklyn Eagle* during the time that Tumblety was advertising heavily in the paper. He had a biting, cynical style which he does not seem to have used on Tumblety despite the size of the target.[10]

At the end of the year, Tumblety was back in Hot Springs, where he made a donation to St. Joseph's Infirmary in response to its appeal. This was a hospital run by the Sisters of Mercy that had been opened in an old hotel in 1888 at 1 Cedar Terrace. The Sisters of Mercy was an order founded in Ireland to serve the poor, the sick and the uneducated. Tumblety would have a growing relationship with them over the final years of his life, being both donor and patient.[11]

This pattern of charitable giving continues into the next year as the *New York Herald* announced its intention to create a new charity for the poor. On May 29, 1892, it stated its intention to distribute free ice to the tenements of New York in the coming summer and solicited donations. On the thirtieth, the day after the announcement, Dr. Tumblety went to the *Herald* bureau in Baltimore and gave then a $20 bill for the cause. Later the *Herald* reported that Tumblety sent a telegram on June 5 saying that he was sending another $40 for the ice charity. In the following year, Tumblety gave $100 to this same charity, and his was one of the largest single donations of any reported.[12]

All of these contributions to charity may have been made because Tumblety, having made a large amount of money, felt a truly charitable impulse to help people, but this does not seem in keeping with his character. These donations may have been part of the role he chose to play as the wealthy and respected philanthropist and his contributions did significantly improve the lives of a number of people. The fact that they were so public and each garnered complimentary notices in the newspapers suggests their purpose for Tumblety. The doctor was ready to publish an updated and modified version of his biography and these press notices would add significantly to his reputation.

The autobiography he published at this time was significantly modified to suit his purposes. It grew from 96 to 156 pages and, like its predecessors, was intended to show how well-known and learned the doctor was. It was simply titled "A Sketch of the Life of Dr. Francis Tumblety," while the rest of the title page touted his success as a physician and his wide circle of prominent friends. It was published in New York but the printer was not listed. There were at least two editions of this issue. In the one I reviewed, dated 1893, the text has two sections. The main section ends with press notices and letters dated to 1891 and is followed by a supplement with letters dated 1891–1893.[13]

Although the earlier edition has not yet turned up, its publication date can be attributed to a narrow period. The latest internal date in the first part of the book is September 1891, based on a testimonial, while it contains a plagiarized section which first appeared in newspapers in December 1891. This section, entitled "How to Live Long," was published in a magazine called the *Youths' Companion* earlier and was reprinted in newspapers at that time. However, in June, the *Olean Democrat* published an edited version of this article which it attributed directly to Tumblety. That newspaper would have gotten the article from the missing edition. Interestingly, several other papers picked up the article from the *Democrat* in later June. Based on the content and the plagiarism, the first edition had to have been published between September 1891 and June 1892.[14]

The first edition was only slightly different from the earlier 1889 biography, adding only 11 pages. In addition to reporting the stowaway story and the free bath ticket giveaway, Tumblety added five pages extolling the health value of parks and fresh air as well as the section on "How to Live Long." As already stated, the latter section was plagiarized and it is likely that the paean to parks was also, but the source has not been identified. Apparently, these sections were well received because in the 1893 edition, he added another 41 pages of essays with titles such as "Philosophy of Life," "Physiognomy," and "Great Men Who Died from Overwork." As with the other sections, these were probably stolen, but their sources remain unknown. The only essay that could be tracked to a source was titled "What a Man Is Made Of" and reports the chemical composition of the human body. This was an article written by Thomas Huxley, possibly for the *Encyclopædia Britannica*, and reprinted in several newspapers. It is highly unlikely that Tumblety wrote any of this material.[15]

The 1893 biography contains one of Tumblety's less well-thought-out lies. He published a letter, dated July 12, 1887, supposedly received from Henry Wadsworth Longfellow, thanking him for the delivery of a private message and verse from Baron Tennyson. This insinuated Tumblety as a messenger between the two most important poets of the era and clearly reflected his acceptance in literary circles. This presents a problem, as Longfellow died in 1882. Being kind, one might suppose that there was a typographical error and the date was actually 1882. However, Alfred Tennyson was not created a Baron by Queen Victoria until 1883, the year after Longfellow died. It is not often that Tumblety can be caught in such a bald lie, but it was probably typical of much of his self-promotional literature.[16]

As with his public charitable contributions, this book was Tumblety's way of keeping his name in front of the public. He thought of himself as a famous and respected physician or that was the image he wanted other people to believe. It is not known how many copies were printed but very few survive today.

Details of Tumblety's travels between 1893 and 1898 have not yet come to light but it is likely that he continued his habit of wintering in the south and summering in the north. However, time was beginning to change Tumblety. From now until his death, people will begin to comment on his shabby manner of dressing and most people who met him thought he was poor. This is so different from everything that we have heard up to this point that we must conclude his mind was beginning to slip. As would be expected from someone his age, he was constantly complaining about his health and had begun to forget things.

During his annual migration, he frequently spent time in Baltimore, where he had several old friends and acquaintances. One of these old acquaintances, William Duvall, had known Tumblety since 1868. At that time he was a clerk in a prominent clothing store, but by 1898, he was set up as a lawyer and real estate broker.[17]

Duvall introduced Tumblety to Robert H. Simpson, a young lawyer with an office in the Law Building in Baltimore. This was a modern, multistory building full of offices for lawyers, brokers, architects and other professionals. Simpson had an office on the fourth floor, no. 415, which he shared with a man named Wilson and Joseph R. Kemp. The office was only 380 square feet but they divided it into three tiny sections. Duvall would eventually take over Wilson's space.

Although they had a very respectable address, these men seem to have bordered on the edge of respectability. Duvall was 52 years old and had somehow, late in life, transformed himself from a clothing salesman into a lawyer and real estate broker. Simpson was a 26-year-old lawyer who seemed to have a minor practice. He was only involved in very small cases and had not spent much time in court.

The most interesting of the three was Major Joseph R. Kemp, who was 62 at the time. Born in Pennsylvania, Kemp enlisted as a sergeant in an infantry regiment during the Civil War and eventually mustered out as a major in the heavy artillery. For most of his life, he was a brickmaker living in Ohio. By 1898, he was living in Baltimore and was on the way to transforming himself into a stock broker. Kemp reported he was a broker for Douglas, Lacey and Co., which dealt in mining stocks. He later went into great detail to explain that Douglas, Lacey and Co. were not regular stock brokers but only dealt with their own stock. They formed mining companies, sold stock and bought property all on their own. He claimed this was to insure that no one lost any money. They were headquartered in New York and had 40 offices across the United States and Canada. Douglas, Lacey and Co. advertised heavily and offered large profits. They claimed to have numerous mining and oil drilling properties. In fact, this operation was little more than a pyramid scheme that bilked millions of dollars from small investors, some 20,000 of whom gave them their entire life savings. They were guaranteed not to lose money yet they inevitably did:

> The best bait in this particular operation was a "trust fund" established for the benefit of stockholders. The proceeds of the better-paying mines were to be applied to pay dividends for those which were less successful. In this way, the various directors of the many Douglas-Lacey Companies explained, it was impossible for the investors to lose. But they did lose. The reorganization, intended to save some of the better properties, wiped out more than seventy per cent of the small stockholders—widows, schoolteachers, stenographers, washwomen, scrubwomen....[18]

Tumblety was introduced into this interesting group of people in 1898 by his friend. Simpson claimed that Tumblety hired him as his lawyer but what he really did was type and edit yet another version of Tumblety's biography, this time entitled "Reminiscences of a Famous Physician." He claimed to have performed "general services" in the preparation of the book from September 1898 to September 1900. Beginning in 1898 and continuing for the entire time, when he was in town, Tumblety was in the habit of dropping in on Simpson, giving him written sections of the book and having him type them up. That he was constantly available to do this suggests that Simpson's law duties were slight.[19]

All three of the men would claim that Tumblety's appearance was that of a threadbare pauper and none of them thought he had any money. Despite that opinion, Simpson kept typing things up without getting paid, Duvall tried to get Simpson to sell Tumblety some of his real estate and Kemp tried to get him to sell the doctor some stock. None of them objected to Tumblety dropping by and spending time at the office. They thought him highly educated and an interesting storyteller. Yet none claimed to have liked him much. All of this was reported in depositions after Tumblety died and a considerable amount of money was at stake.

During this time, Tumblety wrote a letter which seems surprising in its pro–British tone. As was his habit, he was wintering in Hot Springs when he read in the *New York Herald* that a number of British Peers were volunteering to serve in the Transvaal War in South Africa. On December 27, 1899, Tumblety wrote to Viscount Galway, one of those mentioned in the article, expressing his support and admiration. It is very likely that Tumblety did not care about the war or the British. The only thing remarkable about this letter is that it was preserved and provides the other side of a correspondence which Tumblety was fond of publishing. He would send out batches of complimentary letters to notable persons and, if they sent back a cordial response, he could claim them as his personal friend. Since he was preparing his new manuscript, getting additional letters was an essential part of the process.[20]

The manuscript was finished in late 1900 and Tumblety went looking for a printer in Baltimore. Daniel O'Donovan, owner of the United States Engraving Company, recalled his first meeting with Tumblety:

> I think he had been watching our place for a couple of days from the outside, and I thought he was a beggar, and wanted to hold me up. He came in and wanted to buy two or three little things, I don't know what they were, odds and ends of stationary, and he took a lot of my time, and I bothered with him because he appeared to be poor and unfortunate; I thought I was patronizing him, and as subsequent events proved he thought he was patronizing me.[21]

Tumblety presented the manuscript to O'Donovan and told him he wanted to get 1,000 copies printed. He expected to have it set in type, edit the proofs, have corrections made, re-edit it and finally have it printed. However, he did not make this clear to O'Donovan, who assumed that the job was to set the type and print it. He was not interested in doing the job so he introduced Tumblety to Charles T. Kaiss, a typesetter who took on the job as his own project. Tumblety ordered 1,000 copies and asked that they be bound. The book was 92 pages and Tumblety put down a $40 deposit on a total bill of $85. He was told that it would take eight to ten days but it was not completed for a month. The books were ready for delivery on October 21. The doctor must have been very surprised to find that no editorial work had been done and apparently the result was horrible.

Incensed at the poor quality of the book, Tumblety refused to pay the remaining $45 of the bill. Not only would he not pay the bill but he hired Robert H. Simpson to sue for the return of the deposit. Tumblety, who said he was not feeling well, left Baltimore for Hot Springs, leaving the case in Simpson's hands. Either late in 1900 or early in 1901, the case was heard before the Magistrate's Court in Baltimore and Simpson secured a default judgment in favor of Tumblety when the other party did not show up. That should have been the end of it, but the attorney for the United States Engraving Company, instead of appealing the case, made an agreement with Simpson to reopen the case in the Magistrate's Court. It is not certain why Simpson, who had already won the case, agreed to let it be reopened. Perhaps it was his inexperience or perhaps he thought he could get the printing company to redo the book. Tumblety was not happy with this decision and it brought him back to Baltimore in the fall of 1901.

By this time, Tumblety's health and memory were failing quickly. He knew his lawyer was in the Law Building but could not remember his name or where his office was located. Only the year before, he was reported to have been to that office as many as three or four times a week and Simpson must have been in touch with Tumblety for him to know about the new case. Tumblety asked one of the elevator operators to help him find an attorney that "had light hair and was a young man." The boy brought him to the office of Frank Widner, Jr., who apparently fit the description. Tumblety described the man he was looking for to Widner but the attorney could not help him and the doctor went in search of his attorney.[22]

Widner must have made an impression on Tumblety for, ten days later, the doctor came back into his office seeking legal advice. He explained the case to Widner and asked if it was legal for the case to be reopened. Widner replied that the normal course would be for the defendant to appeal the decision. Tumblety sought to hire Widner to represent him but he was reluctant to intrude on the case of another attorney. Eventually they went together to see Simpson, who agreed to accept Widner on the case. According to Widner, the case came to trial and Simpson was out of his depth and, after the payment of his $10 fee, withdrew from the case. In the end, Widner forced the defendant to seek an appeal before the Baltimore City Court and there it languished for a couple of years.

As a result of this case, Tumblety chose Widner for his attorney in Baltimore and began spending time with him. Widner claimed Tumblety would come to his office and propound some point of law, then Widner would look it up and they would discuss it. Perhaps Tumblety was looking for a friend and this was his way of having someone with whom he could talk. This went on, almost daily, while the doctor was in Baltimore.

Tumblety left Baltimore on December 20, 1901, again claiming sickness, and was headed for New Orleans. While he was gone, he kept up a correspondence with Widner. In later depositions, several of these letters were entered as evidence while others were specifically excluded for personal reasons. Widner's replies were always sent to general delivery, where Tumblety would pick them up. The correspondence shows that he continued a long-standing practice of dictating his letters and signing the result. There were three envelopes and two letters entered and only the signatures on the letters and the address on one envelope were in Tumblety's handwriting. Perhaps he had found another young man, like Robert Simpson, to be his secretary.

His letter to Widner from New Orleans states that he was sick with rheumatism but that as soon as he felt better he would come to Baltimore with "all necessary papers," and Widner should have the case continued. The doctor remained in New Orleans from January through March and in April was in Washington. On May 19, he wrote to Widner to apologize for not calling on him yet. He stated that he was recovering from a bad cold and hoped to be in Baltimore soon. Within a week, Tumblety showed up at Widner's office and renewed his former habit of dropping by every day to discuss law. In July, Tumblety announced he was going to Saratoga Springs and was gone from Baltimore until late August. On his return to Baltimore, he was once again a daily visitor to Widner's office. The final time Widner saw the doctor was on October 18, 1902. When Widner had not heard from Tumblety for a month, he wrote a letter in care of Baltimore general delivery on November 19 which was eventually returned as unclaimed. After having been in daily contact with Widner and keeping up a correspondence with him for two years, Tumblety seems to have simply disappeared. So begins the final mystery in a life full of them.

17

Final Act
(1903–1910)

Tumblety left Baltimore in late October 1902 and there is no information on where he went. If he followed his normal course, he headed to Hot Springs for the winter. His health was deteriorating and he may have sought advice at St. Joseph's Infirmary, run by the Sisters of Mercy. Tumblety had been a financial supporter of that institution and they probably knew him well. The infirmary was not set up to handle the kind of heart disease afflicting Tumblety and they may have suggested that he go to St. John's Hospital, in St. Louis, also run by the Sisters of Mercy.[1]

Later reports state that he checked into the hospital on April 26, 1903, under the name of Frank Townsend, the name he assumed when fleeing from England in 1888. While Townsend was the name on the register, the Sisters knew him by his real name. He told them he wanted to conceal his identity. Tumblety knew the seriousness of his condition and he told the Sisters that he chose the hospital because it was a good place to die. It has never been explained why, knowing he was soon to die, he chose to go where no one knew him or why he wanted to hide his identity. Perhaps as his mind deteriorated, a certain amount of paranoia began to trouble him. A simpler explanation is that he knew the trouble his relatives would cause over his estate and just wanted a quiet death.[2]

The hospital where Tumblety engaged his room was not the large, modern facility on Euclid Avenue as has been reported. That facility was not constructed until 1910. At the time Tumblety was there, St. John's Hospital was in part of an old school building at the corner of Morgan and Twenty-Second Streets. The building was L-shaped and five stories high and also housed St. John's Infirmary, an outpatient clinic, and possibly the parochial school. In the 1900 census, St. John's had 29 male patients, 10 female patients, 5 female nurses, 7 female assistants and 6 male assistants. St. Joseph's Convent, next door, was home to 41 nuns, many of whom probably worked in the hospital. While patients of all ages were listed, the majority were elderly and may have been there for long-term care.[3]

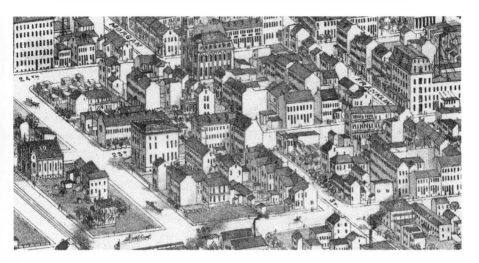

St. John's Infirmary and Hospital (at center, with faint "20"), where Tumblety died. This was a converted school building and Tumblety died in one of the former classrooms. ("Pictorial St. Louis, the great metropolis of the Mississippi valley; a topographical survey drawn in perspective A.D. 1875," Compton & Co., 1876, Library of Congress, Geography and Map Division.)

The doctor who treated Tumblety at the hospital was Dr. Francis A. Temm, who lived nearby on Morgan Street and may have been associated with the hospital. At the time, he was 36 years old, had a wife and three children and appears to have been a general practitioner. Temm claimed to have made 66 visits to Tumblety in the hospital. The number of days from the time Tumblety checked in until his death was 33 so Dr. Temm saw him twice a day, perhaps during his normal rounds. It is likely that Tumblety already knew what was wrong with him but Dr. Temm would have confirmed the diagnosis and treated him according to the standards of the day. Dr. Temm reports making multiple physical and urinal examinations of the patient.[4]

Tumblety was diagnosed as having "valvular disease of the heart," which, like most diagnoses at the time, covered a wide range of possible conditions. Sometimes referred to as rheumatism of the heart, it involved shortness of breath, palpitations of the heart and often severe but intermittent pain in the region of the heart. Frequently, the pain was also felt in the limbs and other parts of the body. After his death, the Sisters referred to his illness as "long and painful." The condition affects other organs in the body which depend on the heart, particularly the kidneys.

One way that doctors charted the progress of the disease was to look at changes in the urine because of the disease's effect on the kidneys. Medical textbooks of the time report that in patients with valvular disease, there was less urine, it was of a higher specific gravity and it contained high levels of

albumin and sugar. Two tests were recommended to gauge the amount of albumin in the urine, the nitric acid test and the heat test. In the first, nitric acid is
added to a test tube of urine and the effect observed. The heat test involves
adding acetic acid to a test tube of urine and boiling the upper part of it. This
could only be achieved by holding the test tube over an intense heat source,
like a gas burner.[5]

After his death, the Sisters of Mercy claimed damages for 'furniture, rugs,
carpets and bed clothes" damaged by fire and the dropping of acids and medicines. Some have suggested that these were the results of some kind of mad
experiments Tumblety was conducting. However, they were more likely the
result of the carelessness of the doctor attending Tumblety and the above mentioned tests for his disease.

By mid May, Tumblety was thinking about making a will to dispose of
his estate. By his own estimation, he had about $140,000, almost all of which
was cash held by the New York firm of Henry Clews & Company. To draw up
the will, Tumblety engaged Thomas D. Cannon, a lawyer with an office in the
Union Trust Building. According to Cannon's record, the first consultation
was held in Tumblety's room at the hospital on May 16 where they discussed
bequests of $65,000 to various people. A will was drawn up that specified
these bequests. That afternoon, they discussed what to do with the remaining
$75,000 and about who should be the executor of the will. This must have been
a difficult decision for Tumblety because they continued to talk about it on
May 18, 19 and twice on May 20. On that day, Cannon wrote a new will that
included the bequests made in the May 16 document, disposed of the rest of
the estate and named the Missouri Trust Company as executor. Despite these
arrangements, the will was still not complete. All of these consultations were
done at St. John's Hospital.[6]

On Sunday, May 24, Dr. Tumblety, having been confined for almost a
month, decided he needed to get out for awhile. Reportedly, he got help getting dressed and then refused to have anyone accompany him while he went
out for a walk. He was gone for awhile and, returning to the hospital, was said
to be tired and to have sat down on the steps to rest. The paper later said he
passed out, fell forward and sustained injuries to his face. Was he simply bored
by being in the hospital? Why did he not allow the attendants to accompany
him? It may be that he wanted to be alone because he went looking for a partner. The report may be true that he passed out on the steps but it is also possible that his attempt at finding a partner went terribly wrong. Whatever the
case, he would not recover from this incident.

Tumblety's injuries were apparently beyond Dr. Temm's experience and
he brought in Dr. A. V. L. Brokaw, whose office was on Taylor Avenue, at the
corner of Washington Avenue, almost 20 blocks away. Dr. Brokaw's bill reveals
that he treated Tumblety for a broken nose and contusions on the face, injuries
consistent with a fall forward or with being hit on the face. Specifically, he

performed a reduction of a fracture of the nose which involved resetting the bones and packing the nasal cavities. He consulted with Dr. Temm at the hospital every day from the twenty-fourth to the twenty-eighth of May.[7]

With his condition worsening, the doctors knew the end was near. Thomas Cannon, who had not seen Tumblety since May 26, brought the will and Tumblety signed it. His witnesses were Dr. Brokaw and lawyer Cannon. Dr. Tumblety died on May 28, 1903, at St. John's Hospital at the age of 73. Newspaper articles stated that there were no relatives nor friends at the bedside and that appears to be the way Tumblety wanted it. There is no indication of any last words nor if his death was peaceful. It would seem a quiet end for such a flamboyant life, but his story was not quite over yet.

Upon the doctor's death, Thomas Cannon began organizing the funeral arrangements and the estate. He sent telegrams to Mary Fitzsimmons and Jane Moore in Rochester, and Henry Clews & Co. in New York. Cullinane Brothers, an undertaker on Dickson Street, were called to take care of the body. It was embalmed, put in a casket and readied for shipment to Rochester.

Cannon filed an application for probate with the court in St. Louis on May 29, presenting Tumblety's will, which had a date of May 16th. This was the document witnessed by Brokaw on the twenty-sixth and it listed legacies to one of Tumblety's sisters, three nieces, and Mark Blackburn and charitable donations to Cardinal Gibbons and Cardinal Hughes of the Catholic Church. These bequests added up to $65,000 but the rest of the estate was not listed. Because there was so much of the estate unaccounted for in the will, the public administrator for St. Louis, Garrard Strode, submitted his own application for probate. In Missouri, the office of public administrator was an elected position which had a four-year term. It was designed to take care of the estates of those people who died intestate, non-residents who died in St. Louis, or people whose heirs were incapable of being executors. It was Strode's responsibility to see that the estate was properly handled and distributed. Cannon was not happy with this turn of events and began one of many legal challenges to Strode's administration.[8]

One of Strode's first responsibilities was to arrange an inventory of Tumblety's possessions. To do so, he had to get three "disinterested householders" to view the goods and provide a monetary value for them. There was no set procedure for selecting these men nor any information on their knowledge of what they were valuing. Arthur Marshall was a law clerk and had been a collector in the assessor's office. Strode had also been in that office and may have known him. A second man, Samuel H. Batavia, seems to have left no record of himself. These two names were filled out on the form before the inventory and they may have accompanied Strode to the hospital. The final man, A. B. Walker, was a retired school janitor and may have been associated with the hospital. While he signed the form, his name is not listed in other parts. None of these men can be shown to have any experience in valuing jewelry nor is there any indication how they came to the assigned values. The personal possessions that these men viewed were few:

One cluster ring of 17 diamond stones	$75.00
One five stone diamond ring	$60.00
Two imitation set rings	$3.00
One old gold watch	$10.00

There are several interesting things about this inventory. There is no mention of Tumblety's clothes or any trunks, bags or other luggage he had with him. Nor is there any indication that Tumblety had personal possessions in any other place. The value of the jewelry is considerably less than reported at other times but there is no way to know if those were inflated values or if these are deflated. When arrested in Washington, 13 years before this, Tumblety had on two diamond rings, each valued at $2,500, as well as a smaller ring worth $200. In certain circles, a great deal has been made of the two imitation set rings which have been suggested as "trophies" taken from one of the Ripper victims. As Tumblety was known to wear many rings and the inventory seems to undervalue these, it is more likely that they were part of his own adornment. The personal possessions were to be auctioned off and this might have answered the question about their value. However, the probate record contains no reference to this and what happened to them remains a mystery.[9]

Tumblety's body was shipped to Rochester in care of his nephew Michael Fitzsimmons and was received by O'Reilly & Sons for burial. He was buried in the Holy Sepulchre Cemetery during the first week of June. There are no details of the funeral but it was probably attended by many of the doctor's relatives. An important topic of conversation both before and after the funeral was likely to have been the estate.

At the time of his death, Tumblety only had one living sibling, his sister Jane Hayes. He left her a bequest of $10,000. He also left similar bequests to three of his nieces. While his other nine brothers and sisters were deceased, they left behind a large number of children, all of whom felt entitled to a part of the estate. The 17 heirs not mentioned in the will determined to have the St. Louis will overturned.

If Strode thought this would be a simple probate, it was not long before he was aware that this was not to be. Within a very short time he would face legal challenges from five separate directions. Almost immediately, T. D. Cannon, the lawyer who drew up Tumblety's St. Louis will, challenged Strode's right to assume control of the estate. In the same way, those relatives who were left bequests in the will attempted to get the will probated in Rochester. The group of relatives not mentioned in the will sued to have the whole thing overturned. Cardinals Gibbons and Hughes, who were each bequeathed $10,000 in the St. Louis will, hired Cannon to defend their interests. Finally, much to everyone's surprise, a second will, written in Baltimore in 1901, surfaced and named Major Joseph Kemp as the executor.[10]

For all the litigants, in one way or another, the issues revolved around two basic questions, where was Tumblety's legal residence at the time of his death and which of the wills, if either, was valid. Answers to these questions would determine who the executor should be and greatly affect the final distribution of the estate. The bankers, Henry Clews and Company, refused to release the money they held until there was some legal settlement of these issues.

Given Tumblety's wandering nature, determining a legal residence would prove to be a difficult task. Mary Fitzsimmons, a niece and one of the legatees, testified that Tumblety had made her home in Rochester his base of operations for the past 20 years while he traveled all over the world. Except for her testimony, there is no indication that Tumblety spent any significant time in Rochester during this period. It should be pointed out that her testimony was in support of having the will probated in Rochester, which his residence would aid greatly. On the contrary, we have seen that he had various residences in New York and that he spent most of the period from 1899 to 1902 living in Baltimore. Major Kemp made this the central issue of his challenge to the St. Louis will and there is much testimony about Tumblety's time in Baltimore. Strode maintained that as Tumblety was in St. Louis when his will was written, the probate of the estate should be there.

Within a few months, the New York courts recognized the priority of the St. Louis court and Henry Clews & Co. transferred Tumblety's money to a St. Louis bank in Strode's name as administrator. The estate paid over $7000 in transfer tax to the State of New York for moving the money. Since Strode seemed to have firm control of the probate, most of the parties shifted their concern to St. Louis and the legal battle would be fought there. However, Kemp was not ready to give up his fight and on August 18, 1903, he filed Tumblety's Baltimore will in the Maryland court. The other parties mounted a legal challenge to having this will entered into probate but late in June 1904, the Maryland court admitted this will, setting up competing administrations. Since Strode actually had the money, this was a minor inconvenience. Kemp would continue to fight for the administration until April 14, 1908, when the St. Louis court denied his final appeal and authorized the estate distribution.

The other issue to be decided was the validity and precedence of the wills. On the surface, neither looks particularly valid. Both seem, at best, to be somewhat shady and the people writing them had motives other than those Tumblety may have wished. It is likely that Strode recognized this from the beginning, which was why he took over the estate. Each of these wills has significant things to say about Tumblety and the people with whom he associated.

The general history of the St. Louis will has already been described. According to Cannon's testimony, he drew up the initial will on May 16 and it included bequests totaling $65,000. Over the next few days he discussed with Tumblety the disposition of the rest of the estate and who should be named executor. On May 20, he claimed to have drawn up a will that outlined these questions. After Tumblety's final accident, Cannon came to see him and one might think that he would have gotten Tumblety to approve the will dated May 20. What Cannon finally submitted for probate was the original will dated May 16 which was not signed by Tumblety until May 26, after his accident. Was this incompetence on Cannon's part or was something else going on? The court recognized the May 16 will as a valid expression of Tumblety's wishes but disallowed Cannon's other arrangements and gave the estate to Strode to administer. Although nothing is stated in the records, we are left with the impression that the court viewed Cannon's arrangements as unsatisfactory.

If the origins of the St. Louis will were shady, those of the Baltimore will were obscure. It was said to have been written for Tumblety by his then lawyer, Robert Simpson, and was witnessed by Simpson, his brother Charles and William Duvall, who all shared an office. The will was described as very simple. It bequeathed $1,000 to Cardinal Gibbons, $1,000 to the Home for Fallen Women of Baltimore City, and all of the doctor's jewelry to Major Kemp. The final provision stated that the residue of the estate was to be divided among Tumblety's blood relations. The determination of who was a relative and how the money was to be distributed was left up to the executor, Major Kemp. It was reported that after the will was completed, Tumblety gave it to Kemp, who kept it in his safe until he heard of the doctor's death.[11]

As part of the ongoing legal proceedings, depositions were recorded in Simpson's office regarding the will. The document was dated October 3, 1901, and Simpson had repeatedly told people both before and after Tumblety died that the will had been drawn up as a joke. They all believed that Tumblety did not have the property to fulfill the terms. The dating of the will is interesting because of what we know of Tumblety's travels. He left Baltimore in October 1900 and did not return until October 1, 1901. During his absence, Simpson had thoroughly botched the case against the United States Engraving Company. Within days of returning to Baltimore, Tumblety hired a new lawyer, Frank Widner, Jr. Is it likely that he would ask Simpson to draw up a will while looking for a new lawyer?

The lack of a signature on the will was a major argument against its being accepted. In his deposition, Major Kemp went to great lengths to suggest that Tumblety often did not sign his name, did not know how to write and was suffering from a nervous disorder that caused his hand to shake. The plaintiffs, on the other hand, deposed Baltimore witnesses who were familiar with Tumblety's writing and introduced several letters and envelopes into evidence to demonstrate his literacy. Kemp also deposed that Tumblety had talked to him about having a will made some time in June, July or August 1901. Since Tumblety was not back in Baltimore until October of that year, it makes the rest of Kemp's deposition suspicious.[12]

That Simpson, who drew up the will, thought of it as a joke might help to explain one of the bequests. It has been suggested that the inclusion of a donation to the "Home for Fallen Women" was an indication of Tumblety's guilty conscience over having killed the prostitutes in London. More likely, Simpson and Kemp were making a joke based on Tumblety's alleged connection to the case. Simpson was young and naive enough to believe Tumblety was a pauper but it is likely that Kemp knew exactly how much money he had. If the will were simply a joke to Kemp, why would he keep it in his safe after not seeing Tumblety for almost a year? The St. Louis court, after reviewing the depositions, refused to transfer the estate to Kemp or to allow co-administrations.

A more serious challenge to the St. Louis will was launched by those of Tumblety's relatives not mentioned in the will. Aside from the named legacies, totaling $65,000, there was no indication what should be done with the bulk of the estate. It may be that those of Tumblety's relatives named in the will believed they could split the rest of the money. However, there were at least 26 other relatives who were afraid they would get nothing. Barely a month after Tumblety's funeral, they had hired a lawyer and were soliciting power of attorney documents from relatives in the United States, England and Ireland. Their only real hope was to challenge the validity of the St. Louis will and, as we have already seen, its status was shaky at best. Their challenge was filed first in the New York courts and then in St. Louis.[13]

As questionable as the St. Louis will might be, the court decided, on June 22, 1905, that it represented Tumblety's final wishes and upheld its validity. The plaintiffs, those relatives not mentioned in the will, immediately filed an appeal and the case drew on for another two years. As many of the people involved in this fight were elderly and many were dying during the time it took to get through the courts, the two sides eventually agreed to a compromise.

A detailed agreement was drawn up on September 27, 1907, and finally agreed to by all parties in December. The plaintiffs agreed to drop their challenge to the will and the legatees agreed to certain points. First, that the named legatees were to get their money without any interest and that the inheritance taxes were to be paid out of their money. The parties agreed that Tumblety died intestate as to the rest of his estate. In return for dropping their claim to the rest of the estate, the five relatives named in the will were given an additional $8,000. Finally, the estate was to pay all inheritance taxes before the rest of the money was distributed. After all of that, the court found that there was still a little more than $47,000 to be distributed. This sum was distributed to the 25 relatives on a share basis determined by how closely they were related to Tumblety. Shares ranged from 1/6 to 1/180 of the total. The court approved the plan for the final distribution on April 15, 1908. Almost five years after Tumblety died, the courts finally closed the books on what had been called a "friendly money fight." Perhaps this explains why the doctor chose to die alone and away from anyone he knew.[14]

In a strange way, Francis Tumblety achieved the archetypical American dream. He came to America as a poor unknown and died a wealthy, famous individual. During the course of his life he had several exciting adventures and narrow escapes. If, in his medical practice, he preyed upon a gullible public, in his private life he was equally preyed upon. Despite a huge amount of advertising, numerous self-promoting biographies, and the large number of press accounts, it is still difficult to know the man inside. Like many of his contemporaries, we are left reading ourselves into the mirror of Dr. Tumblety.

Chapter Notes

Introduction

1. "Ah There! Tumblety," *Bucks County Gazette* (Bristol, PA), December 13, 1888.

2. The first modern interest in Tumblety was the publication of the books by Evans and Gainey in the 1990s. Evans and Gainey, *The Lodger*, 1995, and Evans and Gainey, *First American Serial Killer*, 1998. There is a very extensive literature on the Whitechapel murders. For anyone interested in learning more about the case, the website www.casebook.org is a great place to start. It has reviews of all the books published on the case since the actual events took place and an extensive set of newspaper transcripts.

3. Dunham's story about Tumblety was first published in the *New York World* on December 1, 1888. A full length biography of Dunham's amazing life has recently been published; see Carman Cumming, *Devil's Game: The Civil War Intrigues of Charles A. Dunham*, 2004.

4. Rothstein, *American Physicians in the Nineteenth Century*, 1992.

Chapter 1

1. Only one direct statement by Tumblety exists on his age and place of birth. In his 1872 Memorial to the Joint Claims Commission, he states that he was born in 1831 in the city of Dublin. As there was no reason for him to lie (and many to tell the truth) in this context, we may accept it at face value. Other evidence exists that supports this as well. There are six instances where he or his immediate family reported his age. These include an 1847 passenger list, several census reports, a pass issued during the Civil War and his tombstone. Based on these benchmarks, his year of birth varies between 1825 and 1835. However, two of the earliest and the final one all indicate a date of c. 1830–1831.

Martin McGarry reported that Tumblety told him, in 1882, that he had been born near Dublin. *New York World*, December 5, 1888.

2. When looking at Dr. Tumblety and his family, one is immediately struck by the variety of spellings evident in the records. It seems like no two people could spell the name the same. Such variations as Tumathy, Tumilty, Tomalty, Tumbleton, Tumuelty, etc. are common. Dr. T consistently referred to himself as Tumblety, and that is how the name will be spelled in this study.

One of Tumblety's sisters stayed in Ireland; two ended up in Liverpool. Other family members ended up in Rochester, New York; Waterloo, New York; and Vallejo, California. Tumblety claimed to have an uncle with the same name in Liverpool but no record of this person has been found. Tumblety, *A Few Passages*, 1866, p. 51.

The 1844 Rochester city directory lists Lawrence Tumblety as boarding on South Sophia Street at the corner of Clarissa. South Sophia Street was close to the Erie Canal and this was an early focus of Irish settlement in Rochester. McKelvey, "The Irish in Rochester," 1957, p. 3.

3. The passenger list for the *Ashburton*, which arrived in New York on June 21, 1847, lists the family as Tumbleton (microfilm M237, roll 267). On the list, there are four Tumbletons. Margaret Tumbleton is listed as a 52-year-old female. She was accompanied by James, who is listed as a 24-year-old male, Ann, a 22-year-old female, and Francis, a 17-year-old female. There are several problems with identifying those on this list with the family in Rochester in 1850. Francis at 17 would be the correct age for our subject but is listed as a female. Several other people with men's names are listed as female and it is likely that the clerk was not too careful. Ann is the right age and sex but her mother's age is off by

seven years. The biggest problem is James
Tumbleton. He should be closer to 70 than 24
years old. Another researcher, Joe Chetcuti,
pointed out to me that this is Tumblety's
cousin. How and when James Tumblety, the
father of our subject, came to America is unknown.

Although James Tumblety, the father, was
listed in the 1848/49 city directory, he is not
further recorded. His tombstone lists his death
as May 7, 1851, but he does not show up in the
1850 census or the 1850/51 Rochester city directory.

4. McKelvey, "Irish in Rochester," 1957,
p. 5; McKelvey, *Rochester on the Genesee*,
1993, p. 43.

5. Haywood's description was presented
in an article published in the *Rochester Democrat and Republican* on December 3, 1888.
Streeter's reminiscences of Tumblety were
similarly published in the *Rochester Democrat
and Republican* on the same day.

There has been considerable modern interest in Anthony Comstock because of his stands
against abortion and contraception. Several recent biographies are readily available: Bates,
Weeder in the Garden of the Lord, 1995; Beisel,
Imperiled Innocents, 1997.

6. The subject of nineteenth-century medicine and medical education is well detailed in
Rothstein, *American Physicians in the Nineteenth Century*, 1992. For a discussion of what
Rothstein sees as "medical sects" see pp.
21–24. His description of "heroic therapy" is
on pp. 45–52.

7. Young, *American Health Quackery*,
1992, pp. 57–58; Young, *Toadstool Millionaires*, 1961, p. 70.

8. Atwater, "Medical Profession," 1973.

9. Hoolihan, *Atwater Collection*, vol. 2,
2004, pp. 239–240; Hoolihan, personal communication, 2002.

10. The quote is from Dr. Reynolds' ad in
the 1857 Rochester city directory, p. 15. The
1865 ad for Dr. Lispenard's Hospital is much
more graphic and open than previous expressions. It specifically advertises contraception
and has a lightly veiled claim that some of their
pills will cause a miscarriage. In this ad, Dr. W.
C. Lispenard, consulting physician and surgeon, is described as "one of the most scientific and successful physicians and surgeons
in the United States," not bad for someone who
did not exist. Dr. Reynolds, described as the
proprietor, claims to have cured over 100,000
cases in his 40-year career. As Dr. Reynolds
was only 38 years old, one might question his
veracity. *Rochester Daily Union and Advertiser*, Rochester (NY), April 15, 1865.

11. Hoolihan, *Atwater Collection*, vol. 2,
2004, pp. 239–240.

12. Tumblety's association with Dr. Reynolds and the Lispenard Hospital is based on a
number of anecdotal recollections. Edward
Haywood reported that Tumblety worked at a
drug store kept by Dr. Lispenard. *Rochester
Democrat and Republican*, December 3, 1888.
An earlier article also reported his association
with Dr. Reynolds, the proprietor of Lispenard's Hospital. *Rochester Daily Union and
Advertiser*, April 5, 1881. As early as 1865, his
association with Lispenard's was mentioned in
the press. *Brooklyn Daily Eagle*, May 10, 1865.

13. A history of the Reynolds Arcade is
presented in Barnes and Barnes, "Books to
Multimedia," 1974, pp. 1–40. There is a contemporary illustration of the interior of the Arcade presented in Rosenberg-Naparsteck, "A
Growing Agitation," 1984, p. 15.

14. The itinerary for Lyons' medical excur-
sions was published in the *Rochester Union
and Advertiser* on March 17, 1858.

15. Young, *Toadstool Millionaires*, 1961, p.
39 discusses the impact of these two trends on
medicine in the nineteenth century. I have seen
ads for Dr. Lyons in the *Hornellsville Tribune*
(Hornellsville, NY), September 23, 1858 and
the *Central City Daily Courier* (Syracuse,
NY), January 1, 1859. In Ohio, Dr. Lyons kept
up his traveling ways with stops in nine cities
in Michigan and Ohio, *Elyria Independent Democrat* (Elyria, OH), February 25, 1863.

16. *Elyria Independent Democrat*, February 25, 1863.

17. The recollection of a direct association
between Tumblety and Dr. Lyons was published in the *Rochester Daily Union and Advertiser*, May 9, 1865. There are numerous
similarities between the 1850s ads of Dr. Lyons
and the 1860s ads of Dr. Tumblety that go well
beyond their both being botanic healers. Dr.
Lyons often published the phrase, "The poor
shall be liberally considered," which became a
standard part of Tumblety's ads. Dr. Lyons
used the saying, "A tree is known by its fruits.
So is a good physician by his successful
works." Over the years in Canada and the
United States, Tumblety used this or a variant
of this. Perhaps most importantly, Tumblety
used what he referred to as "Our Motto,"
which figured prominently in his newspaper
ads and was published in his pamphlets. This
was also part of Dr. Lyons' advertisements.

18. *Rochester Daily Union and Advertiser*,
May 9, 1865.

19. Hoolihan, *Atwater Collection*, vol. 2,
2004, pp. 391–392. A copy of Tumblety's
"Guide to the Afflicted" is preserved in the
Toronto Public Library.

20. For the mobility of Rochester doctors
see Atwater, "Medical Profession," 1973, p.
224.

21. A short biography of Mayor Charles J. Hayden is presented in McKelvey, "Rochester Mayors before the Civil War," 1964, pp. 17–18. An almost identical testimonial, but with different names, was published by Dr. Lyons in Syracuse in 1859. *Central City Daily Courier*, Syracuse (NY), January 1, 1859. The first publication of Tumblety's Rochester testimonial appears to be in the *Toronto Globe* on March 9, 1857. It was also published in the *Montreal Pilot* of October 30, 1857.

22. *Rochester Daily Union and Advertiser*, May 9, 1865.

23. Edward Hayward claimed to have met Tumblety in Detroit in 1855. *Rochester Democrat and Republican*, December 3, 1888. There is a persistent report that Tumblety was in Ontario as early as 1853. This cannot be true for a number of reasons. The testimonial clearly shows that he did not leave Rochester until 1855. No ads or testimonials were reprinted from that period. Finally, if he were in Ontario at that time, his association with Dr. Lyons, whom he copied in so many ways, could not have happened. In 1888, Fred Ward, a San Francisco newsman, stated that he knew Tumblety in New York City in 1855. There are problems with this dating as well. That story is discussed in the chapter on his 1861 residence in New York City. Another story places Tumblety in Boston in 1855. That story is discussed in the section on his 1860–61 time in Boston. Based on the testimonials, Tumblety's progress was as follows: London, April–May 1856; Hamilton, June–August 1856; and Brantford, August–October 1856.

24. Information on Tumblety's travels and advertisements during this period is based on editorials and testimonials republished in major city newspapers: *Toronto Globe*, January–September 1857; *Montreal Pilot*, September–December 1857.

25. *London Free Press*, May 6, 1857.

Chapter 2

1. On the importance of newspapers see Young, *Toadstool Millionaires*, 1961, p. 39. Tumblety published his first ad in the *Toronto Globe* on November 17, 1856, and continued publishing through September 17, 1857.

2. Advertising rates for the *Toronto Globe* were listed daily on the front page. For Tumblety's ads, all of which were more than ten lines, the first insertion cost 4d per line and each subsequent run cost 1d per line. For example, his ad first published on January 27, 1857, was 22 lines long and likely cost 7s 4d to insert. That ad was repeated 43 times in the next few months. Each repetition cost 1s 10d and the total cost of the ad's run was £4 6s 2d.

The prices for the other items were taken from contemporary advertisements in the *Toronto Globe*.

3. *Toronto Globe*, November 17, 1856.

4. *Toronto Globe*, November 20, 1856. The conflict between "regular" doctors and "alternative" doctors is described in Rothstein, *American Physicians*, 1992, pp. 21–24 and the use of mercury, pp. 49–52. Dr. Lyons also used the phrase "the poor will be liberally treated." In fact, this was a standard come-on in the medicine business. Young, *Toadstool Millionaires*, 1961, p. 67.

5. Thomsonian medicine has been described as democratic and anti-elite. It was the first of the medical sects to arise in opposition to the perceived harshness and arrogance of the regular doctors. It had a deep streak of socialism in its attitudes. The literature on Samuel Thomson and his followers is extensive. Good summaries are available in Rothstein, *American Physicians*, 1992, pp. 128–146 and Vogel, *American Indian Medicine*, 1970, pp. 130–132. Lyons' ad is in the Rochester city directory 1853.

6. *Toronto Globe*, December 13, 1856. St. Lawrence Hall was designed and built by William Thomas, a famous English architect. A good description of the building and its significance can be found in his biography in Brown et al., *Dictionary of Canadian Biography*, vol. 8,1994, p. 875.

7. *Brooklyn Daily Eagle*, May 10, 1865. Like many aspects of Tumblety's career, these details are based on a none too favorable newspaper report well after the event. There is no way to determine the source or reliability of these details. The use of an Indian informant, real or fictional, was a common part of the presentation of an Indian herb doctor. Young, *American Health Quackery*, 1992, p. 54.

8. *Toronto Globe*, January 6, 1857. Testimonial letters were an important part of advertising in the nineteenth century, particularly in the patent medicine business Young, *American Health Quackery*, 1992, p. 27; Young, *Toadstool Millionaires*, 1961, p. 188.

9. *Toronto Globe*, January 6, 1857; *St. Thomas Weekly Dispatch* (St. Thomas, Ont.), March 28, 1861; Chase, *America's Music*, 1992, pp. 150–51.

10. O'Brien testimonial, *Toronto Globe*, February 13, 1857; Reynolds testimonial, *Toronto Globe*, February 14, 1857; Toronto city directory, 1856.

11. Large ad, *Toronto Globe*, March 6, 1857; *Montreal Pilot*, October 2, 1857; McCullough, "'Dr. Tumblety, the Indian Herb Doctor,'" 1993, p. 57.

12. Reynolds' and Lispenard's advertisements in the Rochester city directories all offer

to provide medical advice for a dollar in a post-paid letter.

13. *Toronto Globe*, March 28, 1857; Gevitz, *Other Healers*, 1988, pp. 17–19.

14. *Toronto Globe*, May 6, 1857. Of course, Tumblety was not above paying for favorable notices.

15. Young, *American Health Quackery*, 1992, pp. 57–58.

16. *Toronto Globe*, December 8, 9, and 10, 1856; *New York Herald*, April 15, 1857.

17. The initial report on the incident was in the *Toronto Globe*, December 8, 1856. The hearing was reported in the same paper on December 12.

18. Leggett, Conaway & Co., *History of Wyandot County*, 1884, p. 709. Tumblety's medical enterprise in Toronto became known as the "Medical Institute" as early as April 1858 and it was to this institution that Jones refers. Based on census records, Jones was born in 1835. At the time he came to be Tumblety's student, he was 21 years old.

19. Denison, "Reminiscences of a Police Magistrate," 1920, p. 259.

20. The first of the mail order ads in the *Boston Pilot* was published on June 6, 1857. The ads appeared weekly for the rest of 1857 and through 1858.

Chapter 3

1. McCullough, "'Dr. Tumblety, the Indian Herb Doctor,'" 1993, pp. 49–66.

2. *Montreal Pilot*, September 16, 1857.

3. *Montreal Pilot*, October 2, 1857; McCullough, "'Dr. Tumblety, the Indian Herb Doctor,'" 1993, p. 57.

4. *Montreal Pilot*, September 23, 1857. There is no explanation for why Tumblety asked about the girl's religion. Both religions were against abortion. While Tumblety was a Catholic, it seems unlikely that this would stop him from dispensing the drugs. Perhaps Simard was trying to discredit Tumblety further by implying that causing abortions in Protestants was acceptable to him.

5. The meeting in Coursol's office is described in the *Montreal Pilot*, September 30, 1857.

6. Brown et al., *Dictionary of Canadian Biography (DCB)*, vol. 11, 1881–1890, pp. 206–207.

7. Details on the meeting between Tumblety, Simard and Dumas were published in the *Montreal Pilot* on September 23, September 25, and September 30.

8. For a short biography of Devlin, see *DCB*, vol. 10, 1871–1880, pp. 229–230; for Drummond, see *DCB*, vol. 11, 1881–1890, pp. 281–283; McCullough, "'Dr. Tumblety, the In-

dian Herb Doctor,'" 1993, p. 59–60 attempts to demonstrate this is a political case.

9. *Montreal Pilot*, September 30, 1857.

10. The testimony of John Birks was published in the *Montreal Pilot* on September 25, 1857. The testimony of Copeland, the druggist who made Tumblety's pills, was published in the *Montreal Pilot* on September 26, 1857.

11. Sources for the use of various medicinal herbs include Ellingwood, *American Materia Medica*, 1919 and Felter and Lloyd, *King's American Dispensatory*, 1898.

12. Refusal of bail for Tumblety, *Montreal Pilot*, September 26, 1857; Denial of *habeas corpus* writ, *Montreal Pilot*, September 28, 1857; Devlin's argument before Judge Gray, *Montreal Pilot*, September 30, 1857.

13. Editorial, *Montreal Pilot*, October 2, 1857. Other editorials are mentioned in McCullough, "'Dr. Tumblety, the Indian Herb Doctor,'" 1993, p. 57.

14. Published in the *Montreal Pilot*, October 13, 1857.

15. *Montreal Pilot*, October 21, 1857.

16. *Montreal Pilot*, October 10, 1857.

17. Dr. Larue's report was published in two issues of the French newspaper *Le Courier du Canada* on November 4 and 6, 1857. I consulted a translation of these reports shown in the Press Reports section on the Casebook website, www.casebook.org.

18. *Montreal Pilot*, October 24, 1857; *Toronto Globe*, October 27, 1857.

19. The address and testimonials were first published in the *Montreal Pilot* on October 30, 1857.

20. *Montreal Pilot*, October 30, 1857; *Montreal Pilot*, December 14, 1857; *Montreal Pilot*, February 6, 1858. Lyman, Brothers & Co. ad is in the 1856 *Toronto* city directory.

21. Tumblety's claim to a medical degree was published in *La Minerve*, September 29, 1857, and reported in McCullough, "'Dr. Tumblety, the Indian Herb Doctor,'" 1993, p. 59.

22. *Devlin v. Tumblety* (1858) 2 L. C. J. 182 (SC).

23. *Montreal Pilot*, November 19, 1857.

24. *Montreal Pilot*, December 2, 1857.

25. The early report of such rumors was in the *Montreal Commercial Advertiser*, December 3, 1857, as reported in Tumblety, *Narrative*, 1872, p. 7. The presentation of the petition was reported in the *Montreal Gazette*, December 5, 1857, as cited in McCullough, "'Dr. Tumblety, the Indian Herb Doctor,'" 1993, p. 50. Tumblety's decline of the nomination was printed in the *Montreal Commercial Advertiser*, December 7, 1857, as reprinted in Tumblety, *Narrative*, 1872, p. 7.

26. *Montreal Pilot*, December 21, 1857.

27. The parody of Tumblety is reported in

the *Boston Globe*, November 27, 1888; the "Carrier's Address" was published in the *Montreal Pilot*, January 4, 1858.

Chapter 4

1. *Toronto Globe*, December 19, 1857.
2. *Toronto Globe*, December 24, 1857.
3. *Toronto Globe*, January 15, 1858.
4. *Toronto Globe*, January 22, 1858; *Toronto Globe*, February 6, 1858; *Toronto Globe*, March 6, 1858;
5. *Rochester Daily Union and Advertiser*, March 11, 1858.
6. *Rochester Democrat and Republican*, December 3, 1888.
7. *Toronto Globe*, March 24, 1858; *Toronto Globe*, April 20, 1858.
8. *St. Thomas Weekly Dispatch*, March 28, 1861; *Rochester Daily Union and Advertiser*, May 9, 1865.
9. A full description of the Eclectic Medical College of Pennsylvania and Dr. Buchanan is presented in Abrahams, *Extinct Medical Schools*, 1966. A later reference to Tumblety as a "Buchanan graduate" indicated his purchase of a fake diploma. Englehard & Co., *Medical Standard*, December 1888, 4(6):191.
10. *Toronto Globe*, June 8, 1858.
11. *Toronto Globe*, June 24, 1858.
12. *Perth Courier*, October 16, 1858–February 18, 1859; *Markham Economist*, November 11, 1858–July 14, 1859.
13. *Buffalo Morning Express*, January 12, 1859.
14. The line about a good tree was also used by Dr. Lyons in his advertisements. *Elyria Independent Democrat*, February 25, 1863.
15. *Buffalo Morning Express*, January 12, 1859; *Buffalo Morning Express*, January 15, 1859; the Montreal circular was printed in the *Montreal Pilot*, December 21, 1857.
16. *Buffalo Morning Express*, January 14, 1859.
17. *Buffalo Morning Express*, February 4, 1859; *Buffalo Morning Express*, February 5, 1859; *Buffalo Morning Express*, February 8, 1859; *Buffalo Morning Express*, February 15, 1859.
18. *Brooklyn Daily Eagle*, May 10, 1865.
19. *Buffalo Morning Express*, February 23, 1859.

Chapter 5

1. *Boston Pilot*, September 17, 1859–January 17, 1860; *Boston Evening Transcript*, October 18, 1859–January 30, 1860.
2. While there is no definite reference, there are indications that this poem was around in the 1840s. The same poem was widely used

by herbalists. Dr. Lyons, Tumblety's preceptor, used it into the 1870s. *Iowa State Reporter*, February 5, 1873. Dr. A. C. Jackson, the "Celebrated Indian Botanic Doctor," published it in the *Hornellsville Tribune*, March 18, 1858.
3. The consumption ad first appeared in the *Boston Evening Transcript*, September 30, 1859.
4. O'Connor, *Fitzpatrick's Boston*, 1984, p. 33; Newcomb, *Reminiscences of an Astronomer*, 2007, p. 220.
5. A good description of the development of the Old Tremont and other luxury hotels is Sandoval-Strausz, *Hotel: An American History*, 2007.
6. The purchase of the Montgomery House by the Massachusetts Horticultural Society and the society's intention to build Horticultural Hall on the site is reported in its publication in September 1863. Hovey, ed., *Magazine of Horticulture, Botany and All Useful Discoveries*, p. 361.
7. *Chicago Tribune*, November 22, 1888.
8. Boston testimonials are listed in Tumblety, *A Few Passages*, 1866. As in most other places, Tumblety's practice in Boston was very successful. The editor of the *Boston Medical and Surgical Journal* reported "...nor did we ever ... witness a more thoroughly uneducated man, more idolized ... by the public than he ... guineas were poured into his lap by parties who paid with grudge the smaller fees demanded in ordinary practice by the regularly-educated physician," 63(9):187.
9. Drake, *Dictionary of American Biography*, 1872 [2006], 255.
10. Wesley and Uzelac, eds., *William Cooper Nell*, 2002, p. 591.
11. New Brunswick had a licensing law for physicians as early as 1816. An interesting discussion of the status and regulation of medicine in early nineteenth-century Canada can be found in Mitchinson, *The Nature of Their Bodies*, 1991.
12. An example of the favorable editorial notice was in the *Morning Freeman*, July 19, 1860, where the editor comments that Tumblety is successful in "alleviating the distresses and bodily sufferings to which mortals are, more or less, subject."
13. The poem is reported to have been published in the *St. John Albion* in 1860. It was reprinted in Tumblety's first biography, *A Few Passages*, 1866, pp. 10–12.
14. A short biography of Kerr is published in the *University of New Brunswick Law Journal*, Marquis, "A Hard Disciple of Blackstone," 1986, pp. 182–187.
15. Tumblety's conviction was reported by the St. John *Morning Freeman* on August 11, 1860; the editorial praising Tumblety's herbal

medicines ran in the *Morning Freeman* on August 2, 1860.

16. The letter from Dr. T. W. Smith was published in the St. John *Morning Freeman*, September 18, 1860.

17. Parker's decision in the case was reported in the St. John *Morning Freeman*, September 13, 1860.

18. St. John *Morning Freeman*, September 29, 1860.

19. Information on James Portmore and Tumblety comes from the inquest testimony of Mrs. Portmore which was published in the St. John *Morning Freeman*, September 29, 1860.

20. Ibid.

21. Dr. Humphrey testified that Portmore died of "acute inflammation of the stomach." Contemporary medical books define this as a disease most often caused by the ingestion of a mineral acid or an acrid herbal. Wood, *A Treatise on the Practice of Medicine*, 1858, pp. 563–566. None of Tumblety's medicines were of an "acrid herbal" nature.

22. Inquest testimony published in the St. John *Morning Freeman*, September 29, 1888.

23. Ibid.

24. Jask's report is in the *St. Thomas Weekly Dispatch*, March 28, 1861. The description of Tumblety hiding in the bushes was in the St. John *Progress*, December 15, 1888.

25. Barker's testimony on the contents of the drugs was published in the St. John *Morning Freeman*, September 29, 1860. A contemporary reference which discusses most of these medicines is Dunglison, *General Therapeutics and Materia Medica*, 1857.

26. St. John *Morning Freeman*, September 29, 1860.

27. Letter of William Smith to James Barber, December 1, 1888, quoted in Daniel F. Johnson, "Jack the Quack," *New Brunswick Reader*, 1995, www.new-brunswick.net/new-brunswick/ghoststory/ghost1.html.

28. Tumblety's letter was originally printed in the *Eastport Sentinel* and reprinted in the St. John *Morning Freeman*, October 16, 1860.

29. St. John *Progress*, December 15, 1888.

30. Ibid.

Chapter 6

1. Morris, *Incredible New York*, 1975, pp. 6–7.

2. Tumblety, *A Few Passages*, 1866, p. 12

3. Tumblety's office is listed in the *New York Herald*, February 20, 1861, as being at 933 Broadway. This continues through early April. On the twelfth, his office is advertised as being at 499 Broadway, which continues into October 1861.

4. New York testimonials are listed in Tumblety, *A Few Passages*, 1866, pp. 67–68.

5. Markham, *Financial History of the United States*, 2002, p. 201; Chemical National Bank, *History of the Chemical Bank*, 1913. As Mackellar was an editor of the *New York Daily News*, the trial was covered in detail through late March and early April 1861.

6. Mackellar was a close friend and advisor to Benjamin Wood, editor and publisher of the *New York Daily News*. Blondheim, *Copperhead Gore*, 2006, pp. 15, 36; Mackellar's association with the *National Police Gazette* is in Abbott and Abbott, *Reports of Practice Cases*, 1867, pp. 459–465.

7. The *National Police Gazette* story was referenced during the trial. *New York Daily News*, April 4, 1861. The title of the article is reported in the *Boston Globe*, November 27, 1888.

8. Mackellar's testimony is in *New York Daily News*, April 3, 1861.

9. In his letter to the press on June 9, 1865, after his release from the Old Capitol Prison, Tumblety refers to having had only one man in his employ over the past five years. Tumblety, *A Few Passages*, 1866, p. 27. The information on Blackburn and his family is from the 1860 U.S. census.

10. Tumblety filed his memorial to the Joint High Claims Commission on January 16, 1872. The original and associated papers are on file in the National Archives of Great Britain in record group FO305/49.

11. Both references to Tumblety are in a column entitled "Editors Table" which appeared monthly in the *Knickerbocker* and was written by Charles F. Hoffman. May 1861, 57(6):570; July 1861, 58(1):90.

12. *Vanity Fair*, August 3, 1861.

13. Tumblety's Pimple Banisher ads appeared in *Harper's Weekly* from August 31 to October 19, 1861, in *Frank Leslie's Illustrated Newspaper* from August 31 to October 5, 1861, and in the *New York Illustrated News* from July 6 to October 21, 1861.

14. *New York Times*, August 2–3, 1861; *Philadelphia Inquirer*, August 24, September 28, October 5 and 12, 1861.

15. Tumblety advertised in the *Baltimore Sun* from September 14 to October 7, 1861.

16. Hart's story was published in the *San Francisco Daily Examiner*, November 23, 1888.

17. There seems to be no full biography of Fred H. Hart. Some details about his life can be found in Loomis, "Hart's Tall Tales from Nevada," 1945, pp. 216–217.

18. Burchard's role in the election of 1884 is recounted in Johnson and Johnson, *A Funny Thing Happened on the Way to the White House*, 1983, p. 65.

Chapter 7

1. Leech, *Reveille in Washington*, 1941, p. 121.

2. *Buffalo Express*, November 15, 1861; *British American Journal*, December 1861, pp. 574–575.

3. *Boston Medical and Surgical Journal*, January 2, 1862, 65(22):458.

4. Rafuse, "Typhoid and Tumult," 1997; Haller, *American Medicine in Transition*, 1981, p. 122, 186.

5. Sears, *George B. McClellan*, 1999, pp. 136–137.

6. The story about Tumblety and Robert Lincoln is in *Newark Advocate*, November 28, 1861.

7. Haywood's story is part of a larger article printed in the *Rochester Democrat and Republican*, December 3, 1888.

8. The Willard Hotel is described in Sandoval-Strausz, *Hotel: An American History*, 2007, pp. 253–254.

9. The history of this building is reported in the HABS/HARE file entitled "Central National Bank Building, 631 Pennsylvania Avenue Northwest, Washington, District of Columbia, DC," HABS No. DC-229, on record at the Library of Congress. At the time of the report in 1981, the upper floors of the building were abandoned and the lower floor was the Apex Liquor Store. Since then the building became the offices of the National Council of Negro Women, Inc., and has been beautifully restored. The 1860s arrangement of offices is based on listings in the city directories and on ads in the *Washington Star*.

10. *National Intelligencer*, January 10, 1862; February 14, 1862; March 25, 1862.

11. Ibid., March 21, 1862; March 29, 1862; May 24, 1862.

12. Information on Father Constantino L. Egan is found in Corby, *Memoirs of Chaplain Life*, 1992.

13. *Frederick Daily News*, November 20, 1888.

14. Joe Chetcuti first found references to this episode in the National Archives in Record Group 94, Turner-Baker papers. An interesting discussion of the discharge process and the taking of unauthorized leaves is in Lande, *Madness, Malingering, and Malfeasance*, 2003, pp. 131–137.

15. *National Intelligencer*, March 2, 1863.

16. *Rochester Democrat and Republican*, December 3, 1888; *Daily Inter Ocean*, November 20, 1888.

17. William Pinkerton, the detective, described Tumblety's rides on the Avenue in *Daily Inter Ocean*, November 20, 1888.

18. Eicher and Eicher, *Civil War High Commands*, 2001, p. 547.

19. The Lincoln letter is first mentioned in Tumblety, *Passages*, 1866, p. 20 and reproduced in Tumblety, *Narrative*, 1872, p. 17.

20. The skit was first advertised in the *Washington Star*, December 2, 1861, and repeated until December 9, 1861. This same skit was performed by Bryant's Minstrels in New York from October 8 to 31, 1861, at 472 Broadway, only a short distance from Tumblety's office at the time.

21. The original Canterbury Music Hall is described in Kift, *Victorian Music Hall*, 1996, pp. 17–18; the description of Washington's version of the music hall is in Leech, *Reveille in Washington*, 1941, p. 276.

22. The performance took place on March 7, 1862, and Tumblety filed suit the next day. *Evening Star*, March 10, 1862.

23. *Washington Evening Star*, March 3, 1862.

24. Tony Pastor is advertised from March 5 to 7, 1862. The "Carte-de-Visite Album" is printed in Pastor and Anthony, *Tony Pastor's Book of Six Hundred Comic Songs*, 1867, p. 74.

25. The suit is first reported in the *Evening Star*, March 10, 1862, and the judgment is reported on March 12, 1862.

26. Dunham's article was printed in the *New York World*, December 1, 1888, and reprinted as part of a larger article in the *Rochester Democrat and Republican*, December 3, 1888.

27. Dunham's movements in the summer of 1861 are chronicled in Cumming, *Devil's Game: The Civil War Intrigues of Charles A. Dunham*, 2004, pp. 27–29.

28. *Evening Journal*, June 23, 1865.

29. A version of the story by "Col. Sothern" is in the *Boston Globe*, November 26, 1888.

Chapter 8

1. The quote from the *Philadelphia Press* was found in the *St. Louis Republican*, May 14, 1865.

2. *Philadelphia Press*, May 21, 1863.

3. The origin of the black servant is uncertain. One wonders if the description of him being followed by a "black servant" is somehow a corruption of the name Blackburn.

4. *St. Louis Republican*, May 14, 1865.

5. *North American and United States Gazette*, Philadelphia, July 2, 1863.

6. Tumblety regularly advertised in the *Brooklyn Daily Eagle* beginning on October 3, 1863, and ending July 9, 1864.

7. *Brooklyn Daily Eagle*, April 19, 1864.

8. Ibid., October 3, 1863.

9. Ibid., May 10, 1864.

10. Ibid., May 6, 1864.

11. Ibid., May 4, 1865.

12. Ibid.

13. The fire and B. R. Farrell's role in it was in the *Brooklyn Daily Eagle*, April 4, 1862.

14. The passenger list for the *George Cromwell* is in the *New York Times*, December 4, 1864.

15. Tumblety, *Passages*, 1866, pp. 29–30.

Chapter 9

1. The first ad noted was in the *Missouri Republican*, January 5, 1865. Tumblety's first ad in the *Missouri Democrat* was printed on January 11, 1865.

2. *Missouri Republican*, May 6, 1865.

3. Barns, *Commonwealth of Missouri*, 1877, pp. 462–463.

4. *Missouri Republican*, May 6, 1865.

5. *Missouri Democrat*, March 11, 1865

6. Tumblety, *Passages*, 1866, pp. 21–22.

7. *Missouri Democrat*, March 21, 1865.

8. Leonard, *Lincoln's Avengers*, 2004, pp. 34–36.

9. *Missouri Republican*, April 22, 1865; Tumblety, *Passages*, 1866:22–23

10. *Brooklyn Daily Eagle*, May 4, 1865; *New York Times*, May 5, 1865.

11. *Brooklyn Daily Eagle*, April 28, 1865.

12 The special orders recording Tumblety's arrest and his transfer to Washington are in the Records of the St. Louis Provost Marshal, State and District Offices, Provost Marshal General's Bureau (Civil War), RG 110.1, National Archives and Records Administration, Washington.

13. Tumblety, *Passages,* 1866, pp. 22–23; 1872 Claims Memorial.

14. Tumblety was arrested on May 5, 1865, and both the *Missouri Democrat* and the *Missouri Republican* reported it on May 6, 1865. Neither paper was sure why he was arrested. The following day, the *Missouri Republican* reported he was arrested "on the strength of the telegraph dispatches of the Associated Press"; Tumblety, *Passages*, 1866, p. 23.

15. John P. Baker to Charles Dana, May 6, 1865, MS on file, National Archives, War Department Records, Judge Advocate-General Office, File "B," Document 261, quoted in Evans and Gainey, *First American Serial Killer*, 1998, p. 204.

16. Oregon Wilson was a young, reportedly talented artist who died before his potential was reached. His most famous painting was "A Woman's Devotion," or "Angel of the Battlefield." He died in Santa Barbara in 1873 at 28 years of age. *San Francisco Bulletin*, October 1, 1873.

17. *Missouri Democrat*, May 6–7, 1865.

18. *Brooklyn Daily Eagle*, May 10, 1865.

19. *Missouri Democrat*, May 11,1865.

20. *New York Times*, May 7, 1865; for a history of yellow fever in the United States see Murphy, *An American Plague*, 2003.

21. Testimony of the inquest held in Bermuda was reported in the *New York Times*, May 16, 1865.

22. Blackburn's arrest in Toronto, *New York Times*, May 22, 1865; testimony of W. W. Cleary, *New York Times*, May 26, 1865; for more information on the real Dr. Blackburn see Baird, *Luke Pryor Blackburn*, 1979.

23. *New York Tribune*, May 12, 1865.

24. A good source for the Old Capital Prison is Leech, *Reveille in Washington*, 1941, pp. 134–143; Colby's account of the prison is reprinted in Colby, *Civil War Papers*, 2003, pp. 267–268.

25. Tumblety's description of his prison stay is in Tumblety, *Passages*, 1866, pp. 24–25; The story, as told by Colby, is reprinted in Colby, *Civil War Papers*, 2003, pp. 272–273.

26. Tumblety reproduced the type of letter he sent out to many papers in Tumblety, *Passages*, 1866, pp. 27–28.

27. Lomax, *Old Capital*, 1867.

28. The article is reproduced in Tumblety, *Passages*, 1866, pp. 30–31.

29. Tumblety, *Passages,* 1866, pp. 48–51.

30. Ads for Doctor Blackburn ran in the *Cincinnati Commercial* from September 26 through November 7, 1865.

Chapter 10

1. Tumblety had ads in the *Cincinnati Commercial*, almost continually from December 13, 1865, through May 5, 1866.

2. Stevens, *City of Cincinnati*, 1869, p. 24.

3. Tumblety, *Passages*, 1866, p. 77.

4. Ibid., pp. 78–80; the cholera article was printed in the *Cincinnati Commercial*, April 10, 1866; Fowler's ads begin in early April in the same newspaper and are done by April 12.

5. Tumblety's autobiography was published privately in Cincinnati in 1866. It is not known how many were printed but there are 28 libraries that currently have copies of the pamphlet. Other narratives include Greenhow, *My Imprisonment*, 1863; Boyd, *Belle Boyd*, 1865; Lomax, *Old Capital*, 1867.

6. Tumblety, *Passages,*1866, p. 4.

7. Ibid., p. 23.

8. Ibid., p. 6.

9. Ibid., p. 75.

10. Ibid., p. 54; a good summary of the Lincoln administration's difficulties with civil liberties, and Stanton's part in it, can be found in Neely, *Fate of Liberty*, 1991.

11. Tumblety, *Passages,* 1866, p. 48. For a discussion of the negotiations leading to the

Joint High Claims Commission see Cook, *The Alabama Claims*, 1975.

12. Receipts for all of these people are printed in Tumblety, *Narrative*, 1872.

13. Cutter was once a noted American poet but is not talked about much any more. A brief sketch of his life may be found in Townsend, *Kentucky in American Letters*, 1913; Anderson and his part in laying the transatlantic cable is detailed in Hearn, *Circuits in the Sea*, 2004.

14. Both men were members of the Royal College of Surgeons. A short description of John Abernethy's life is in Stephen and Lee, *Dictionary of National Biography*, 1908, vol. 1, pp. 50–52; Astley Cooper's life is detailed in vol. 4, pp. 1062–1064.

15. Tumblety, *Passages*, 1866, pp. 39–40.

16. New York City marriage certificate #3104 lists the marriage of Mark A. Blackburn and Olivia B. Young. She was from Hamilton County, Ohio, and her parents were Charles B. Young and Lusina Ellis. His parents are listed as Mark Blackburn and Martha Simpson. In the 1870 census, Olivia is living back with her mother in Cincinnati and Mark Blackburn is not listed.

17. The 1867 Pittsburgh city directory lists Tumblety as boarding at the Merchant's Hotel, with his office at 194 Liberty Street. *Pittsburg Commercial*, October 24, 1866.

18. In the era when coffins were handmade and did not come in standard sizes, there are frequent references to finding the corpse too long for the coffin. A way around this problem was to cut off part of the legs. From this came a folktale which combined the fear of being buried alive with this problem. Tumblety, never one to turn down a good story, probably adapted this to himself. There is no evidence that this actually happened.

19. John A. Best ads run in the *Pittsburgh Commercial* from February 2 through February 20, 1868.

20. There were eight separate ferries from New York that docked at Exchange Place, see Cudahy, *Over and Back*, 1990.

Chapter 11

1. Tumblety, *Narrative*, 1872, pp. 16–17, 56–58.

2. Description of the *Nebraska* is from www.theshiplist.com. Cost of the ticket was advertised in the *New York Times*, July 11, 1869. The line of credit is referenced in Tumblety, *Narrative*, 1872, p. 58.

3. *New York Times*, July 15, 1869; *New York Times*, July 24, 1869. Dr. Barter is reported in Tumblety, *Narrative*, 1872, p. 58.

4. Metcalfe, *Rise and Progress of Hydropathy*, 1906, pp. 120–141.

5. A description of Aghadoe House and the estate is in Hamilton, *National Gazetteer*, 1868.

6. The quote concerns the estate in 1807, when Lord Headley's father was alive. It was reprinted in Wiseman, "English Tourists in Ireland," 1837, pp. 401–427.

7. The Langham Hotel produced its own guide to London, which describes the hotel, as early as 1867. See Langham Hotel Company, *The Langham Hotel Guide to London*, 1907. Although I have not seen the earlier guidebook, I believe it likely that Tumblety adapted his description of London from this source.

8. Tumblety, *Narrative*, 1872, pp. 61–63.

9. An interesting account of the awarding of the Legion of Honor and of the rest of his experience in Paris can be found in Carson, *The Dentist and the Empress*, 1983.

10. The letter from London is in Tumblety, *Narrative*, 1872, pp. 59–61.

11. National Archives microfilm M237, roll 318, list 1062, line 6. A sketch of the life of the Rev. Milburn is in Herringshaw, *Encyclopedia of American Biography*, 1902, p. 656.

12. A vast amount of primary source material on the transcontinental railroad, including timetables, schedule and ticket prices can be found at the website for the Central Pacific Railroad Photographic History Museum, cprr.org/Museum.

13. For the story of A. D. Jones see Nelson, *Union Pacific Railroad*, 1871.

14. Twain's opinion of the hotel is in Taper, *Mark Twain's San Francisco*, 2003, p. 41; a description of the Occidental Hotel is in Smith, *San Francisco's Lost Landmarks*, 2005, pp. 209–210.

15. Smith, *San Francisco's Lost Landmarks*, 2005, contains numerous references to Montgomery Street as the financial and social center of San Francisco. It was exactly the kind of location Tumblety looked for when he came to a new place.

16. A description of the Lick House is in Smith, *San Francisco's Lost Landmarks*, 2005, pp. 210–211.

17. Samuel Thomson originated much of the system; see for example Comfort, *The Practice of Medicine on Thomsonian Principles*, 1859.

18. *San Francisco Chronicle*, April 7, 1870.

19. Tumblety's date of leaving San Francisco was reported by C. F. Smyth in the *San Francisco Daily Examiner*, November 23, 1888.

20. A large number of stories appeared in the San Francisco papers between November 18 and 25, 1888. Lees' and O'Donnell's stories are in the *San Francisco Daily Examiner*, November 20, 1888.

21. Quoted from the *San Francisco Daily Examiner*, November 23, 1888.

22. *Brooklyn Daily Eagle*, November 18, 1870; Tumblety, *Narrative*, 1872, pp. 74–75, 83.

23. An interesting discussion of the negotiations and politics of the "Alabama Claims" is presented in Mahin, *One War at a Time*, 1999.

24. Tumblety's memorial to the Joint High Commission is on file in the records of the Foreign Office in the British National Archives, Ref # FO 305/49; Tumblety's petition was considered in the U. S. House in 1876, U. S. Congress, House of Representatives, "Journal of the House of Representatives of the United States," p. 669.

25. Tumblety, *Dr. Tumblety's Narrative*, 1871.

26. Tumblety, *Narrative*, 1872.

27. The description of Tumblety's medals was published in the *New Orleans Picayune*, March 25, 1881.

28. Margaret Tumblety died on May 27, 1873; see Evans and Gainey, *First American Serial Killer*, 1998, p. 260. The 1900 census shows that Blackburn married Elizabeth in 1873. It was her second marriage and she already had two children. They had their first child together in 1877.

Chapter 12

1. Tumblety arrived in Liverpool on the *SS Idaho* on July 21, 1873. *Liverpool Mercury*, July 22, 1873.

2. Information on Carr and his family is from the 1871 British census.

3. Pinkerton's poor memory of Tumblety was reported in the *Daily Inter Ocean*, November 20, 1888.

4. Caine's life has recently been chronicled in Allen, *Caine*, 1997.

5. Tumblety's letters are stored in the Caine Collection of the Manx National Heritage Library, MS0952; Allen, *Caine*, 1997.

6. *Liverpool Mercury*, September 1, 1874; Tumblety ran ads in the *Mercury* from September 1, 1874, through January 15, 1875.

7. For the evolution of Duke Street see Muir and Muir, *History of Liverpool*, 1907, p. 180.

8. Tumblety, *Sketch*, 1893, p. 42.

9. The ad was published in the *Liverpool Mercury*, November 2, 1874. Tumblety had a poster printed that set forth his side of the suit and a copy is preserved in the Caine Collection of the Manx National Heritage Library, MS0952.

10. Information on the Hanratty case is from the *Liverpool Mercury*, January 19, 1875.

11. Dr. Bligh's testimony was reported in the *Liverpool Mercury* on January 28, 1875.

12. The verdict of the grand jury was reported in the *Liverpool Mercury* on January 28, 1875.

13. The result of the libel suit was reported in the *Liverpool Mercury* on February 24, 1875.

14. Information on the Margaret Street address is from the 1871 and 1881 British census. Tumblety reports moving from this address in a letter to Caine dated February 8, 1875. Caine Collection of the Manx National Heritage Library, MS0952.

15. Tumblety's pamphlet was to be entitled "Passages from the Life of Dr. Francis Tumblety." *Liverpool Mercury*, February 2, 1875.

16. Tumblety wrote letters from Glasshouse Street from February 8 through May 14, 1875. Information of the Glasshouse address was derived from the 1871 and 1881 British census. Piccadilly Circus as a hangout for homosexuals is described in Cook, *London and the Culture of Homosexuality*, 2003, p. 25.

17. Details of the pamphlet are from an ad in the *Liverpool Mercury*, March 15, 1875,

18. For a detailed biography of Thomas Holloway and his medicines see Harrison-Barbet, *Thomas Holloway*, 1994.

19. Letter of Tumblety to Caine, from 5 Glasshouse Street, London, Caine Collection of the Manx National Heritage Library, MS0952.

20. Tumblety is listed as a passenger on the *SS Greece*. *Passenger Lists of Vessels Arriving at New York, New York, 1820–1897*, micropublication M237, roll 400, list 851, line 8, National Archives, Washington, D.C.

21. The failure of the Bank of California was reported in the *New York Times*, August 27, 1875. Ralston's suicide was reported in the *New York Times*, August 28, 1875. The Hibernia Bank was mentioned as getting a large influx of gold in the *Atlanta Constitution*, September 16, 1875.

22. Background for Tumblety's relationship with Lyons was reported as part of the recollections of William P. Burr, the lawyer that represented Mrs. Lyons, and published in the *Rochester Democrat and Republican*, December 3, 1888.

23. The description of the 1878 trip to Rome is in Tumblety, *Sketch*, 1893, pp. 55–56.

24. Reference to Tumblety's letters to Lyons was reported in the *Rochester Democrat and Republican*, December 3, 1888.

Chapter 13

1. *Rochester Democrat and Republican*, December 3, 1888.

2. Ibid.

3. For a discussion of wages in the 1880s see Levasseur, "The American Workman," 1900.

4. "Decisions in the Courts," published in the *New York Times*, July 24, 1880.

5. Daly, *Reports of Cases Argued*, 1887, pp. 176–178.

6. Pryor's recollections are in the *Pittsburgh Daily Chronicle and Telegraph*, November 27, 1888.

7. Guiteau's time in New York and his work on the speech are detailed in Ackerman, *Dark Horse*, 2003.

8. Tumblety's arrival at the Rossin House was published in the *Toronto Globe*, October 2, 1880. The original Rossin House was built in 1857 and Tumblety would have seen its opening. That building was burned in 1862 and an even more impressive structure was built in 1863; see Filey, *More Toronto Sketches*, 1993, p. 109.

9. Tumblety's arrest on the charge was reported in the *Toronto Globe*, October 15, 1880. The details of the case and the verdict were reported in the *Toronto Globe*, October 19, 1880.

10. The landlady's description of Tumblety was reported in the *New Orleans Picayune*, March 25, 1881.

11. Govan's testimony was detailed in the *New Orleans Picayune*, March 25, 1881.

12. For Dominick O'Malley see Koenigsberg, *King News*, 1941, pp. 85–86 and Asbury, *The French Quarter*, 2003, p. 413.

13. The description of the medals found on Tumblety was published in the *New Orleans Picayune*, March 25, 1881.

14. Ibid.

15. McGarry's somewhat confused recollections were printed in the *New York World*, December 5, 1888.

16. For a discussion of attempts to license and regulate physicians see Walsh, *History of Medicine in New York*, 1919.

17. Details of the collision were reported in the *Daily Inter Ocean*, May 23, 1887; the De Puy letter was published in Tumblety, *Sketch*, 1893, p. 95.

18. The description of Tumblety is in a letter from Frederick Douglass to Amy Kirby Post, dated June 10, 1887, in the Post Family Papers, Dept. of Rare Books, Special Collections and Preservation, University of Rochester Libraries.

19. *Washington Evening Star*, November 21, 1888.

Chapter 14

1. Tumblety's confessed familiarity with Whitechapel was reported in Palmer, "Tumblety Talks," 2007. These charges are detailed in Evans and Gainey, *First American Serial Killer*, 1998, pp. 270–271. A printed version of the charges, copies of the laws under which he was charged and a discussion of their meaning can be found in the casebook message boards under the Tumblety thread, www.casebook. org.

2. A relatively contemporary description of the concept of police bail is reported in Renton et al., *Encyclopædia of the Laws of England*, 1909, vol. 1, p. 661.

3. Hedge case reported in the *London Times*, February 12, 1886; De Tatum case reported in the *London Times*, April 30, 1891.

4. The name Frank Townsend is on the passenger list for *La Bretagne* dated December 3, 1888, where he is described as being 45 years old. Interestingly for a person on the run, he had four bags with him. *Passenger Lists of Vessels Arriving at New York, New York, 1820–1897*. Micropublication M237, roll # 528, list 1616, line 36, National Archives, Washington, D.C. Numerous articles were published in the New York papers regarding Tumblety's arrival in New York. See, for example, *Brooklyn Daily Eagle*, December 4, 1888; *New York Herald*, December 4, 1888. It is clear from the New York press reports that Tumblety was expected and followed by the New York police.

5. *San Francisco Chronicle*, November 18, 1888.

6. For a discussion of the "Maiden Tribute" articles and their impact see Schults, *Crusader in Babylon*, 1972; for the Labouchère Amendment see Cook, *London and the Culture of Homosexuality*, 2003.

7. Statistics on arrests and convictions in London for sodomy and gross indecency can be found in Cook, *London and the Culture of Homosexuality*, 2003.

8. The *London Times* covered the case of Burleigh and Widdows on March 28, April 5, and May 2, 1888.

9. The story of the man posing as a detective appeared in the *London Times* on October 26, 1886.

10. *Daily Inter Ocean*, November 20, 1888.

11. *New York Times*, November 19, 1888.

12. Palmer, "Tumblety Talks," 2007, p. 4.

13. Evans and Gainey report that there is not one mention of Tumblety in the surviving police or Home Office files in the Public Records Office. *First American Serial Killer*, 1998, p. 250. While many of those close to the case made statements or wrote memoirs mentioning the case, not one even hinted at Tumblety being a suspect.

14. San *Francisco Chronicle*, November 18 and November 20, 1888; *New York Times*, November 19, 1888; *New York Herald*, November

19 and November 20, 1888; *Washington Evening Star*, November 19 and November 20, 1888.

15. *New York Herald*, November 21, 1888.

16. Dunham's article was printed in the *New York World*, December 1, 1888, and reprinted as part of a larger article in the *Rochester Democrat and Republican*, December 3, 1888.

17. Tumblety's flirtation with the women of Brooklyn was reported by the *New York Times*, November 19,1888; his conquest of the "heiress of one of the richest families on the Heights" was mentioned in the *Brooklyn Daily Eagle*, May 4, 1865.

18. The discovery and importance of the Littlechild letter is detailed in Evans and Gainey, *First American Serial Killer*, 1998.

19. Ibid., p. 180.

20. Krafft-Ebing's *Psychopathia Sexualis* was reprinted in 1998; for a consideration of Krafft-Ebing's impact see Oosterhuis, *Stepchildren of Nature*, 2000.

21. Macnaghten, *Days of My Years*, 1914, p. 54.

22. Griffiths, *Mysteries of Police and Crime*, 1898, vol. 1, pp. 28–29.

23. The questionable club to which Tumblety belonged was called the "Busy Bees" as reported in *The Medical Standard* 3 (1888):191; *New York Times*, November 19, 1888; *Brooklyn Daily Eagle*, April 27, 1890.

24. Batty Street and its connection to the Whitechapel murders are discussed in Evans and Gainey, *First American Serial Killer*, 1998, pp. 119–128.

25. Sims' postscript to the story was reported in "Addendum—Part II," Evans and Gainey, *First American Serial Killer*, 1998, pp. 267–268.

26. The "black bag" incident is discussed in Evans and Gainey, *First American Serial Killer*, 1998, pp. 115–118; the auction sale for the Innkeepers' Act was advertised in the *London Times*, September 22 and 24, 1888.

27. On November 23, 1888, the *San Francisco Daily Evening Bulletin* reported that "On the 19th inst. Chief Crowley sent a dispatch to the London detectives informing them that he could furnish specimens of Tumblety's handwriting." The *New York Times* article, also on November 23, 1888, lists its source as a report from San Francisco and repeats the same language as the original but changes the "19th inst." to "Oct. 29" for unknown reasons.

28. The full factor list is in Evans and Gainey, *First American Serial Killer*, 1998, p. 251.

29. Ibid., p. 47.

30. Tumblety, *Narrative*, 1872, p. 32; *Washington Evening Star*, November 20, 1888; see chapter 12 for a discussion of what Tumblety's medicine was like.

31. For the height of Londoners in the nineteenth century see Johnson and Nicholas, "Male and Female Living Standards in England and Wales," 1993, and Bliss, *Encyclopedia of Social Reform*, 1897, p. 412.

32. Evans and Gainey, *First American Serial Killer*, 1998, pp. 234–235.

Chapter 15

1. Both the *New York World* and the *New York Herald* described Tumblety's arrival in New York on December 4, 1888.

2. Inspector Byrnes is quoted in the *New York World*, December 4, 1888.

3. Shaw, whose real name was Hoddington, was arrested as he got off the ship. In his pocket was a printed account of the Whitechapel murders. The papers suggested that he matched the description of the murderer, see the *Frederick News*, November 26, 1888. Shaw was finally released on November 27, see the *New York Times*, November 28, 1888.

4. An example of Mrs. McNamara's changing story was reported in the *New York Tribune* of December 4, 1888.

5. The "English detective" is mentioned by both the *New York World* and the *New York Herald* on December 4, 1888. No other papers talk about him and he is not mentioned again.

6. A good review of Inspector Andrews' trip to Canada, including the fact that it was planned even before Tumblety went missing, is in Vanderlinden, "On the Trail of Tumblety? Part 2," 2005, pp. 23–47.

7. Tumblety's flight from Mrs. McNamara's was reported in the *New York World* on December 6, 1888; his "discovery" was reported in the *New York Sun* on January 28, 1889.

8. De Puy's letter is reprinted in Tumblety, *Sketch*, 1889, p. 89; Bible House was a well-known landmark in New York City, see Wosh, *Spreading the Word*, 1994.

9. Hammond's letter is reprinted in Tumblety, *Sketch*, 1889, p. 88; biographical information on Hammond can be found in Blustein, *Preserve Your Love for Science*, 2002.

10. *Brooklyn Daily Eagle*, January 28, 1889.

11. Palmer, "Tumblety Talks," 2007; *New York Sun*, January 29, 1889; *New York World*, February 3, 1889.

12. *Brooklyn Daily Eagle*, February 2, 1889; *Olean Democrat*, February 7, 1889.

13. If the February edition of the pamphlet does exist, it has not yet been identified.

14. Information on the development of Turkish baths in Manhattan and the people involved can be found on the web at http://www.victorianturkishbath.org.

15. An interesting study of the events is Kranzberg, *The Siege of Paris*, 1971.

16. Carson, *The Dentist and the Empress*, 1983.

17. This sermon was reprinted in the *Frederick News* on September 23, 1889.

18. For more information on DeWitt Talmage and his sermons see Banks, *T. DeWitt Talmage*, 1902.

19. For Washington Square and the neighborhood as a cruising area see Chauncey, *Gay New York*, 1994, p. 196. A description of the confrontation between Tumblety and Davis was printed in the *St. John Globe* of St. John, New Brunswick, on June 10, 1889.

20. Tumblety's no-show was reported in the *Brooklyn Daily Eagle*, June 25, 1889; Assistant District Attorney Grosse is quoted in the *New York Times*, August 10, 1889.

21. *Olean Democrat*, August 8, 1889.

22. Tumblety's arrest and the subsequent events were reported in the *Washington Post*, November 18 and 19, 1890; for Ninth Street as a cruising area see Muzzy, *Gay and Lesbian Washington*, 2005, p. 79.

23. Tumblety's description was reported in the *Washington Post*, November 18, 1890; *Brooklyn Daily Eagle*, November 18, 1890.

Chapter 16

1. General background on the area can be found in Hanley, *Hot Springs, Arkansas*, 2000. Information on the Plateau Hotel is from Cutter, *Cutter's Guide to the Hot Springs of Arkansas*, 1890, pp. 44–45, and the gracious assistance of Ms. Sharon Shugart, Museum Specialist, Hot Springs National Park.

2. An interesting exposé of the profession of "hotel thief" is presented in Farley, *Criminals of America*, 1873, pp. 480–481.

3. Reports of the thefts were printed in the *Daily Picayune* on April 16, 1891.

4. Details of Tumblety's loss were published in the *Arkansas Gazette*, April 19, 1891.

5. In listing New Yorkers who arrived at Richfield Springs, the *New York Times*, July 16, 1891, includes "F. Tumblaty."

6. Frank Sherman's case is presented in the *New York Times* on July 21, 1891; a report of his release was printed in the *New York Times* on July 22, 1891.

7. Tumblety's letter to the *New York Herald* was published on July 22, 1891; Sykerman's true past is reported in the *New York Times* on July 25, 1891; his final release was printed in the *New York Times* on August 4, 1891.

8. A report on the "bath crisis" was printed in the *Boston Globe*, August 27, 1891.

9. The story of Tumblety's bath donation and the quote by Joseph Howard, Jr., are printed in Tumblety, *Sketch*, 1893, pp. 103–104.

10. For a biography of Howard see Johnson and Brown, *Twentieth Century Biographical Dictionary of Notable Americans*, vol. 5, 1904.

11. Tumblety's contribution to St. Joseph's Infirmary is evidenced by a letter from Sister M. Aloysius reprinted in Tumblety, *Sketch*, 1893, p. 113. Information on the history of St. Joseph's Infirmary can be found on the website of St. Joseph's Mercy Health Center, www.mercy.net.

12. The initial notice of the Ice Fund was published in the *New York Herald*, on May 29, 1892; Tumblety made his donation in Baltimore on May 30, 1892. Tumblety, *Sketch*, 1893, p. 112; *New York Herald*, June 6, 1893.

13. I have found no copy of the 1891–1892 edition but the 1893 second edition is commonly available. One version is online at Google Book Search.

14. The earliest printing I have found of the "How to Live Long" essay was in the *New Haven Register*, December 26, 1891; *Olean Democrat*, June 2, 1892.

15. An example of the piece by Huxley was printed in the *Reno Gazette*, January 14, 1889.

16. A useful biography of Longfellow is Gale, *Henry Wadsworth Longfellow Companion*, 2003. A classic study of Tennyson's life and work is Ricks, *Tennyson*, 1972.

17. William Duvall gave a deposition on his relationship to Tumblety and the doctor's time in Baltimore on March 20, 1905. See Case #29083, St. Louis City Probate Court.

18. For information on Douglas, Lacey and Co. see Hough, "Gold Brick and the Gold Mine," 1910, pp. 44–55; Kemp's deposition was taken on March 20, 1905, and filed in Case #29083, St. Louis City Probate Court.

19. Simpson's testimony is in a deposition taken on March 20, 1905, Case #29083, St. Louis City Probate Court.

20. The letter to Lord Galway is preserved in Papers of the Monckton-Arundell Family, Viscounts Galway of Serlby Hall, Nottinghamshire, Early 13th Century–1958, Ga C11/1–11/309, held at the Nottinghamshire University Library.

21. O'Donovan's testimony is in a deposition taken on March 20, 1905, Case #29083, St. Louis City Probate Court.

22. Widner's testimony is in a deposition taken on March 20, 1905, Case #29083, St. Louis City Probate Court.

Chapter 17

1. Tumblety's contribution to St. Joseph's Infirmary is evidenced by a letter from Sister

M. Aloysius reprinted in Tumblety, *Sketch*, 1893, p. 113.

2. Information on Tumblety's intention to die was reported in the *St. Louis Post Dispatch*, May 29, 1903.

3. Information on the history of St. John's Hospital can be found on the website for St. Johns Mercy Medical Center, www.stjohns-mercy.org.

4. Dr. Temm's claim on the estate, detailing his services, was filed on February 16, 1904. See Case #29083, St. Louis City Probate Court.

5. Contemporary descriptions of how to test for albumin in the urine were common. See, for example, Keating, *How to Examine for Life Insurance*, 1891, pp. 200–206; The Sisters of Mercy filed their claim on the estate on March 23, 1904. See Case #29083, St. Louis City Probate Court.

6. Canon filed a detailed claim, on June 1, 1903, with the probate court for services rendered. See Case #29083, St. Louis City Probate Court.

7. Dr. Brokaw detailed his treatment of Tumblety in a claim filed in June 1904. See Case #29083, St. Louis City Probate Court; *St. Louis Post Dispatch*, May 29, 1903.

8. An explanation of the purpose and function of the public administrator is in Fair, *Government and Politics in Missouri*, 1922, pp. 118.

9. Information on Arthur Marshall and A. B. Walker comes from the 1900 census and the St. Louis City directories. The assessment was made on July 16, 1903, and is included in Case #29083, St. Louis City Probate Court.

10. The various challenges to the St. Louis will and Garrard Strode's administration of it are detailed in Case #29083, St. Louis City Probate Court.

11. Information on the Baltimore will is in the deposition of Joseph Kemp taken on March 20, 1905, Case #29083, St. Louis City Probate Court; see also George, "The Cardinal and the Ripper Suspect," *Ripperologist*, 1999, pp. 21–24.

12. Kemp's deposition was taken on March 20, 1905, and filed in Case #29083, St. Louis City Probate Court.

13. The other heirs had hired Nelson E. Spencer of Rochester to represent them by August 1, 1903. The case was filed in St. Louis on January 16, 1904. Details of the heirs' case are to be found in Case #29083, St. Louis City Probate Court.

14. The final settlement was approved in December 1907. See Case #29083, St. Louis City Probate Court. It was called a "friendly money fight" in the *New York Times*, June 26, 1903.

Bibliography

Public Records

National Archives of Great Britain. 1872. "Archives of the British and American Claims Commission," FO305/49.

National Archives and Records Administration. 1865. Records of the St. Louis Provost Marshal, State and District Offices, Provost Marshal General's Bureau (Civil War), RG 110.1, National Archives and Records Administration, Washington, D.C.

Post Family. n. d. Post Family Papers, Dept. of Rare Books, Special Collections and Preservation, University of Rochester Libraries.

St. Louis City Probate Court. 1903–1908 Probate Papers Related to the Estate of Francis Tumblety, case no. 29083.

Secondary Sources

Abbott, Benjamin V., and Austin Abbott. 1867. *Reports of Practice Cases Determined in the Courts of the State of New York.* New series, vol. 2. New York: Diossy & Cockcroft.

Abrahams, Harold J. 1966. *Extinct Medical Schools of Nineteenth-Century Philadelphia.* Philadelphia: University of Pennsylvania Press.

Ackerman, Kenneth D. 2003. *Dark Horse: The Surprise Election and Political Murder of James A. Garfield.* New York: Carroll & Graff.

Allen, Vivien. 1997. *Caine: Portrait of a Victorian Romancer.* Sheffield, England: Sheffield Academic Press.

Asbury, Herbert. 2003. *The French Quarter: An Informal History of the New Orleans Underworld.* Reprint of 1936 edition. New York: Thunder Mouth Press.

Atwater, Edward C. 1973. "The Medical Profession in a New Society, Rochester, New York (1811–60)." *Bulletin of the History of Medicine* 47 (3): 221–235.

Baird, Nancy Disher. 1979. *Luke Pryor Blackburn: Physician, Governor, Reformer.* Lexington: University Press of Kentucky.

Banks, Louis A. 1902. *T. DeWitt Talmage: His Life and Work.* London: O. W. Binkherd.

Barnes, Joseph W., and Robert W. Barnes. 1974. "From Books to Multimedia: A History of the Reynolds Library and the Reynolds Audio-Visual Department of the Rochester Public Library." *Rochester History* 36 (4): 1–40.

Barns, Chancy R., ed. 1877. *The Commonwealth of Missouri: A Centennial Record.* St. Louis, MO: Bryan, Brand & Co.

Bates, Anna Louise. 1995. *Weeder in the Garden of the Lord: Anthony Comstock's Life and Career.* Lanham, MD: University Press of America.

Beisel, Nicola Kay. 1997. *Imperiled Innocents: Anthony Comstock and Family Reproduction in Victorian America.* Princeton, NJ: Princeton University Press.

Bliss, William D. P., ed. 1897. *The Encyclopedia of Social Reform.* New York: Funk & Wagnalls Co.

Blondheim, Menahem. 2006. *Copperhead Gore: Benjamin Wood's Fort Lafayette and Civil War America*. Bloomington: Indiana University Press.

Blustein, Bonnie Ellen. 2002. *Preserve Your Love for Science: Life of William A. Hammond, American Neurologist*. Cambridge: Cambridge University Press.

Boston Medical and Surgical Journal. 1862. "Medical Intelligence." January 2, 1862, vol. 65 (22): 458.

Boyd, Belle. 1865. *Belle Boyd in Camp and Prison, Written by Herself*. New York: Blelock.

British American Journal. 1861. "Tumblety Tumbled Up Again." December 1861: 574–575.

Brown, George W., Ramsay Cook, and Jean Hamelin, eds. 1994. *Dictionary of Canadian Biography*. 15 vols., Toronto: University of Toronto Press.

Carson, Gerald. 1983. *The Dentist and the Empress: The Adventures of Dr. Tom Evans in Gas-lit Paris*. Boston: Houghton Mifflin.

Chase, Gilbert. 1992. *America's Music: From the Pilgrims to the Present*. Urbana: University of Illinois Press.

Chauncey, George. 1994. *Gay New York: Gender, Urban Culture and the Making of the Gay Male World, 1890–1940*. New York: Basic Books.

Chemical National Bank. 1913. *History of the Chemical Bank, 1823–1913*. Privately printed.

Colby, Newton T. 2003. *The Civil War Papers of Lt. Colonel Newton T. Colby, New York Infantry*. Ed. William E. Hughes. Jefferson, NC: McFarland.

Comfort, John W. 1859. *The Practice of Medicine on Thomsonian Principles Adapted as Well to the Use of Families as to That of the Practitioner*. Lindsay & Blakiston.

Cook, Adrian. 1975. *The Alabama Claims: American Politics and Anglo-American Relations, 1865–1872*. Ithaca, NY: Cornell University Press.

Cook, Matt. 2003. *London and the Culture of Homosexuality, 1885–1914*. Cambridge: Cambridge University Press.

Corby, William. 1992. *Memoirs of Chaplain Life: Three Years with the Irish Brigade in the Army of the Potomac*. Ed. Lawrence F. Kohl. New York: Fordham University Press.

Croufutt and Eaton, 1870. *Great Trans-Continental Railroad Guide Containing a Full and Authentic Description ... from the Atlantic to the Pacific Ocean*. Chicago: Croufett & Eaton.

Cudahy, Brian J. 1990. *Over and Back: The History of Ferryboats in New York Harbor*. New York: Fordham University Press.

Cumming, Carman. 2004. *Devil's Game: The Civil War Intrigues of Charles A. Dunham*. Urbana: University of Illinois Press.

Cutter, Charles. 1890. *Cutter's Guide to the Hot Springs of Arkansas*. St. Louis, MO: Slavison.

Daly, Charles P. 1887. *Reports of Cases Argued and Determined in the Court of Common Pleas for the City and County of New York*. Vol. 13. New York: Banks and Brothers, Law Publishers.

Denison, George T. 1920. "Reminiscences of a Police Magistrate." *Canadian Magazine* 54:259.

Drake, Francis S. 1872 [2006]. *Dictionary of American Biography*. Boston: J. R. Osgood.

Dunglison, Robley. 1857. *General Therapeutics and Materia Medica: Adapted for a Medical Text Book*. 2 vols. Philadelphia: Blanchard and Lea.

Eicher, John H., and David J. Eicher. 2001. *Civil War High Commands*. Stanford, CA: Stanford University Press.

Ellingwood, Finley. 1910. *The American Materia Medica, Therapeutics and Pharmacognosy*. Chicago.

Englehard, G. P. 1888. *The Medical Standard*. Vol. 4. Chicago.

Evans, Stewart P., and Paul Gainey. 1995. *The Lodger: The Arrest and Escape of Jack the Ripper*. London: Century.

_____. 1998. *Jack the Ripper: First American Serial Killer*. New York: Kodansha America.

Fair, Eugene. 1922. *Government and Politics in Missouri*. Columbia, MO: Walter Ridgway.

Farley, Philip. 1873. *Criminals of America, or, Tales of the Lives of Thieves: Enabling Everyone to Be His Own Detective*. Author's edition. New York.

Felter, Harvey W., and John U. Lloyd. 1898. *King's American Dispensatory.* 18th ed. Cincinnati: Ohio Valley.

Filey, Mike. 1993. *More Toronto Sketches: The Way We Were.* Toronto: Dundurn Press.

Gale, Robert L. 2003. *A Henry Wadsworth Longfellow Companion.* Westport, CT: Greenwood Press.

George, Christopher H. 1999. "The Cardinal and the Ripper Suspect." *Ripperologist* 21:21–24.

Gevitz, Norman. 1988. *Other Healers: Unorthodox Medicine in America.* Baltimore: Johns Hopkins University Press.

Greenhow, Rose O'Neal. 1863. *My Imprisonment and the First Year of Abolition Rule at Washington.* London: Richard Bentley.

Griffiths, Arthur. 1898. *Mysteries of Police and Crime: A General Survey of Wrongdoing and Its Pursuit.* 2 vols., London: Cassell.

Haller, John S. 1981. *American Medicine in Transition: 1840–1910.* Urbana: University of Illinois Press.

Hamilton, Nicholas E. S. A., ed. 1868. *The National Gazetteer of Great Britain and Ireland.* London.

Hanley, Ray. 2000. *Hot Springs, Arkansas.* Charleston, SC: Arcadia Publishing.

Harrison-Barbet, Anthony.1994. *Thomas Holloway: Victorian Philanthropist.* London: Royal Holloway College, University of London.

Hearn, Chester G. 2004. *Circuits in the Sea: The Men, the Ships and the Atlantic Cable.* Westport, CT: Praeger.

Herringshaw, Thomas W. 1902. *Encyclopedia of American Biography of the Nineteenth Century.* Chicago: American Publishers Association.

Hoffman, Charles F., ed. 1861. "Editors Table." *Knickerbocker* 57 (6): 570.

_____. 1861. "Editors Table." *Knickerbocker* 58 (1): 90.

Holbrook, Stewart H. 1959. *The Golden Age of Quackery.* New York: Macmillan.

Hoolihan, Christopher. 2001, 2004. *An Annotated Catalogue of the Edward C. Atwater Collection of American Medicine and Health Reform.* 2 vols. Rochester, NY: University of Rochester Press.

Hough, Emerson. 1910. "The Gold Brick and the Gold Mine: Fake Mining Schemes That Steal the People's Savings." *Everybody's Magazine* 23 (1): 44–55.

Hovey, C. M., ed. 1863. *Magazine of Horticulture, Botany and All Useful Discoveries and Improvements in Rural Affairs* 29 (9): 361.

Johnson, Daniel F. 1995. "Jack the Quack." *New Brunswick Reader.* On the web at www.newbrunswick.net/new-brunswick/ghoststory/ghost1.html.

Johnson, David E., and Johnny R. Johnson. 1983. *A Funny Thing Happened on the Way to the White House.* Lanham, MD: Taylor Trade.

Johnson, Paul, and Stephen Nicholas, 1993. "Male and Female Living Standards in England and Wales, 1812–1857: Evidence from Criminal Height Records." *Melbourne Papers in Economic History*, paper no. 2. Melbourne: Department of Economic History, University of Melbourne.

Johnson, Rossiter, and John H. Brown, eds. 1904. *The Twentieth Century Biographical Dictionary of Notable Americans.* Vol. 5. Boston: Biographical Society.

Keating, John M. 1891. *How to Examine for Life Insurance.* Philadelphia: W. B. Saunders.

Kift, Dagmer. 1996. *The Victorian Music Hall: Culture, Class, and Conflict.* Cambridge: Cambridge University Press.

Koenigsberg, Moses. 1941. *King News, An Autobiography.* Philadelphia: F. A. Stokes.

Krafft-Ebing, Richard von. 1998. *Psychopathia Sexualis: With Especial Reference to the Antipathic Sexual Instinct: a Medico-forensic Study.* New York: Arcade.

Kranzberg, Melvin. 1971. *The Siege of Paris, 1870–1871: A Political and Social History.* Westport, CT: Greenwood Press.

Lande, R. Gregory. 2003. *Madness, Malingering, and Malfeasance.* Washington, D.C.: Potomac Books.

Langham Hotel Company. 1907. *The Langham Hotel Guide to London.* London: Langham Hotel Co.

Leech, Margaret. 1941. *Reveille in Washington, 1860–1865*. New York: Harper & Brothers.

Leggett, Conaway & Co. 1884. *History of Wyandot County, Ohio*. Chicago: Leggett, Conaway.

Leonard, Elizabeth D. 2004. *Lincoln's Avengers: Justice, Revenge and Reunion after the Civil War*. New York: W. W. Norton.

Levasseur, E. 1900. "The American Workman." Trans. Thomas S. Adams. *Johns Hopkins University Studies in Historical and Political Science*. Vol. 22. Baltimore.

Lomax, Virginia. 1867. *The Old Capital and Its Inmates*. New York: E. J. Hale.

Loomis, C. Grant. 1945. "Hart's Tall Tales from Nevada." *California Folklore Quarterly* 4 (3): 216–238.

Macnaghten, Melville L. 1914. *The Days of My Years*. London: Longmans, Green.

Mahin, Dean B. 1999. *One War at a Time: The International Dimensions of the American Civil War*. Dulles, VA: Brassey's.

Markham, Jerry W. 2002. *A Financial History of the United States*. New York: M. E. Sharpe.

Marquis, Greg. 1986. "A Hard Disciple of Blackstone." *University of New Brunswick Law Journal* 35:182–187.

McCullough, Michael. 1993. "'Dr. Tumblety, the Indian Herb Doctor': Politics, Professionalism, and Abortion in Mid-Nineteenth Century Montreal." *Canadian Bulletin of Medical History* 10 (1): 49–66.

McKelvey, Blake. 1957. "The Irish in Rochester: An Historical Retrospect." *Rochester History* 19 (4): 1–16.

_____. 1961. "Rochester's Part in the Civil War." *Rochester History* 23 (1): 1–24.

_____. 1964. "Rochester Mayors before the Civil War." *Rochester History* 26 (1): 1–20.

_____. 1993. *Rochester on the Genesee: The Growth of a City*. Second ed. Syracuse, NY: Syracuse University Press.

Metcalfe, Richard. 1906. *The Rise and Progress of Hydropathy in England and Scotland*. London: Simkin, Marshall, Hamilton, Kent.

Mitchinson, Wendy. 1991. *The Nature of Their Bodies: Women and Their Doctors in Victorian Canada*. Toronto: University of Toronto Press.

Morris, Lloyd. 1975. *Incredible New York*. New York: Arno Press.

Muir, Bryce, and John Ramsay. 1907. *A History of Liverpool*. Liverpool: University Press of Liverpool.

Murphy, Jim. 2003. *An American Plague: The True and Terrifying Story of the Yellow Fever Epidenic of 1793*. New York: Houghton Mifflin Harcourt.

Muzzy, Frank. 2005. *Gay and Lesbian Washington, D.C.* Charleston, SC: Arcadia.

Neely, Mark E. 1991. *The Fate of Liberty: Abraham Lincoln and Civil Liberties*. Oxford: Oxford University Press.

Nelson, Thomas. 1871. *The Union Pacific Railroad: a trip across the North American continent from Omaha to Ogden*. New York: T. Nelson.

Newcomb, Simon. 2007. *Reminiscences of an Astronomer*. Reprint of 1903 edition. Kessinger.

O'Connor, Thomas H. 1984. *Fitzpatrick's Boston, 1846–1866: John Bernard Fitzpatrick, Third Bishop of Boston*. Boston: Northeastern University Press.

Oosterhuis, Harry. 2000. *Stepchildren of Nature: Krafft-Ebing, Psychiatry and the Making of Sexual Identity*. Chicago: University of Chicago Press.

Palmer, Roger J. 2007. "Tumblety Talks." *Ripperologist* 79 (2): 2–6.

Pastor, Tony, and Henry B. Anthony. 1867. *Tony Pastor's Book of Six Hundred Comic Songs and Speeches: Being an Entire Collection of the Humorous Songs, Stump Speeches, Burlesque Orations and Funny Dialogues, as Sung and Given*. New York: Dick & Fitzgerald.

Rafuse, Ethan S. 1997. "Typhoid and Tumult: Lincoln's Response to General McClellan's Bout with Typhoid Fever during the Winter of 1861–62." *Journal of the Abraham Lincoln Association* 18 (2): 1–16.

Renton, Alexander W., Maxwell A. Robertson, Frederick Pollock, and William Bowstead. 1909. *Encyclopædia of the Laws of England with Forms and Precedents by the Most Eminent Legal Authorities*. 17 vols. London: Sweet & Maxwell.

Ricks, Christopher. 1972. *Tennyson.* New York: Macmillan.

Rosenberg-Naparsteck, Ruth. 1984. "A Growing Agitation: Rochester before, during and after the Civil War." *Rochester History* 46 (1–2): 1–40.

_____. 1998. "The Development of Gas and Electricity in Rochester." *Rochester History* 61 (4): 1–24.

Rothstein, William G. 1992. *American Physicians in the Nineteenth Century.* Baltimore: Johns Hopkins Press.

Sandoval-Strausz, A. C. 2007. *Hotel: An American History.* New Haven, CT: Yale University Press.

Schults, Raymond L. 1972. *Crusader in Babylon: W. T. Stead and the Pall Mall Gazette.* Lincoln: University of Nebraska Press.

Sears, Stephen W. 1999. *George B. McClellan: The Young Napoleon.* New York: Da Capo Press.

Smith, James R. 2005. *San Francisco's Lost Landmarks.* Sanger, CA: Word Dancer Press.

Stephen, Leslie, and Sidney Lee, eds. 1908. *The Dictionary of National Biography.* Vols. 1–22. London: MacMillan.

Stevens, George E. 1869. *The City of Cincinnati: A Summary of Its Attractions, Advantages, Institutions, and Internal Improvements with a Statement of Its Public Charities.* Cincinnati: George S. Blanchard.

Taper, Bernard, ed. 2003. *Mark Twain's San Francisco.* Berkeley, CA: Heyday Books.

Townsend, John W. 1913. *Kentucky in American Letters, 1784–1912.* Cedar Rapids, IA: Torch Press.

Tumblety, Francis J. 1857. *Guide to the Afflicted, containing at a glance the most common symptoms of certain diseases which arise from the abuse of the genital organs or contagion, together with the means of relief, being the result of great research and study.* Privately published.

_____. 1866. *A Few Passages in the Life of Dr. Francis Tumblety, The Indian Herb Doctor.* Privately published, Cincinnati.

_____. 1871. *Dr. Tumblety's narrative, how he was kidnapped, by order of the infamous Baker, his incarceration and discharge, an exciting life sketch: with important letters and ... constituting the great sensational work of the day.* Privately published, Brooklyn.

_____. 1872. *Narrative of Dr. Tumblety: How He Was Kidnapped during the American War, His Incarceration and Discharge.* Privately published, New York.

_____. 1889. *Dr. Francis Tumblety: A Sketch of the Life of the Gifted, Eccentric and World-Famed Physician....* New York: Press of Brooklyn Eagle Printing Department.

_____. 1893. *A Sketch of the Life of Dr. Francis Tumblety. Presenting an Outline of his Wonderful Career as a Physician ... Reminiscences of Foreign Travel, etc., etc.* Second ed. New York.

United States Congress, House of Representatives. 1876. "Journal of the House of Representatives of the United States, being the second session of the Forty-fourth Congress; begun and held at the City of Washington, December 4, 1876, in the one hundred and first year of the independence of the United States." *United States Congressional Serial Set.* Vol. 1740. Washington, D.C.: U. S. Government Printing Office.

Vanderlinden, Wolf. 2005. "On the Trail of Tumblety? Part 2." *Ripper Notes* 24:23–47.

Vogel, Virgil J. 1970. *American Indian Medicine.* Norman: University of Oklahoma Press.

Walsh, James J. 1919. *History of Medicine in New York: Three Centuries of Medical Progress.* 3 vols. New York: National Americana Society.

Wesley, Dorothy Porter, and Constance Porter Uzelac, eds. 2002. *William Cooper Nell: Selected Writings 1832–1874.* Baltimore: Black Classic Press.

Wiseman, Nicholas P. 1837. "English Tourists in Ireland." *Dublin Review* 2:401–427.

Wood, George B. 1858. *A Treatise on the Practice of Medicine.* 2 vols. Philadelphia: J. B. Lippincott.

Wosh, Peter J. 1994. *Spreading the Word: The Bible Business in Nineteenth Century America.* Ithaca, NY: Cornell University Press.

Young, James Harvey. 1961. *Toadstool Millionaires.* Princeton, NJ: Princeton University Press.

_____. 1992. *American Health Quackery.* Princeton, NJ: Princeton University Press.

Index

Numbers in **bold italics** indicate pages with photographs.

231

Milton Keynes UK
Ingram Content Group UK Ltd.
UKHW041828121124
451104UK00011B/45

9 780786 444335